THE
CHICKEN
BOOK

THE CHICKEN BOOK

Page Smith
and
Charles Daniel

The University of Georgia Press

Athens

Published in 2000 by the University of Georgia Press
Athens, Georgia 30602
© 1975 by Page Smith and Charles Daniel
All rights reserved

The paper in this book meets the guidelines for
permanence and durability of the Committee on
Production Guidelines for Book Longevity of the
Council on Library Resources.

Printed in Canada
04 03 02 01 00 P 5 4 3 2 1

Library of Congress Cataloging-in-Publication Data
Smith, Page.
The chicken book / Page Smith and Charles Daniel.
p. cm.
Originally published: 1st ed. Boston : Little, Brown, 1975.
Includes bibliographical references (p.).
ISBN 0-8203-2213-X (pbk. : alk. paper)
1. Chickens. I. Daniel, Charles, 1933– II. Title.
SF487 .S67 2000
636.5—dc21   99-051834

The author is grateful to the following publishers and magazines for
permission to reprint previously published copyrighted materials:

Daedalus, Journal of the American Academy of Arts and Sciences, Boston,
Massachusetts, for "Deep Play: Notes on the Balinese Cockfight,"
by Clifford Geertz, as published in the Winter 1972 issue entitled
Myth, Symbol, and Culture.
The University of Oklahoma Press, for excerpts from *Aldrovandi on Chickens:
The Ornithology of Ulisse Aldrovandi*, volume 2, book 14, by L. R. Lind.
Copyright © 1963 by the University of Oklahoma Press.
101 Productions, San Francisco, California, for three recipes
from *Manna: Foods of the Frontier*, by Gertrude Harris.
Copyright © 1972 by Gertrude Harris.
Holt, Rinehart and Winston, Publishers, for "A Blue Ribbon at Amesbury"
from *The Poetry of Robert Frost*, edited by Edward Connery Lathem.
Copyright © 1963 by Robert Frost. Copyright © 1964 by Lesley Frost
Ballantine. Copyright © 1969 by Henry Holt and Company. Reprinted by
permission of Henry Holt and Company, LLC.
And for the recipes of "Brunswick Stew" and "Smothered Chicken" from
The Williamsburg Art of Cookery by Helen Bullock, published by
The Colonial Williamsburg Foundation and distributed by
Holt, Rinehart and Winston, Inc. Copyright 1938,
© 1966 by The Colonial Williamsburg Foundation.

To the students in Cowell 144AT, Spring, 1972,
our collaborators,
and to Alan Chadwick,
who understands so well the order of things.

THIS BOOK is appropriately dedicated to the students in a course on the chicken, taught in Cowell College, University of California, Santa Cruz, in the spring of 1972. It was they who by their ingenious researches developed the subject in all its range and variety. They are partners in the venture.

In addition we had the assistance of many others, chicken fanciers like ourselves or simply interested and helpful friends. Clarence Boles gave us much useful information. Ed Mannion of Petaluma put his large archive of material relating to the rise and decline of the poultry industry in that city at our disposal. Vernon Miller of Santa Cruz did likewise and added his own sage comments from his long experience of the poultry business. Mrs. Dorothy Steele made a most important contribution.

Wendy Watson's assistance was indispensable. She dispatched a stream of books and articles from one of the great strongholds of chickendom, Iowa.

Mary Holmes, David Stanford (student in the course but an active contributor to chicken lore outside it as well), Barbara Embree, Beth Brown, Gertrude Harris, Frances Rydell, Gerald Grant, Dilip Basu, Bert Kaplan, Richard Randolph, Jasper Rose, Louise Cain, and Donald Clark all made valuable contributions. Many others deserve our gratitude for patiently enduring our odd enthusiasm for chickens.

CHARLES DANIEL
PAGE SMITH

Santa Cruz, 1975

Acknowledgments

viii

Introduction   3   *Contents*

PART ONE   *ix*

1. The Origin(s) of the Chicken   9
2. The Global Chicken   27
3. Aldrovandi   41
4. The Cock   51
5. Cockfighting   69
6. Cockfighting Continued   98
7. The Chicken Apothecary   125
8. The "Folk" Chicken   135

PART TWO

9. The Hen and Her Egg   159
10. The Egg and the Chick   189
11. The Century of the Chicken   204
12. The Decline of the Chicken   232
13. The Industrialization of the Chicken   250
14. The Fall of the Chicken (and Almost
       Everything Else)   264

PART THREE

15. On Keeping Chickens   303

16. The Culinary Chicken (and Egg)   343

    Bibliography   373

    Index   375

ILLUSTRATIONS

"Colonel Mordaunt's Cock Match"   93

Contents

x

Illustrations at the heads of chapters are from the following sources:

Chapters 1, 7, 9, 12, 13, 14, 15, and 16 from *The People's Practical Poultry Book*, by William M. Lewis (New York, 1871).

Chapters 2, 6, and 11 from *Ornamental and Domestic Poultry*, by the Reverend Edmund Saul Dixon and J. J. Kerr, M.D. (Philadelphia, 1851).

Chapters 3, 4, 8, and 10 from *Aldrovandi on Chickens: The Ornithology of Ulisse Aldrovandi* (1600).

Chapter 5 from the Museo Archeologico Nazionale di Napoli.

Oh, who that ever lived and loved
Can look upon an egg unmoved?
— CLARENCE DAY

THE
CHICKEN
BOOK

Something must be said about the genesis of this work, which began, as most things should, with the particular. The authors, it turned out, shared an affection for chickens, kept them, enjoyed them, and wished to know more about them. A reasonable way to learn more about them seemed to be to teach a class on the chicken. Some adventurous if quizzical students were rounded up, and, since the teachers knew very little more about chickens at this stage than the students, the venture was largely a cooperative one. The class was divided into small groups, each of which pursued a particular aspect of that remarkable fowl — the biology and embryology of the chicken, the chicken in art, in song, in folklore and literature, in its historic and economic and anthropological aspects, the history of the chicken, the keeping of ornamental birds, the history of cockfighting, the cooking and eating of the chicken and the egg. The real work of the class centered on these groups who reported their progress periodically. Guest lecturers who were experts on one aspect or another of the chicken assisted us in our efforts.

At the end of the class we had a "chicken festival" — a celebration of the cosmic chicken. The students who had concentrated on the culinary aspects of the chicken and the egg fed us a splendid meal; those who had taken the chicken in music as their topic sang us chicken songs while we festooned a statue of the cosmic chicken with garlands of flowers.

At this point, starting out quite naïvely — it should be said that we scandalized many of our colleagues by teaching so unorthodox a course — we found that we had stumbled upon several important discoveries. First, a splendid way for a scientist (Charles Daniel is a biologist) and a humanist (Page Smith is a historian) to cooperate in a teaching venture is to choose a topic, like the chicken, upon which scientist and humanist — or perhaps better scientist and nonscientist — can focus their attention. In such a venture the boundaries between science and the humanities, if they exist at all, fade into insignificance and it becomes evident that these "disciplinary areas" are simply different perspectives on the same "thing." The result, we feel, is a great sense of liberation, an exhilarating leap beyond the limits of our respective disciplines. In consequence we, and I think most of the students, found the course both delightful and illuminating.

Second, we discovered in the course of our academic excursion that we were, quite unwittingly, following in the footsteps of the great Italian Renaissance natural historian Ulisse Aldrovandi, who, like us, insisted on perceiving the chicken as part of a much larger "order of things." Aldrovandi, in seeing the chicken historically, scientifically, anthropologically, and gastronomically — one might say, naturally — had anticipated us by almost four centuries. We realized that in the intervening period, Aldrovandi's "Universal" consciousness had been replaced by the much narrower consciousness of the expert, most characteristically the scientist and his imitators who insisted understanding was only possible by pulling unities to pieces and examining the pieces. Remarkable achievements followed from this "pulling apart" of the world, natural and human, but it occurred to us that this procedure has also been destructive, and we were confirmed in this feeling by reading a book called, in English translation, *The Order of Things*, by the French philosopher Michel Foucault.

Foucault makes much in his book of our intellectual ancestor, Aldrovandi. Indeed his principal thesis is that need to recover the Italian naturalist's sense of the "order of things," and with it an awareness of the unity and coherence of life, without, meanwhile, abandoning the advantages to be gained by "pulling apart."

So besides being a kind of informal, preliminary blueprint for a truly comprehensive work on the chicken, this book is intended to suggest a new way of thinking — or an old way retrieved — and a new way of teaching in order that that which is divided (including, please God, the chicken) may once more be made whole.

PART ONE

PART ONE

T<small>HE</small> R<small>EVEREND</small> E<small>DMUND</small> S<small>AUL</small> D<small>IXON</small>, rector of Intwood-with-Keswick, wrote in the introduction of his *Treatise on the History and Management of Ornamental and Domestic Poultry*, published in London in 1849, "Poultry has been too much undervalued as a means of study and a field of observation. Insignificant, and, to us, valueless wild animals, brought from a distance, about whose history and habits we can learn little or nothing, are received with respectful attention by men of education and ability, are embalmed in spirits, treasured in museums, and portrayed by artists; but a class of creatures inferior to few on the face of the earth in beauty — useful, companionable, of great value in an economical point of view — are disregarded and disdained.

"It is possible," Mr. Dixon continued, "that any one claiming to be considered as an educated gentleman, may be thought to have done a bold thing in publishing a book on Poultry, and giving his real name on the title page." The author of the most authoritative earlier work on chickens, Dixon pointed out, had "only ventured to meet the public criticism under the shelter of an assumed title."

Mr. Dixon was especially interested in what might be learned about the development of "organic life" by studying the chicken. In addition "the history of the animated races now inhabiting this planet" was "closely connected with the creatures we retain in domestication, and can scarcely be studied so well in any other field. Poultry living under our very roof, and, by the rapid succession of their generations, affording a sufficient number of instances for even the short life of man to give time to take some cognisance of their progressive succession, — poultry afford the best possible subjects for observing the transmission or interruption of hereditary forms and instincts."

Mr. Dixon's observations provide an appropriate introduction to this study of the chicken. The origins of the domestic fowl (*Gallus domesticus*, as the Romans named it) go back tens of thousands of years. Charles Darwin, observing the Red Jungle Fowl of southeast Asia, identified it as the progenitor of the modern barnyard chicken. Some present-day archeologists assume the time of domestication to be in 3000 B.C. and, following Darwin's lead, the place India, or the Indus valley. Others prefer Burma and others the Malay Peninsula. There is evidence that chickens were known in Sumer in the second millennium and the Sumero-Babylonian word for the cock was "the king's bird."

The remarkable similarity in appearance between the wild jungle fowl and the domesticated game bird, and the obvious differences in appearance between the latter and many other breeds of chicken, raise the strong possibility that other wild birds, such as the grouse and some relatives of the now extinct dodo, may well have been involved in the development of the various breeds of domestic chicken. This at least was the conjecture of Dixon, who, after discussing the theory of Erasmus Darwin, father of Charles, that the Red Jungle Fowl was the ancestor of the domestic chicken and commenting on the absence of fossils of chickens that would make it possible to trace their evolution, gave it as his opinion that "even subspecies and varieties are much more permanent, independent, and ancient, than is currently believed at the present day." Dixon opted for the notion of "distinct species . . . produced by a Creative Power."

J. J. Kerr, M.D., Dixon's American editor, gave it as his opinion, based on a careful reading of Dixon (who, incidentally, made no such claim), that the keeping of poultry was "coeval with the keeping of sheep by Abel, and the tilling of the ground by Cain. . . ." In Dr. Kerr's view it was to Gomer, son of Japhet, who took his surname from the cock, "that Western Europe stands indebted for a stock of Fowls from the Ark itself."

What is perhaps most striking about Dixon's hypothesis is that there is a growing feeling today that domestic chickens have, indeed, had a multiple origin rather than all being, as Darwin maintained, descended from the Red Jungle Fowl. Recently John Morepark has argued that four species of jungle fowl have contributed to the modern bird — the Java, the Ceylon, the Jungle Grey, and the Jungle Red. Morepark's experiments have indicated that these four strains are not simply variations on a single species — the Red Jungle Fowl — but are distinct species between whom interbreeding is almost impossible. Thus was born what cockfighters today claim to have been the human race's oldest spectator sport. (They are probably right, too. Although cockfighting is illegal today in almost every country of the world, it continues, in defiance of courts and police, to be one of the most deep-rooted as well as most ancient entertainments of the race.) It is likely that female game birds were, at some time in the early history of man, perceived as a source both of meat and of eggs. Men discovered that by removing from the nest eggs that they did not wish to have hatch (or that they simply wished to eat), they could induce the female jungle fowl to lay additional eggs and, indeed, to continue to lay eggs through an extended laying season.

The various species of birds are identified by the molting pattern of the tail feathers. In the subfamily of the Phasianidae (pheasant) the molt is centrifugal — the feathers molt in order from the center to the outside. The molt of the second subfamily is centripetal — the feathers molt from the outside inward. In the third family, the birds molt from the third pair of feathers outward and inward alternately. And in the fourth family the molt is from the sixth pair of feathers outward. The tail molt in the chicken or fowl (*Gallus domesticus*) is from outside to inside. In this respect it is similar to several species of pheasants, differing primarily in the fact that it has a comb (hence the name "gallus").

The major distinctions between Eastern and European chickens lie in the color of eggs, size and shape of comb, rate of maturity, and color of shanks (legs) and bone. The pea comb is Asian and is dominant over the single comb. Birds with feathered shanks are Asian in origin. Asian birds are also often characterized by rumplessness (the lack of the last segments of the spinal column). The lobes of the ears of European chickens are commonly white, while those of Asian fowl are generally red.

There are four principal species of chicken in India and southeast Asia. *Gallus gallus* is found from northwest India through Cambodia and down to Sumatra. Its eggs are buff-colored. *Gallus lafayetti* is found only in Ceylon and lays spotted eggs. *Gallus sonnerati* makes its home on the Indian peninsula and lays spotted or plain white eggs. Most wild jungle fowl lay plain white eggs, as do their first cousins, birds of the present day. The feather-shanked birds of China and the East, especially the Cochin China, are very heavy-bodied, slow to mature, and conspicuously lacking in wing length and flying capacity. It seems clear they are the result of centuries of selective breeding.

In sharp contrast to the jungle fowl of India, breeds of Asiatic fowl developed that were heavy and dark-boned. Such birds were (and are) found throughout the Asian subcontinent and on the islands of the Pacific. The set breeds of chicken were domesticated very early in China and much later in Japan. The spread of the jungle fowl from the Indian subcontinent to the Mediterranean basin was apparently through military and commercial contacts between those two regions of the ancient world. When Persia conquered India in the fourth century B.C. it acquired from the Indians an interest in cockfighting and an attendant concern with raising chickens for meat and eggs.

From Persia cockfighting (and chickens) spread, in turn, to Greece, and finally to Rome. The Greeks were familiar with cockfighting. Homer speaks of cocks as models of courage and hardihood, and the Greeks seem to have developed a taste for chickens as food as well as enjoying their eggs. In the *Phaedo*, as the hemlock moves along his limbs, Socrates reminds Crito, "We owe a cock to Aesculapius."

In Egypt we find mention of chickens as early as the Second Dynasty. Ikhnaton's "Hymn to the Sun," written in the early fourteenth century B.C., refers to the chicken in one of its stanzas. In the annals of Thutmose III a record of tribute from the East reads: "Lo! four birds of this land, which bring forth every day." A scene in the tomb of Rekhmara at Thebes, which apparently depicts the giving of tribute, shows among other animals a cock. Since there seem to be no subsequent references to chickens until 50 B.C. there have been conjectures that chickens were introduced briefly into Egypt, perhaps as a sacred royal bird, and thereafter disappeared. But references in Greek writings of the fourth century B.C. to the fact that the Egyptians kept chickens and, moreover, that they were able to incubate large numbers of eggs, seem to refute this idea completely.

Indeed, it was no accident that Egypt, like ancient China, was a mass society which mastered the technology of large-scale incubation. Some four thousand years ago the Egyptians invented incubators capable of hatching as many as ten thousand chicks at a time. Undoubtedly there was a relationship between the huge labor force required to build the pyramids and the organization and mass production of food — in this case, chickens. Similarly the Chinese may well have learned to incubate large numbers of eggs in order to feed the workers who built the Great Wall of China.

The Egyptians built incubators of clay brick in which fires were kept burning by an attendant who, without any kind of thermometer other than his own skin, adjusted constantly burning fires to maintain the temperature at the level required for incubation of the eggs (around 105 degrees Fahrenheit). Not only were eggs incubated and hatched in these structures in large numbers — ten or fifteen thousand at a time — they served as brooders to keep the young chicks warm until they were ready to fend for themselves. This process of incubation was one of the most remarkable technological accomplishments of the people who built the pyramids; it is only in the last sixty years that modern incubators have been built that could incubate more eggs and incubate them better.

What is interesting about the Egyptian incubators, aside from their technical sophistication, is, of course, the social and economic arrangements that made both practical and desirable to the Egyptians a method of raising chickens so radically different from any employed elsewhere in the ancient world. Egypt was probably the first urban, mass society in history, and it is clear that the consciousness which conceived large-scale irrigation projects and organized the labor forces that constructed the pyramids and monuments of the middle dynasties created also a mass food source. In a sense, the development of Egypt foreshadowed modern technological society, where people must be organized and social arrangements rationalized in order that the state may carry out vast collective projects.

Specialization and technology thus appeared in Egypt millennia before they established themselves elsewhere in the world. Egyptian incubators were the accomplishment of a social and political order in which the mass production of food was already highly organized. To incubate ten or fifteen thousand eggs at a time requires that very large flocks of chickens already be available and that the methods of procuring and identifying fertile eggs be far more advanced than the mythology-science that flourished in Greece and later Rome. There must, in addition, have been well-established procedures for caring for large flocks, collecting and distributing the eggs, and marketing those birds sold for meat. When we recall that fewer than fifty years ago a flock of three or four thousand hens was a large-scale enterprise in the United States and western Europe, we will get some notion of the degree of organization and technological skill reached by the Egyptians long before the Christian era.

The Egyptians may have been no match for the Greeks in the area of abstract thought and speculation, but they were clearly their superiors in the practical aspects of agriculture and animal husbandry. One Greek author wrote of the Egyptians: "Among the Egyptians there is a large supply of chicks. For there the hens do not incubate their eggs, but they warm the eggs in ovens, with heat applied gradually so that with marvelous skill and dispatch the chicks are produced within a few days [wrong, of course] and raised; they sell them not by numbers but by the measure."

If the Persians taught the Greeks the pleasures of cockfighting, it was doubtless from the Egyptians that they acquired breeds developed for meat and eggs.

From Greece, the chicken spread to Rome and there, it might be said, it came into its own. Not only was it domesticated and bred on a greater scale than anywhere else in the Mediterranean world, it was a central creature in religious rituals.

When the Romans conquered Britain, they brought chickens with them, most notably a five-toed bird which was apparently the ancestor of the English Dorking. But they also found domestic fowl already there, for Julius Caesar notes in his *Gallic Wars:* "The inland parts of Britain are inhabited by those whom fame reports to be natives of the soil. They think it unlawful to feed upon hares, pullets, or geese; yet they breed them up for their diversion and pleasures."

Whether the Greeks were introduced to chickens by the Persians or the Egyptians or both, poultry made up an important element in their life. It was said of Socrates that when Alcibiades asked him why he did not turn out his shrewish wife (the same wife whose naggings were reputed after all to have made him philosophical about life), Socrates replied, "Why don't you drive out hens that are noisy with their wings?" When Alcibiades answered, "Because they lay eggs," Socrates replied, "A wife bears children for me." And it was Plato, the student of Socrates, who defined man as "a biped without feathers." When Diogenes, the leader of the Cynics, brought a plucked cock to the Academy and asked Plato if this were not his "man," Plato revised his definition: man was a biped without feathers and with broad nails. Still not a very satisfactory description, one might think;

but many philosophers have made the attempt without much greater success.

By the sixth century B.C. the Greeks were using chickens for religious purposes and for cockfighting, and by the third century B.C. they had apparently produced breeds of chicken in whom both flying and fighting were subordinated to egg laying qualities and to meat, although the strains of fighting bird were still carefully maintained.

It was apparently a common practice at this time to offer a cock or a hen as a sacrifice to Aesculapius, the god of medicine, to ward off disease, to thank Aesculapius for a recovery, or on one's deathbed. Only hens with black legs, black beaks, and unequal toes were permitted. Chickens were also sacred to Hercules and his last wife, Hebe, the daughter of Jove, and hens were maintained in the temple of Hebe and cocks in the temple of Hercules. A river flowed between, and the birds were kept separate until the males "at their time . . . stimulated with lust, flew across the river and after they had impregnated the females, they returned to their god and to their purified dwelling, purged by the river that ran between by which each sex was divided."

Aristotle was the premier student of the chicken, as of so many other aspects of the natural and human world. And as in almost every field of learning, Aristotle's observations of the chicken were taken as irrefutable truth by philosophers of subsequent ages. To Aristotle belongs the honor of having performed the first experiment in embryology by opening a hen's eggs at each day of their incubation and describing the development of the embryos.

Aristotle's writings on the chicken are a characteristic combination of close observation and wildly inaccurate conjecture. Certainly he was an accurate observer when he wrote, "The chickens crow when the males have won a fight; their crest and tail are erected so that it is not easy to tell whether they are females or not. Sometimes also small spurs grow out on them." The Roman philosopher Julius Alexandrinus confirmed Aristotle, noting, "I have myself seen some hens now and then who have taken the spirit of the males, and having once experienced victory over the cocks, have grown accustomed to mount the males to coition, in fruitless attempt, of course, but one to which they nevertheless grow accustomed."

If the chicken was important in Greek culture it reached its apotheosis in Rome. There, as food, as a sacred bird, as medicine, as the subject of philosophical inquiry, the chicken had no serious rival. Among the Latin authors, Columella, a first-century writer on agriculture, deals at greatest length with the chicken in his *De re rustica* (*Of Rural Matters*). The *Oxford Encyclopaedia* says of him that his "Latin is facile and elegant," and his information "surprisingly accurate."

Pliny the Elder, A.D. 23–79, who was a friend of the Emperor Vespasian, wrote an encyclopedic work on natural history — *Historiae naturalis* — which is a fascinating compilation of information and misinformation. He, like Columella, had much to say about the chicken, until the curiosity of the scientist drew him to the erupting Vesuvius, where the smoke and gas asphyxiated him.

Varro (circa 116–27 B.C.) was the father of Roman natural history, a legate of Pompey. Later, after Pompey's defeat, he was reconciled to Caesar, who made him director of the public library. His output of writings was estimated at 620 volumes, surely a record, and he had, not surprisingly, a good deal to say about the chicken in *De re rustica*.

The writings of Columella, Pliny, and Varro mark a substantial advance over the Greeks in accuracy and systematic observation. Their work indeed calibrates the difference in the consciousness of the dominant cultures of the ancient world.

Columella took note of the popular breeds of fighting cocks — the Rhodian, Chalcidian, and Median. When the hens of these breeds, who were indifferent mothers, laid eggs, their owners placed them "under their local hens and raise the chicks hatched from them." Columella himself preferred "nostrum vernaculum" ("our common sort") for such practical purposes as meat and egg production. "But the Adriatic hens [apparently Bantams]," he wrote, "are small indeed; but they lay every day. They are ill-tempered, and frequently kill the young. And they are of all sorts of colors." Columella had special praise for those breeds that had five toes and white ears, a characteristic of the modern breeds of Dorking and Spanish, suggesting the origin of those birds.

"Hens," Varro wrote, "are of three kinds: country-villa hens, rural, and African." Varro also advised that "the eggs you place under them [hens] should be rather those of older hens than of pullets."

There was certainly much that was fanciful in ancient accounts. Pliny, for example, reported hens that laid "sixty times, some once a day, some twice, and others so much that they become exhausted and die." Pliny was apparently speaking of gamecocks when he observed: "Of chickens, some are born only for battle and constant fighting and have thus ennobled their native lands of Rhodes and Tanagra. . . ."

There is general agreement among all ancient writers that the frequent handling of incubating eggs was to be avoided. Nevertheless, Florentinus instructed the farmer to turn the eggs each day "so that they may be warmed equally" by the heat of the hen. More gratuitous advice could hardly have been given. The hen herself takes care of this chore better than any human intervenor could do. She turns her eggs approximately three times a day with her beak and she certainly does not need any assistance in doing so. One wonders how many indignant hens had to suffer presumptuous interference by their owners as a result of Florentinus's advice. Fortunately, farmers seldom read philosophers; thus we are probably safe in assuming that the great majority of hens set in peace. Only those few whose masters had scholarly pretensions were disturbed in their uxorious duty.

The unfortunate hen whose master had studied such authorities as Varro and Columella must have been kept in a constant state of agitation, not to say fury, because both writers declared that fresh straw must frequently be placed under the setting hen to prevent the growth of lice "and little creatures of this kind which do not allow the hen to rest." The fact is the hen's rest was much more threatened by officious experts than by lice. Indeed, with so much interference by chicken-raisers it is a wonder that any eggs hatched at all and that the hens, their competence so called into question, did not simply abandon their nests with an angry cluck, suggesting to their masters that they hatch the damned eggs themselves. Undoubtedly many hens did just that.

Among the Romans much attention was given to the proper selection of eggs for incubation. A prudent farmer chose a steady, experienced hen of proven reliability to be the mother. She had also, of course, to be in the mood for motherhood — that is, broody. Columella thought, wrongly, that the eggs to be placed under a hen should be no more than a day or two old. Actually, a hen can reliably hatch eggs that are as much as three weeks old.

Among a number of examples of fable or fancy accepted as fact by the classical authors perhaps one will suffice. Aristotle declared that hens in "a sort of ritual" sprinkle themselves and their eggs with water after they have laid their eggs. Theophrastus affirmed the same story, as did Pliny; but all that can be said about the tale with confidence is that none of those famous philosophers and naturalists had ever seen a hen sprinkle herself and her eggs with water, nor has any other observer.

The ancients, and doubtless their predecessors as well as their successors, placed wooden troughs or baskets for the hens to lay their eggs in. Apuleius in his *Metamorphoses* calls out, " 'Hey there, boy, get a basket for the hens to lay in and put it in the corner where it is usually put.' When the boy had done as he was ordered, the hen refused to go to her nest. . . ." Very henly behavior, it might be said! The ancients had also discovered the utility of the nest egg (usually made of stone or marble), an egg placed in the nest to suggest to the hen that it was an appropriate place to lay an egg. The power of the nest egg to suggest to the hen both the place for and the laying of the egg raises some fascinating conjectures about the psychology of that infinitely mysterious bird.

Ancient writers, among them Varro, believed that in those instances where eggs were not "fecundated" or fertilized by a cock, the hen "conceived" from the wind. Such eggs were called by the Greeks, in consequence, *hypenemia oa* or wind-eggs. Albertus Magnus, the thirteenth-century theologian and editor of Aristotle's works, wrote that zephyrean eggs were conceived in the autumn when the south wind "opens the bodies of the birds, moistens and fecundates them." Pliny, on the other hand, had believed that infertile eggs were conceived "by a mutual imagination of lust among themselves," as well as, on occasion, dust. Aristotle also believed that an infertile egg could be made fertile if the hen would copulate with a cock after the egg was formed in the ovary, but before it changed from yellow to white, or before the albumin had surrounded the yolk — a reasonable enough supposition.

The Roman natural historians advised farmers to collect fertile eggs and keep an account of their number. Only, in their opinion, odd numbers of eggs should be placed under a hen following the theory of Pythagoras, who placed the *summum bonum*, or greatest good, in unequal numbers. There remained the question of the number of eggs that a hen could best incubate and care for. Florentinus said not more than twenty-three; Varro and Pliny cast their vote for twenty-five as the maximum number. Columella was closer to the mark in advising that no more than fifteen eggs be placed under a hen in her first laying period of the year in January, no fewer than nineteen in the second period in March, and twenty-one thereafter.

The distinction between those hens raised for the production of eggs and those raised for meat goes far back. Pliny wrote, "The people of Delos began to fatten hens, whence arose the revolting practice of devouring fat birds basted in their own gravy." And Cicero noted also that "at Delos at the time of its prosperity a number of people were in the habit of keeping large numbers of hens for trade purposes. These poultry keepers used to be able to tell which hen laid an egg by merely looking at it."

The practice of fattening hens just for the table was looked down upon by most Romans and taken as a measure of the decadence and effeminacy of the Delians. Indeed, in 161 B.C. a law was passed which forbade "the serving of any fowl except a single hen not fattened for the purpose." This law remained on the books for centuries, but it is clear that many farmers fattened hens in spite of it. Martial wrote: "The hen is easily fattened with sweetened meal; it fattens also in the dark. Gluttony is ingenious."

Cocks were caponized, or castrated, very early and Pliny wrote that the way to evade the sumptuary laws "was discovered by feeding cocks also with foods soaked in milk; in this way they are much more acceptable. To make them fatten quickly, they were placed in small cages so that their heads and tails protruded at each end so that their dung would not foul the cage and their motions were confined and they could do nothing but eat." According to Varro, some farmers fattened hens with wheat bread soaked in wine; "they grow fat and tender in twenty days." Varro wrote that birds were also stuffed with paste balls made from barley flour and flaxseed. Another authority recommended lizard fat mixed with barley meal and cumin seed, adding that "with this food men also grow so fat that they burst."

The Roman philosophers also agreed on what all modern manuals on chicken-raising affirm: that year-old or two-year-old hens are best for laying, take the best care of their eggs, and are the most skillful and competent mothers. Varro and Aristotle agreed that hens laid all year around with the exception of two months in the winter. Some hens lay even in those barren months of midwinter.

Much attention was given to the cackling of the hen who has just laid an egg. Columella, we note, believed that laying an egg pained the hen, a not unnatural assumption when one compares the size of the egg with the orifice from which it emerges. "Hens about to lay indicate that fact by a frequent [sobbing] interrupted by a shrill cry," he wrote. Ambrosius, a contemporary of Aldrovandi, observing the same phenomenon centuries later, speculated that hens sob, "not because the egg in passing out has injured them but because the place made empty when the egg has been laid has received cold air. Thus when they void urine the bladder, while empty, receives some air which gives them pain." The fact is that hens rarely announce their intention to lay an egg and often are silent afterwards so that the famous cackle of triumph is by no means a universal cry.

The Latin naturalists all agreed that a plentiful supply of fresh water is essential to the health of the birds. Columella stated that henhouses should be regularly fumigated and cleared of manure. Oregano in the drinking water helped to save the hens from getting the pip. Garlic and onions were popular ancient remedies for sick chickens. Garlic boiled in human urine and used to wash off the hen's head, "taking the greatest possible care that none of the liquid flows into the hen's eye," was another treatment. Pteriasis was an affliction of mites and fleas and this was best cured by the ashes remaining from the manufacture of lye soap. For sore eyes cocks and hens were to have their eyes bathed in mother's milk. For diarrhea a handful of meal, moistened with wine and made into little balls, was recommended; for hens weak from setting, dried grapes and the cooked egg whites. Constipated chicks should have their anuses opened with a feather.

Hawks were the classic enemies of chickens, and Columella advised farmers to have ample yards covered with nets to keep out the predatory birds.

The specifications given by Varro for building a henhouse are worth repeating for they are as sensible and practical today as they were in the first century B.C. He recommended that three adjacent chambers twelve feet square and twelve feet in height should be built to form an entire building for some two hundred birds. It should face east and in the middle chamber a seven-foot door should be cut. Facing the door should be a fireplace with ducts leading to the two adjoining chambers. Each room should be divided into floors or lofts; the first floor seven feet above ground level, each pair of floors then a foot apart with four feet between the top floor and the ceiling (this would allow for only two floors by my calculations). The lofts should have small windows on the east side to serve as an opening for light and as a means of access to the birds when they went to roost at night.

Once the birds had gone to roost, all the windows should be shut "so that the birds may remain in greater safety." The walls should be so thick that nesting places may be cut in them for the hens to lay eggs or hatch their chicks. Alternating small wicker baskets can be fastened to the walls for the hens to lay in but there must be perches or "vestibules" before each nest so that the hen can step easily into her nest and not have to jump down, thereby breaking her eggs. From each nest there should be a plank for the hen to descend to the floors and these "should be roughened a little with steps formed on them so that they are not slippery. . . ."

The houses should be kept well plastered at all times "so that cats or snakes may have no access to the birds and that similarly harmful pests may be excluded." The birds should not roost on a floor since dung cakes on their feet and, according to Varro, causes gout. But they should have sturdy perches, rather square than round so that they can get a better purchase on them with their feet. The perches should be a foot above the floors and two feet from each other.

The ancient writers differed on the proper size of the poultry houses and the number of chickens a particular-size house could accommodate. A less ambitious scheme than Varro's involved two smaller coops ten feet long and five feet wide, with fenced-in runways where the chickens could exercise and take dustbaths during the day. The runs should be open to the south to get as much sun as possible during the winter and have ample shade to protect the chickens from "the fierce heat of summer." As the recommendations suggest, chickens are very vulnerable to extremes of heat and cold. Young chicks will die from relatively brief exposure to the direct rays of the sun. Black chicks will die first, since they absorb the sun's heat more rapidly. Adult birds will, on hot days, pant like dogs with their beaks open, looking utterly miserable.

Florentinus recommends a portico made of poles

and cross-members covered with vines and roofed with shingles or tiles, and there is general agreement that every properly equipped area for chickens needs dust and ashes for the chickens to "bathe" in. Sulfur, asphalt, and pitch should be used to clean the hen-houses and the hens themselves.

The writings of the Roman naturalists on the chicken represented a considerable advance over the speculations of the Greeks, and many of the Roman prescriptions are as useful today as when their authors first made them. It was in the classical world that the chicken first became an object of scientific scrutiny rather than a taken-for-granted resident of the barnyard.

Tᴴᴇ ꞯᴜᴇꜱᴛɪᴏɴ of the distribution of chickens
throughout the world and the roles they play in various cultures is one that falls most appropriately into
the discipline of anthropology.

We have already discovered references to chickens
in ancient India, in China and the Far East, as well
as in Egypt and the Mediterranean basin. The
Brahma, Cochin, and Langshan are the three most important Asiatic breeds, followed by the Malay, Aseel,
and Black Sumatra. The Rose Comb Black Bantam
also originated in the East. It is the smallest of all
fowl (there are even miniature Bantams), while the
Brahma is the largest domestic fowl. Although biologists and anthropologists have argued that *all* domestic fowl originated in the Asiatic breeds, most such
statements have a defensive tone about them. In modern times, since, say, the fifteenth century, Asiatic
breeds have been deliberately crossed with various
European breeds but there is no solid evidence that
the chicken in the earliest stages of its development
as a domestic fowl originated exclusively in Asia. The
exception would, of course, be the game bird, who, it
is perfectly clear, had either one (or four) common
ancestors in the area of India, Java, and Malay and
was carried throughout the world for the primary if

not exclusive purpose of providing a sporting spectacle for men of all races and nations.

Chickens have also been found on islands scattered across the Pacific Ocean. Captain Cook's expedition observed pigs, dogs, and fowl on all the inhabited islands. The chickens "roamed about at pleasure through the woods, and roosted on fruit-trees." In Tahiti tradition had it that fowls had inhabited the islands as long as the people. They were made, Cook's men were told, by the god Taarva at the same time men were made. In Hawaii the voyagers were told that when, in ancient times, there was nothing but water where the islands stood, "an immense bird settled on the water and laid an egg, which soon bursting produced the island of Hawaii. Shortly after this, a man and a woman, with a hog and a dog, and a pair of Fowls, arrived in a canoe from the Society Islands, took up their abode in the eastern shores, and were the progenitors of the present inhabitants."

The first explorers to reach the Sandwich Islands found chickens there which were seldom eaten but valued for their eggs. In the words of Cook, "There is only one tame species of birds, properly speaking, in the tropical islands of the South Sea, viz. the common Cock and Hen: they are numerous at Easter Island, where they are the only domestic animals; they are likewise in great plenty in the Society Isles and Friendly Isles, at which last they are of prodigious size; they are also not uncommon at the Marquesas, Hebrides, and New Caledonia; but the low isles, and those of the temperate zone, are quite destitute of them."

The chickens of Polynesia clearly show Asiatic origins. Marquesans call the chicken *kuku* instead of the Polynesian name of *moa*. *Kuku* comes from the Sanskrit. The Marquesans also use the Chinese word *hei* as a name for fowl. The most ancient game known to Tahitians was cockfighting, and the Polynesians had special gods for the sport.

Marquesans believed that a man named Haii had brought chickens to the islands twenty generations earlier. Since *hei* is the Chinese name for chicken the story points very clearly to the Chinese origins of the birds, and some of their physical characteristics confirm this.

In the Easter Islands chickens had great importance. There they were small birds with long legs, similar in conformation to the Mediterranean chickens. Their feathers were used in headdresses and ornamentation, and they were one of five gifts given to especially honored persons. The tale of the arrival of the great benefactor of the island includes the chicken among the list of things he introduced. On Easter Island the chicken was used extensively in magic and in religious rituals. Sorcerers used white cocks to conjure an enemy to death. In the Hawaiian Islands white chickens were also used for divination and other forms of magic.

Anthropologists have argued heatedly and rather inconclusively about whether chickens preceded Columbus to the New World or whether the Spanish and Portuguese brought chickens with them when the explorer Vicente Yáñez Pinzón landed on the coast of Brazil in 1500, followed by Pedro Alvares Cabral.

Certainly there is no substantial evidence to indicate that there were chickens on the Caribbean islands. The early European explorers found no chickens there, and quite clearly introduced them along with the most modern methods of breeding and raising them. "Those [chickens]," Capa wrote, "called 'from Castille,' were with the famous explorers in the island of Gallo, and they increased so that there was an abundance of eggs in all the viceroyalty, which was no small assistance to the traveler and merchant, because of the scarcity of other foods in the Indian towns. The Spanish worked hard to multiply so useful a bird, imposing tribute of chickens and eggs."

With the South American mainland the case seems quite different. The fact is that the first widespread mention of chickens in South America comes scarcely thirty years after Pinzón's original landfall. Considering the relative slowness with which keeping of the chicken had spread from India westward through the Mediterranean and then into northern Europe and Africa and eastward from China to the Pacific islands, it is, as George Carter has noted, most unlikely that the Spanish explorers introduced the chicken to the New World. For one thing, if Vicente Pinzón and Cabral carried chickens with them (and most voyagers did, since the chicken was a good traveler and provided a self-perpetuating supply of meat and eggs on long sea voyages), they would hardly have been willing to part with them, especially in sufficient quantity to have made any impact on so vast a land mass. If they had, with reckless generosity, given up a substantial part of their food supply, the Indians would certainly have had little idea of what to do with them.

We have already assigned the earliest chickens, at least tentatively, to India, the Chinese mainland, southeast Asia, and, by diffusion over sea-lanes, to the Pacific islands. But by the time of the Spanish conquest of Mexico the Incas were thoroughly familiar with chickens and the name of the last Inca, Atahualpa, was the Quechua name for chicken. Thus evidence and common sense are strongly on the side of the "pre-Columbian chicken." The only question that remains (and one that probably cannot be answered with any certainty) is whether the chicken was indigenous to America — that is to say whether birds closely related to the chicken were domesticated by tribes of the Americas or whether they had been brought across the ocean by Polynesian sailors or even, perhaps, by the Egyptians themselves.

In support of the "indigenous chicken" it might be pointed out that grouse and chickens are so closely related as to be almost indistinguishable in their bone structure. Certainly, the South American Araucanas have a decidedly grouselike appearance. In addition the Araucanas bear a striking resemblance to Asiatic breeds. The pure Araucanas are rumpless and melanoid (black in pigmentation). I suspect that chickens were in fact brought to the west coast of South America by venturers whose voyages are unrecorded in any historical annals. These birds may very well have mated with native grouse.

What is most striking of all, and perhaps gives the strongest support to the theory of indigenous South American chickens, is the fact that the Araucanas are unique among breeds of chicken in the world for their blue and green eggs. Moreover they take their name from the ruggedly independent Indians of the Chilean mountains, who remained remarkably free of Western influences until the end of the nineteenth century, when the first Araucana chickens were identified.

Perhaps the last word can be left to José de Acosta, a Jesuit missionary who wrote in 1590: "I must say I was astonished at the fowls which without doubt were kept there even before the coming of the Spaniards, this being clear by the fact that the natives have names of their own for them, calling a hen *gualpa* and an egg *ronto*." A later visitor noted, "In the first accounts we have of the conquest, we frequently hear of hens and the name leads us to believe that they were like our own; this, however, is not so and only the birds of Paraguay and Tucumán were somewhat similar to ours."

In many Indian tribes of the tropical forests of South America, chickens and eggs were used largely for religious and ceremonial purposes and their feathers are valued for ornamentation, especially those of white chickens.

Throughout China, southeast Asia, India, Tibet, and the islands of the Pacific, the chicken has been, for more years than can be counted, of great economic importance for its meat and, above all, for its eggs. Equally, it has been a creature of enormous religious and magical potency. We know that the Greeks and Romans used chickens for purposes of divination. It is less well known that the same is true of the peoples of the Asiatic continent and more particularly southern China and southeast Asia. In many rites bamboo splinters were inserted in the perforations of chickens' bones and the prophecy made on the basis of the angle at which the splinters projected. The Karen people of upper Burma, the Lolo, still use this form of divination. Other forms of divination using chickens are common in African tribal life. E. E. Evans-Pritchard, in his study of the magic practices of the Azande in Zandeland in the Sudan, observed the use of the "poison-chicken oracle." In this ritual, a chicken is fed poison and then asked questions. If the chicken dies the answer is taken to be affirmative; if it lives, negative.

Chicken divination also survives among Thai tribes and the Khmer of Cambodia. For them the cock is a sacred bird, a messenger of the gods, and it is for this reason (and his value as a clock) rather than for meat or eggs that chickens are kept by these tribes. In many parts of the world where tribal life persists, eggs are also used for divination, sometimes by dropping them and interpreting answers according to whether or not the egg breaks and sometimes by deliberately breaking an egg and studying its color and conformation. The Khasi of the Assam hills consult the egg oracle for favorable signs before undertaking a hunt, and among the Lolo the witch doctor rubs an ill person with an egg, then breaks the egg and inspects it for any sign of blood or streaks which might indicate the nature of his patient's sickness.

Some of the more primitive people of southeast Asia interbreed domestic and wild (or jungle or game) fowl, believing, as do the Palaung of Burma, that the bones of the jungle fowl are better suited for divination by virtue of having more perforations. For many tribal peoples in southeast Asia there is little to distinguish between domestic and wild fowl. Domestic fowl, like the wild fowl, come and go unconfined, roost in trees, and have, doubtless, the same casual relationship to human beings that chickens had for centuries and perhaps millennia before they were reared "scientifically." The chief distinction between domestic and wild fowl lies in the fact that wild fowl (like all wild birds) do not lay a surplus of eggs. Most commonly they lay only in the spring when they are ready to raise a brood of chicks. The same thing is usually the case with domesticated game hens.

Who first prevailed on domesticated hens to produce a surplus of eggs over and beyond any they intended to set and hatch and by what strange blandishments they brought off one of the most notable coups in history will never be known. A natural assumption would be that having discovered the appealing quality of eggs as food, men began by robbing the nests of baffled fowls, who kept on laying eggs in the hope of accumulating sufficient to set upon and raise a respectable brood. What seems more likely is that particularly fecund hens were encouraged, by selective breeding, to produce more and more eggs, and the laying of these eggs was increasingly divorced from the hatching of baby chicks by actively discouraging or preventing some hens from setting on eggs.

In some tribes chickens are thought to be poisonous to pregnant women. One tribe (the Sema Naga) imposes taboos on the kinds of chicken women can eat.

They cannot eat chickens that "lay here and there in different places" for fear that the women will be promiscuous. Among the Kamar of Chhattisgarh in India women are not allowed to eat chickens, and eggs are forbidden to girls of the Ao Naga after they have been tattooed, apparently on sexual grounds.

In southeast Asia and the islands of the Pacific some native peoples prefer eggs in which the fetus is already formed. In Cochin China (South Viet Nam), where one of the classic breeds of chicken was developed, hens were set to incubating eggs ten days before a feast so that the embryo would be well developed by the time of the festival. The Tagal of Malaysia also prefer "developed" eggs, as do many tribes of the Philippines. One anthropologist has speculated that this preference for brooded eggs may go back to the time of the domestication of the chicken, when eggs were taken from under fowl who were setting on them. Or, in his words, "primitive man may have been afraid to eat them before they had developed into some recognizable form of life. . . ."

Orthodox Hindus are among the few people in the world who regard chickens with active distaste, doubtless both because they are a favorite of their religious rivals, the Moslems, and because of the fact that in many parts of India human waste makes up a substantial part of a chicken's diet. The Ho of Chota Nagpur, apparently as a consequence of their relation to Hindus, refuse to eat chickens or eggs, but do keep birds for religious sacrifices.

The attitude of Buddhism toward chickens and eggs has been ambivalent. The teachings of the Buddha have, it seems, been modified to suit preexisting local customs. A Javanese Buddhist priest writing in the fourteenth century listed birds and eggs as permissible food "according to the holy writings of antiquity," but the lamas of Tibet are forbidden to eat chickens, and many Tibetans eschew eggs as well.

The ban on chickens is based on the fact that "they eat worms, which makes them sinful and their flesh unclean."

How and when the chicken appeared in China is obscure. There is evidence that it was present in the Shang era (c. 1520–1030 B.C.), and it was early on one of the great staples of the Chinese cuisine. As we have already noted, remarkably sophisticated techniques were developed in China for incubating and brooding large numbers of chicks. Eggs were so important as a food that hens were seldom eaten until their laying days were over. Mass-produced eggs were an item of export in China from centuries before Christ down to the twentieth century and the Chinese perfected methods of preserving and shipping eggs that were far in advance of the rest of the world. In those areas of the Eastern world most directly affected by Chinese culture — Manchuria, Mongolia, Formosa, and Korea — chickens and eggs are important both as food and for religious purposes. In Japan the emphasis has been on raising and breeding rare and exotic birds, usually valued more aesthetically than gastronomically. While the Japanese are reluctant to kill and eat birds whose primary value is as pets, they have no prejudice against chickens and eggs. In Japan as in China, chickens have, traditionally, been expensive and thus only rarely available to the poor.

In India and Iran chickens and eggs are dietary staples and the same is true throughout most of the Middle East. Yet here and there prejudice is still found against chicken flesh or eggs as items of diet. In much of the Arabian world, despite the persuasive Moslem faith, eggs are looked down upon by the well-to-do as the food of the poor, and in certain villages in Saudi Arabia along the Red Sea, although natives do keep chickens, apparently for religious or magical purposes, they never eat flesh or eggs. In the oasis villages of the Sahara, chickens are a common sight, but here again some tribes who keep chickens refuse to eat them. The Moors will have nothing to do with chickens at all.

It was undoubtedly from Egypt that the keeping of chickens spread through the northern part of the African continent. From there they spread, perhaps along the Nile and by Sahara caravan and ocean-going transport, west and, more slowly, south. In Africa, as in the tribes of southeast Asia and the Pacific islands, one finds a great variety of attitudes and beliefs in regard both to chickens and eggs. In the words of one anthropologist: "The Walamo of Ethiopia . . . regard fowl as sacred. Pastoralists among the Nyoro keep a cock to wake them in the morning. In the last century the Pondo reared fowl, but only for feathers and head ornaments." The Uzinza of Uganda, the Hangaza of Urundi, the Maji of Ethiopia, the Azande of the Sudan, and the Nyoro all keep chickens for the purpose of augury or prophecy.

Some tribes consider eggs as the excrement of hens, and a German explorer, Eduard Vogel, in the nineteenth century, may have been killed because he violated a taboo against eating eggs. The Kafa of Ethiopia punished women who transgressed a law against eating chicken by making them slaves, and the Walamo went somewhat further by executing anyone who defied the rule against eating sacred chickens.

Obscure as the origins of the avoidance of chickens and eggs as food may be, two things are clear: first, certain recurrent tribal attitudes are remarkably similar in widely separated parts of the world; second, the taboos against eating eggs or chickens rest, primarily, on the sacredness of the chicken and on sexual anxieties, particularly in regard to the eating of eggs by women. What seems to have occurred is a widespread diffusion of taboos originating in an "ur" area,

_The Global
Chicken_

_36_

such as Egypt, and then spreading through adjacent peoples.

But what is not so clear is whether taboos were disseminated with the spread of domesticated fowls or whether they grew up in response to local needs or fears. The argument against the dissemination of classic practices of avoidance is that the picture is so extraordinarily mixed. Tribes living in proximity to each other may have entirely different customs in regard to eating chickens or eggs. Since the keeping of chickens for sacred rituals and/or for food is almost universal, a natural assumption is that certain archetypal attitudes toward the chicken have existed since earliest times. That the hen with her eggs and the cock with his insatiable sexual appetite should be highly potent sexual symbols is hardly surprising. Different practices in regard to the chicken and the egg may have served to accentuate tribal distinctions as well as to inhibit the freedom of women and symbolize masculine domination by the denial to the woman of a desired object.

Of course, chickens and eggs are by no means the only food surrounded by taboos. For tribal peoples food is full of potency, capable of hurt as well as life-giving. To take an obvious example, pork is forbidden to orthodox Jews on the grounds that it is "unclean," a judgment very similar to that of Hindus in regard to the chicken, although the Hindu ban on chicken meat is not as severe as that of the Jews against pork.

Even in the matter of chicken-for-divination or magic versus chicken-for-food, the pattern is strangely mixed. The Vedda of Ceylon do not like to eat chicken, apparently because of the sacred nature of the bird. The Sabimba, a division of the Orang Laut of Malaya, refuse to eat fowl, though other closely related tribes consider it a great delicacy. The Batak of Sumatra very rarely eat eggs, though they keep chickens; and on Buka and Bougainville in the Solomon Islands

chickens are raised in order to have a supply of cocks'
tail feathers, which are used in ceremonial headdresses.

What is fascinating is that in so many tribes where
the eating of chickens or eggs is of very great importance or entirely prohibited, chickens have been
kept for many centuries, probably millennia, thus
leading Berthold Laufer to theorize that their original
use was for magic and divination, and only at a later
stage were their eggs and flesh important as food.
Such speculations are as fragile as eggshells and far
less nourishing than eggs. What is more interesting is
this differentiation of function and the fact that the
chicken in some domesticated form is probably common to more living groups — from the simplest tribal
societies to so-called high cultures — than any other
animal, the dog perhaps excepted.

Among races and cultures for whom the chicken is
an important symbolic bird are the Jews. For some
orthodox Jews the second day prior to Yom Kippur
is the day of the *kapparah* (often *kappores*), or the
atonement. Men use cocks and women hens. In the
words of one writer, "The homes are usually noisy.
The fowls, their legs tied, cluck and crow at the tops
of their voices. It generally happens, too, that a
rooster gets excited and begins to run and fly all over
the house, despite his bound feet, and there follows a
long struggle to subdue him.

"First the fowl . . . is held in the hand and everyone reads selections from certain Psalms, beginning
with the words, 'Sons of Adam.' Then the fowl is cir-
cled about the head nine times, the following being
recited at the same time: 'This is instead of me, this
is an offering on my account, this is in expiation for
me; this rooster, or hen, shall go to his, or her, death
. . . and may I enter a long and healthy life.' " This
rite is followed by the slaughter of the chickens by
the *shochet*, or ritual slaughterer.

The *kapparah* is such a universal ceremony that a person's blank stare is compared to the gaze of the cock at the words "sons of Adam," and a great clamor is often referred to as a *kappores*.

The *kapparah*, which dates back among the Jews to the Gaonic period, has many analogies in tribal societies, ancient and modern, whose members believe that it is possible to relieve human pain or sin by transferring it to an animal or a stick or stone.

The view was widely held that a cock or hen when sacrificed would drive away evil, the cock because his crowing announced the light and evil spirits could not tolerate light; the hen because she shared the magical qualities of the cock. In addition the bright red comb of the cock was considered an anathema to devils. But the image was ambiguous. In Jewish folklore, the devil was usually depicted as having a cock's feet.

In some non-Christian ritual practices, the birds, once the illness or evil had been transferred to them, were chased off into the forest or thrown into a nearby stream to be carried away. The Jews, on the other hand, gave the sacrificial birds to the poor, after having thrown the entrails on the roof to be carried off by carrion birds.

Jews, the Talmud says, had a cock and hen carried before the bride and bridegroom in the marriage procession, "as if to say, Be fruitful and multiply like fowls." The Talmud also told the faithful, "If one sees a cock in a dream he may expect a male child; if several cocks, several sons; if a hen, a fine garden and rejoicing." (An odd conceit, as hens and fine gardens are certainly not compatible.) Polish Jews in medieval times made a cock and a hen fly over the bridal canopy to encourage sexual vigor. The Palestinian Arabs still follow a custom, inherited apparently from the Jews in ancient times, of carrying a cock at the head of a procession designed to produce rain; the cock is encouraged to crow to God for rain.

Presently, the United States and other, European countries who have taken some responsibility, often through the United Nations, for trying to improve the agricultural methods and, thereby, the diets of native populations in "emerging" countries have been trying to break down tribal taboos against the eating of chickens or eggs. Chickens are so rich in protein and so prolific when properly cared for that they have an irresistible attraction for planners. The efforts to promote chickens as food are not, of course, confined to so-called backward, emerging, or developing nations. After World War II, Point-Four planners launched a concerted campaign to try to prevail on the Greeks to consume more chickens. Eggs were a staple of the Greek diet, but the meat of chickens was not popular. American agricultural agents introduced modern methods of poultry management with the result that there was soon a large surplus of meat birds. The Greek government intervened by establishing first one and then two days a week when butchers were allowed to sell only chickens. The result was a substantial increase in the consumption of chickens by the Greeks.

In this preliminary discussion of the "anthropology" of the chicken we have said little about the magical properties of the cock as distinguished from the hen and her egg. That is a subject so vast that it requires a chapter of its own.

Between Pliny and Columella in the first century A.D. and Ulisse Aldrovandi, fifteen hundred years intervened. During this period, the chicken dropped from the consciousness of the learned community in the Western world. Or at least it received no special attention. There were a number of reasons, of course, for the eclipse of the chicken. The classical writers, starting with Aristotle, had, it was assumed, said everything there was to say about that remarkable bird.

Under the influence of Christianity the attention of Western man shifted from the practical and the worldly (which had so preoccupied the Romans especially) to the visionary and unworldly. Science — the careful observation of the natural world — gave way to theology, which concerned itself primarily with "ultimate" matters such as the relation of God to man and the prospects of immortality.

Thus the chicken, that most practical and mundane of creatures, was neglected. But its neglect by the learned and scholarly world made no difference to the chicken. Like its master, the farmer, it went on year after year, decade after decade, century after century, a generation to a year, roughly speaking, for many more than a thousand generations. It went on through its own Dark Ages, laying eggs beyond counting, rewarding uncounted husbandmen generously or meagerly, according to their deserts. One might say it moved from the stage of history to the dimly lit arena of anthropology.

With the advent of the fifteenth century there came an awakening of interest in classical learning, in ancient philosophy (science) and literature. We know the period as the Renaissance and while there were many renaissances, Italy has certainly the best claim to have been the locus of the great intellectual revolution that produced a new kind of human consciousness — a new way of looking at the world and with it a new philosophy (science) which, though much indebted to the philosophy of the ancients, went far beyond it.

One of the exemplars of the new spirit was Ulisse Aldrovandi. The classical tradition of the chicken in Italy made it appropriate that the most comprehensive modern work on that bird should be written by an Italian. Aldrovandi was born in Bologna in 1522. Like all those who have written on the chicken prior to the most recent decades of the twentieth century, he loved chickens and was a patient lifelong observer of them and an indefatigable reader about them in the works of the classical authors. He reported that in his country house he "raised a hen who, in addition to the fact that she wandered the whole day alone through the house without the company of other hens, would not go to sleep at night anywhere except near me among my books, and those the larger ones, although sometimes when she was driven away she wished to lie upon her back." His researches, which extended over decades, were supplemented by paintings which he commissioned from various artists. The stipend which he received as professor of natural history at the University of Bologna was inadequate to support the expenses of his research and more particularly of the publication of his *magnum opus* — a nine-volume treatise on animals — consequently he was forced to make frequent application to patrons, and he was seventy-seven before his first volume was published (1599). Five volumes followed before his death in 1605. Aldrovandi's interests extended far beyond chickens. He was an accomplished ornithologist, and chickens occupied only one volume of a three-volume work on the history of birds. A volume on insects followed, and successive volumes on fish and on quadrupeds were published after his death.

Aldrovandi began his volume on chickens by noting, "No proof is required, for it is clear to all, how much benefit the cock and his wives provide for the human race. They furnish food for both humans who are well and those who are ill and rally those who are almost dead. Which condition of the body, internal or external, does not obtain its remedies from the chicken? . . . The cock and the hen, desirous of generating offspring, make their genus eternal under the leadership of Nature."

Aldrovandi's science, like the science of the ancients, was rather hit-or-miss by present-day standards. The inclination was more to theorize than to observe. Yet where observations were made they were often made with great attention and accuracy. The hen's egg, of course, provided an almost ideal opportunity to view the generative progresses of life. It was clear enough even to a relatively casual observer that a living creature was developing in a chicken's egg and doing so in a progressive fashion over a period of days. A farmer, in the ordinary course of tending his farm, saw eggs broken at various stages of incubation and could readily piece together a rough notion of the development of the embryo. As we have noted, Aristotle systematically opened eggs at successive points in their incubation and described what he saw. Thereafter philosophers mainly preferred to speculate about the development of the chicken embryo. Perhaps this was because it did not occur to anyone that the observations of Aristotle might be improved upon. Indeed, there is little indication that any one looked systematically at the chicken embryo from the time of Aristotle to that of Aldrovandi, who may be said to have revived the study of the egg almost two thousand years later.

In Aldrovandi's treatise he gives an eloquent account of tracing the development of the embryo and compares his observations with those of the man he refers to reverently as "the Philosopher." Doubtless it was as mysterious to Aldrovandi as it is to us that he was treading in his master's footsteps after so long a passage of time and noting phenomena that men had been for many ages willing to accept on authority when they might so simply and easily have made the same observations themselves.

At the end of his experiments with the embryos, Aldrovandi wrote: "All these facts observed by me grew daily more evident as time passed, just as they appeared in the perfected chick. On the twentieth day the shell was broken by the parent hen, and on the twenty-second day the chick came out of the egg of its own accord." Aldrovandi had completed a journey that was, in its own way, as significant as the sailing voyages that for a century past had been carrying European seamen to a New World. The Italian naturalist cannot be given credit for inventing the new age of science but he was certainly among the early scientific voyagers of modern times and he sailed on his own course as stoutly and indefatigably as his countryman Columbus had earlier sailed on his.

Aldrovandi's description of his investigation of the egg, simple and brief as it is, is the most striking part of his often turgid treatise. As the story of a symbolic moment when legend, fable, and ancient authority lost at last their power over the mind of modern man, it deserves a place in every account of the development of modern science. And most appropriately, it was the egg of the humble and familiar chicken that was the subject of Aldrovandi's examination.

Having completed the account of his investigation, Aldrovandi added: "I pass over now that trite and thus otiose . . . question, whether the hen exists before the egg or vice versa. It is stated in the sacred books that the hen existed first. . . . Both time and space prevent me from dwelling longer upon it."

In such cavalier fashion Aldrovandi dismissed the ancient and inscrutable question of which came first — the chicken or the egg. Stated now as a joke, it was once a question so crucial that men staked their lives upon the proper answer, and the proper answer — or the dogmatic answer of the Church — was that the Bible said that God created man and woman and all the creatures of the earth, all the breeds, varieties, and species. The heterodox who argued that the living world began with seeds (and eggs) also professed to find support for their arguments in Scripture, but the "chicken-firsters" held the fort against the sporadic attacks of the "egg-firsters" for centuries.

A major part of Aldrovandi's treatise was concerned with anatomical study of the chicken. Here he was, on the whole, a careful and accurate observer, though it is clear that his principal interest in the anatomy of the chicken was due to the medicinal properties attributed to virtually every portion of the bird, from the windpipe — "helpful to those who urinate in their bedclothes" — to the stones in the gullets of cocks — a remedy for kidney stones. Aldrovandi was especially interested in dissecting the chicken, searching out thereby "the secrets of Nature in order to discover her admirable artifices in generating eggs."

One of the controversies among ancient writers concerned the question of whether cockerels were born of round eggs and hens of pointed eggs (a position held by Aristotle) or whether it was vice versa (a position held by Columella). In this case (as to be sure in others) both sides were wrong. Aldrovandi, reporting this dispute at considerable length, added the one sensible word said on the subject: "Whether males come from long eggs, or whether the contrary is true, is a question on which the chicken raiser himself should be consulted." But the Italian women that Aldrovandi consulted solemnly informed him that "males are produced from long eggs and females from round eggs."

Aldrovandi reported that Italian women left the mother hen to take care of her chicks in her own way (which was certainly wiser than following the dubious prescriptions of scholars). In fact he expressed very well the advantages of the chicken in its natural state. "Under the instruction of Nature," the Italian wrote, "[the chickens] learn that they cannot do these things [dust bathing, eating, etc.] best for themselves in any other way. With Nature's leadership, they seek a quiet place in which to lay their eggs and build nests, and sleeping places for themselves; they make as soft a bed as possible as if they knew that the eggs would easily collide with each other if they laid them on a harder surface. But they show their sharpness of wit . . . no less when they have hatched their chicks, whom they know how to protect by the use of their feathers lest they be injured by surrounding cold or heat." The Italian warned that one hen could nurse no more than thirty chicks. Newborn chicks could, moreover, be placed under another hen if it were done in the first few days and preferably at night when the hen is drowsy and inattentive. (A fact.)

Aldrovandi favored hens with "dusky or reddish, yellow, golden, or even black feathers." White hens were "to be avoided as breeders" because they were "very soft and less tenacious of life." More important, their "shining whiteness" exposed them to attacks by eagles, hawks, and kites. "As among other farm ani-

mals, so with fowl," he wrote; "the best are to be kept
and the worst sold or sent to the table; this can best
be done in autumn when their production ceases."
Hens should be disposed of after three years, cocks
kept as long as they are able to impregnate the hens:
advice as good today as when Aldrovandi gave it. In
his summary of the eating habits of chickens, Aldrovandi wrote, "These animals are omnivorous and there
is nothing that they do not devour and consume, assisted by the fierceness of their nature, to such an extent that not only beside almost all kinds of grain
they enjoy the flesh of all land and water animals.
They do not refrain from even human dung or serpents, scorpions, and poisonous creatures of this kind.
In fact, they sometimes dissolve sand and pebbles in
their own crops. . . ."

Aldrovandi calls the "place where the chickens are
kept" the poultry house — *gallinarium*. A contemporary naturalist, Gilbert Longolius, calls it the barnyard workshop. But Julius Pollux called it a hencoop
and Aristophanes the place "where domestic birds go
to sleep." By Aldrovandi's time the commodious "poultry houses" described by the ancients had shrunk to
structures "quite small [that] scarcely ever hold a
flock, often with great loss of them since a large part
are often shut out at night and are left as prey to
thieves and harmful animals." He noted that "those
who wish to make money from raising chickens can
build a henhouse such as I have described" from Columella or Varro.

He had further advice for the commercially-minded:
"Although every woman knows how to raise chickens
there are none the less some precepts laid down by the
most careful ancient writers on agriculture which are
unknown not only to women but also perhaps to the
learned in these matters. He who wishes to gain profit
from these birds should first choose someone he can
trust. For unless the person who takes care of the hens

keeps faith with his master no profit of the poultry house overcomes the expenses. A foster father of this sort who climbs into the henhouse, collects the eggs, incubates and turns them, will be called the caretaker or rightly guardian of the hens."

Aldrovandi was convinced that hens that laid many eggs without intervening periods of incubation grew ill and died before their time. On the other hand his remedy for broodiness was to draw "a little feather through the hen's nostrils, and by sprinkling it with cold water." He also has a word of warning for the person who purchases eggs for the purpose of incubating them under a hen. He should not be deceived "by the sellers of eggs who often sell wind-eggs [infertile eggs] for fertile ones to the unsuspecting public. The chicken raiser should shun small eggs and select the larger ones of those he sees of which there is a large supply; of these he should first eat one so that from its sweet flavor he can judge the other shares of the semen."

One method of incubation recommended by Aldrovandi was to fill a nest with finely crumbled dry chicken dung, cover the dung with chicken down, and then place the eggs to be incubated on the down with their ends up. Another nest similarly prepared is placed over the first and the two placed in a warm place. After the second day the eggs are to be carefully turned until the twentieth day and on the twenty-first removed from the nests and "the chirping chicks" drawn "gently out of the egg."

When Aldrovandi wrote on the subject in the sixteenth century he described a relatively sophisticated incubator four feet high with three trays, each of which could hold a hundred eggs. The interior of the structure was warmed by an oil lantern of three or four wicks, and the temperature had to be frequently checked by taking out an egg and holding it near the eye to judge its warmth, the eye being the most sensitive organ of the body. After the fourth day the eggs had all to be turned daily "and moved around in the nest as the hen does." (Pietro Crescenti, a contemporary of Aldrovandi, told of a certain region in Italy where there were incubators which held and hatched a thousand eggs at a time.)

In addition to his classical learning and his practical knowledge, Aldrovandi had a remarkable familiarity with exotic breeds. He described chickens found in the "city of Quelim in the kingdom of Magnus . . . clothed with hair like that of a black cat" and "Fuch, a large city toward the East," where, it was reported by a missionary, there were white "wool-bearing chickens." Some chickens had "hairy legs and feet as if shod with boots. . . . Again some have a simple crest, others a double crest, some a tail, others no tail." (The hairy and woolly chickens were doubtless the Chinese Silky, and we know the feather-legged and -footed chickens as Cochin Chinas and Brahmas.)

The admirable Aldrovandi was insatiably curious. He saw the world as a divinely appointed order, an intricate unity fashioned by an ingenious God. Every element of that unity was of significance. It fitted with, complemented, or completed other elements. Medicine, for example, was a mixture of folk practices of religion, magic, and philosophy. Every ailment had a specific, natural remedy. Many, as we shall see, derived from the chicken.

When Aldrovandi contemplated the chicken, he saw it as a fascinating totality, an integral part of that ordered world in which man and chicken both flourished, and both, in their own ways, worshipped the Supreme Master of the Universe.

Aldrovandi, considering the chicken as part of that marvelous universe, recorded everything he could discover about the chicken, its names, its parts, its feathers, its organs; the poems, the myths, the legends that clustered about it; its medicinal uses, its symbolism; how to raise it and how to cook it (and its by-product, the egg). To Aldrovandi there was no hierarchy of importance in the information he collected on the chicken. One could not say, or did not need to say, that a study of the internal organs of the hen was more important or scientific than a recipe for stewing a tough cock. Or question the efficacy of a remedy described by Aristotle.

This "wholeness," this encompassing order of which Aldrovandi was still a part, was the residue of that consciousness which had dominated western Europe since the end of classical times. It was essentially religious, and Christian. The order of things was, to be sure, hierarchical, imitating the divine hierarchy; within that general order every particular subspecies had its appropriate place. One aspect of these lesser orders was not considered more scientific than another — a fable about a chicken might thus be more important than a closely observed "scientific" fact.

In the seventeenth century this unitary view of the "order of things" was dissolved in the acid of scientific skepticism, as represented most dramatically by Descartes' "Cogito, ergo sum." In order to understand the world it was necessary to call into doubt everything that had once been believed. Since naïve faith had held that older world together, it could not withstand the cold "objective stare" of the new science. It fell apart instantly, and on its ruins a new and more ruthless orthodoxy was promptly erected. The new orthodoxy began by breaking the old order into pieces. Only pieces could be understood. In this the new orthodoxy proved more exclusive and dogmatic than the old; Aldrovandi was dismissed as credulous, naïve, and "unscientific."

Wh HILE THE HEN has always been considered primarily utilitarian, the cock has captured men's imagination and been considered a creature of remarkable
beauty and power in itself and of great importance as
a symbol of masculine virility.* Aldrovandi quotes the
story of Croesus, "who sat on a high throne shining
brightly with every kind of ornament" and was bold
enough to ask the great lawmaker, Solon, "whether
he had ever seen a more beautiful sight." To which
Solon, rather indiscreetly, replied that "cocks are
clothed in their natural splendor and with incredible
beauty."

Aelian wrote in the same spirit, "The serpent has a
crest; the cock likewise is endowed with surpassing
beauty." "A most splendid ensign," Pliny said, describing the cock's comb; and Aristophanes in *The
Birds* writes, "Just like the great king he struts along,

---

* In many cultures the word for the male chicken has been the
same as the word for the male sexual member, the penis. Thus it
was quite in harmony with the spirit of the so-called Victorian
era that the name "cock," which was an old Anglo-Saxon word
for penis, should have been replaced in general American usage
by the word "rooster," a word which does not even appear in
English dictionaries. It must be said, in their favor, that American
devotees of fighting cocks never showed any inclination to speak
of "fighting roosters," or "rooster-fighting." In most tongues the
word "cock" is remarkably similar: Sanskrit, *kukkuṭa;* Old Slavic,
kokotŭ; Latin, *cucurio* (I crow); German, *Küchlein* (chick); Dutch,
kuiken (chicken). In Old Teutonic the word is spelled *kok;* in
African Senga, *kuku;* in Wisa, *koko;* in Kaffir, *kuku.*

the only bird that has a straight crest on his head."

Only the lion rivaled the cock in majestic power and importance. The Greeks and Romans (and later Christians) believed that the cock could overawe the lion. So potent was he that men smeared with a broth made from cocks, with a little garlic added, would not be touched by lions and panthers.

The question of why the lion, the bravest of beasts, himself "solar" — that is, drawing power from the sun — should fear the cock was one that had caused extensive debate among the ancients. Aldrovandi, recapitulating the various opinions (whether it was the crest or the crow or the cock's spurs that terrified lions), quoted Lucretius's statement that "rabid lions cannot stand before or look at [a cock]; so immediately they think of flight, doubtless because there are certain seeds in the body of the cock, which, sent into the eyes of lions, dig into the pupils and cause harsh pain; fierce as they are, the lions cannot endure it." St. Ambrose, an early Church Father, wrote, "The lion fears the cock, especially a white one."

The awesome basilisk was reputed to be so struck with fear at the crow of a cock that it simply died of terror. A traveler journeying through "the immense wilderness of Cyrene" inhabited by the basilisk was advised to take a cock with him to keep the monster at a safe distance.

The Egyptians sacrificed cocks — sometimes black and sometimes white — to Osiris. Mithra, or Mithras, god of the sun and of light, had a cock as his symbol, as had Ahura Mazda, out of whose worship Mithraism developed in the second century B.C.

Among the Greeks, it was common to sacrifice a white cock to Jove. The philosopher-geometer Pythagoras warned his followers against eating cocks because of the birds' benefactions to mankind and he was reputed to love white cocks so much that whenever he saw one he greeted it like a friend and kept it with him.

In Greece, as well as, later, in Rome, the sexuality of the cock was perhaps its dominant characteristic. A cock was frequently given as a gift of love from an older man to a boy he wished to seduce. The extreme erectness of the cock, straining upward, has suggested to many besides the Greeks the erectness of a tumid penis. The Greeks indeed went so far as to represent in sculptured relief a cock whose neck and head were depicted as a phallus, thus making the symbolism inescapable. There is such a representation of the cock in the Vatican — "a bronze bust the back of whose head has the comb and wattles of a cock, which the front is an erect phallus." The statue is apparently in celebration of the life force, of sexuality as "the Savior of the World," a form of divine power. The intention is not pornographic but religious.

The sexual aspect of the cock was ubiquitous. According to ancient writers crystalline stones called *alectorii* were found in the stomachs of cocks and capons. One such stone was described as smaller than a cherry, weighing 28 carets and spherical in shape. Sometimes they were black, sometimes black and white. Such a stone had magical properties that enabled its owner to have whatever he wished. In the words of a classical writer on minerals: "This stone makes the orator eloquent, constant, pleasing to all in everything. This makes one vigorous for love. It is useful to the wife who wishes to please her husband. In order to produce so many good things, let it be carried encased in a ring." It made gladiators invincible, quenched thirst, and made women attractive to men.

Pliny reports that the right testicle of a cock bound with the skin of a ram was a powerful aphrodisiac. On the other hand, the testicles of a fighting cock smeared with duck grease inhibited "venery." The potency of a cock's testicles was such that if a woman ate them after intercourse she greatly increased her chances of becoming pregnant.

The plant called "cock's comb" or "cock's crest" by the ancients was considered an aphrodisiac "because it looks like a cock's crest, all the more since the cock, a most salacious bird, is rendered unfit for copulation when its crest is removed." (A quite erroneous notion, incidentally.) Cockspur, also called *gallitricus*, was an aromatic plant. Cocksfoot was an herb, noted by Apuleius, whose top was divided like a cock's foot. This herb, when crushed, was thought to stop the flow of blood from a wound most effectively.

There are on Greek sarcophagi numerous representations of cocks as family pets, pets of children as well as adults; of cocks being carried, stroked, and caressed and fed with grapes. The association of cocks with grapes is frequent and again suggests the Dionysian element. There are also a number of scenes of cockfights on Greek tombs. The implication seems to be that the dead one has, like the cock, conquered death. E. R. Goodenough is confident that such cocks symbolize the soul of the departed. The same theme carries over into Roman symbolism. A mosaic floor on the Isle of Wight shows a man with the head and wattles of a cock about to ascend a ladder, presumably to "the inner shrine," or heaven. "It appears," Goodenough writes, "as an offering to the dead, as an object borne by the dead on the way to Hades, under a table with the offering of the mystic mirror, within the vine, poised in fighting, in the arms of a flying Victory, or as an absolute symbol with little setting. . . . I cannot look at the [temple] plaques," Goodenough adds, "with their eagerness, without thinking that these symbols witness the direct hope of the people who used them, hope for immortality, and it is this meaning for the cock which has steadily been emerging out of the usages."

Then there are Socrates' last words that we have already noted: "O Crito, we owe a cock to Aesculapius. Pay it and do not neglect it." Was not Aesculapius, in this context, the healer of souls after death and the corruption of the body? Thus, the sacrifice to him of the cock as a symbol of life hereafter.

So the cock embodied three of the most powerful themes in nature — sexuality, the sun, and the theme of resurrection. It is small wonder that the cock has been among the most powerful and ambiguous symbols in the history of the race. He was, in the deepest sense, a magical bird. Indeed, so awesome were his powers that it was thought his crowing would weaken and splinter wood. It followed that someone who wished to make a fine flute was advised to get wood from an area where the crowing of a cock was never heard and where the trees, in consequence, were sturdy and strong.

For the Romans the cock was the favored creature of Mars. Aldrovandi repeats the story that when Mars was committing adultery with Venus, he set the god Alectryon to guard the door of his bedroom. But Alectryon fell asleep at his post and was, in punishment, changed into a cock charged with perpetually announcing the sunrise.

The cock was also associated with Mercury because of his diligence and watchfulness. Certain representations of the god showed him sitting on a throne, helmeted and crested, holding a cock in his left hand. The cock was also dedicated to Aesculapius, the god of medicine, both as a symbol of vigilance and because from the cock (and hen) "both nourishment and medication suitable for most ills of the body can be drawn." On a marble tablet in the temple of Aesculapius at Rome was reputed to be the following inscription: "God rendered an oracle to Valerius Aprus, the blind soldier, to come and take the blood from a white cock, mix it with honey, and make an eye salve. He was to use it three days on his eyes. Then he saw again; he came and thanked God publicly."

The cock was sacred to Latona, the favored one of Zeus and mother of Apollo and Artemis. In the words of Aelian, "He was in love with Latona, was beside her as she gave birth, and brings about happy childbirths."

The ancients carried on a rather extended and inconclusive debate about whether the song of the cock was melodious or cacophonous, whether it was an expression of the bird's sexuality or of its affinity with the sun. Juvenal and Quintilian discussed the question. The tragic poets often referred to heralds as cocks because they made their announcement stridently. Aldrovandi, mentioning that the cock crows at intervals during the night, notes that "the ancients measured the passage of night and the arrival of days by the cock's crowing when the first sundials had not been discovered. For the beginning of the day commenced from the first inclination of midnight. They called the next point of time the cockcrow because at that time, sensing the light of dawn much before it actually arrives, the cock begins to sing. The third point of time is that when all becomes still, when the birds are silent and men are at rest. The fourth point of time is dawn, when the day is already bright with the risen sun. Thus the second cockcrow comes much before the rising of the sun, as Juvenal mentions when he says: 'Nevertheless, what he does at the crowing of the second cock the nearest merchant will know before day.' The Greeks therefore called the cock 'day-sounding' [*hemerophonos*] since 'he performs the greatest of services to men because they know they must leave their beds when the cock awakens them from a sleep that is often sound.' "

Ovid writes, "Now the light-bringer treads the northern skies and the bird wakes wretched men to their work." Pliny, playing with the conceit that sluggish men would never rise from their beds without the exhortations of "the crested bird," declares that the human race owes all that it has achieved to the cock's song rather than to people's own talents.

Soldiers changed watches by the crowing of the cock, and often they tied a cock to their chariots as a guard, a watchman, a clock, and a symbol of martial spirit.

Cocks were also valued as weather forecasters. The cock was the first to predict rain. He announced its imminence by "an insolent, raucous crowing accompanied by a tireless flapping of the wings."

In Theocritus, Helen of Troy is assured by the twelve Theban girls, "We shall return in the morning when the first singer calls from his nest, lifting his beautiful feathered neck, to sing a new epithalamium of wedding song."

According to Aldrovandi, in the ancient world the only real enemies to the cock and his insistent crowing were the Sybarites, who did not let cocks be kept in their city. "They were," Aldrovandi notes, "a very soft and effeminate people, so delicate that they not only did not allow cocks to be raised in their city but rejected all trades and crafts, such as that of a carpenter, which make a noise." For all subsequent Sybarites, Aldrovandi offers two doubtful remedies for the crowing of cocks. "Pliny promises that the cock will not crow when you place a circle of brushwood around his neck. Albertus says he will be silent if his head and face are smeared with oil." Aldrovandi did not care to vouch for the efficacy of these measures, leaving it to his readers to try the experiment if they wished — and so do the authors of this work.

In addition to those who stressed the cock's affinity with the sun there were those who declared that his song stemmed from his sexual potency. The song was a lovesong: "The bird crows because he is very lusty and has frequent, interrupted slumber; and . . . because his impregnation of the hens is more fertile when he sings." Cicero's explanation of the cock's crowing was much more mundane. Cocks crowed, in his opinion, "when their food has moved down into their crops and been divided and made soft throughout their bodies; then, satisfied and quiet, they begin to crow."

The greatest importance of cocks in the ancient world lay in providing auguries for events to come, most commonly military campaigns. Flocks of birds were maintained at public expense for no other function than, by their behavior and by divination practiced upon their entrails, to foretell the future. Pliny gives a number of examples of the favorable omens deduced from the behavior of cocks. If sacred cocks, coming forth from their coop in the morning, went about eating and, most important, while eating dropped some food from their beaks, the omens were favorable. If they refused to eat, "it was a sad omen." Since healthy cocks emerging from their coops invariably ate, the auguries were, one must assume, almost invariably good. "These [cocks]," Pliny wrote, "daily govern our magistrates; they shut them up in their houses and keep them there; they order battle lines to move or restrain them; theirs are the auspices of all the victories gained throughout the world. These especially rule the earth with their power, and are also with their entrails and guts not otherwise than pleasing to the gods of victory."

The official chicken keeper was a person of great importance. No Roman military leader would enter battle without taking an augury. The chicken keeper was thus summoned and food was thrown to the birds. It seems safe to assume that a wise chicken keeper kept his birds hungry. On at least one occasion, however, we know that the augury on the eve of a battle was unfavorable. When Hostilius Mancinus, about to depart for Spain as consul, called for the chicken keeper and his birds, the pullets flew out of their coop and into the trees, where they evaded capture. The result was that Hostilius was badly defeated by the Numantines. The defeat at Leuctra was foretold to the Lacedaemonians a little before the battle "because . . . the cocks in that place began to crow so lustily that they did not stop. Then the Boeotian augurs said the victory had been won by the Thebans because that bird when conquered is accustomed to keep silent but sings if it has won a victory."

As for the Romans, Pliny wrote of cocks, "They are great Commanders, and Rulers," adding, "These rule our great Rulers every Day: and there is not a mighty Lord or State of Rome, that dare open or shut the Door of his House, before he knows the good Pleasure of the Fowls: and that which is more, the Sovereign Magistrate in his Majestie of the Roman Empire, with the regal Ensigns of Rods and Axes, carried before him, neither sets he forward or recoileth back, without direction from these Birds; they give order to whole Armies to advance forth to Battle, and again command them to stay and keep within the Camp. . . . In one word, these Birds command those great Commanders of all Nations upon the Earth."

Not all Romans were cowed by the auguries. When Claudius Pulcher was about to engage the Carthaginians in the first Punic War, he dutifully consulted the sacred chickens but when the chicken keeper told him that the cockerels would not come out of their coop, he ordered them thrown into the sea, "declaring that as they did not wish to eat, they could drink."

Suetonius tells the story of the emperor Vitellius who, while he was giving judgment at Vienna, had a cock light first on his shoulder and then on his head, which was taken to mean that he could not hold military power by himself. The bird in fact was taken to have predicted the emperor's defeat and death at the hands, as it turned out, of Antonius Primus, who was born in Gaul (hence the cock, *gallus*) and was nicknamed Beccus, cock's beak.

Among the legends involving cocks was that of the young cock which laid an egg in Livia's hand when she was pregnant with Tiberius. Curious as to whether she was to bear a male child or not, she and her servants kept the egg warm by hand until it hatched a cockerel. The bird was taken to portend not only the sex of her unborn child "but also that salaciousness and impudence which [were to make] him notorious."

In view of the ubiquitousness of the cock as a symbol of belligerence and virility, it is not surprising that the ancients often wished to carry talismans of the cock. The right foot of a cock would enable a man to overcome an adversary. A cock's comb with a grain of incense and a bit of deer horn would drive away night fears "and every ill that happens and make the man who carries them intrepid. . . ."

So valued were cocks by the Greeks and Romans that it was not uncommon for a man to bury a pet cock with an elaborate tombstone and epitaph such as the following:

> No more as in the past shall you waken me from my bed in the early morning with the rapid flapping of your wings. For a plunderer crept upon you stealthily and killed you, clutching your throat with his claws.

The story was told of one Polyarchus that he took such pleasure in his dogs and cocks that when they died he gave them public burials and erected monuments in their honor.

Like the human the cock was not without his faults, of course. As Aldrovandi reluctantly admitted, "Braggarts, vainglorious, and stupid men, who are all too arrogant, can also be indicated by cocks."

The intense sexuality of the cock was sometimes a

problem for his admirers. He was frequently described as salacious and licentious. Aldrovandi wrote, "He leaps upon his mother in copulation, as the hippopotamus does, and he likewise cruelly treads upon his father." In Aristophanes' *Clouds*, Pheidippides, the father-beater, compares his act to that of the cock who contends with his father. And in Cicero: "This man boasts about his wealth like a Phrygian cock or some soothsayer weighted down with gold who shouts and is mad."

Not only in Greece and Rome was the cock a bird of great potency and religious significance. In India and Iran as well as in the ancient lands of southeast Asia — the Indochina peninsula — he was the announcer of the new day who frightened off with his lusty crowing the devilish spirits of the dark. In the Kianian Period of ancient Iran (2000 to 700 B.C.), when the Zoroastrian religion prevailed, the cock was described as "the admonisher of mankind to discard sloth, and to wake up early to lead an industrious life." Every devout Zoroastrian had a cock to guard him and to ward off evil spirits with his raucous cry.

Among the Mohammedans were sects who believed that a giant cock held one heaven in his feet and touched the other with his head and that when this huge cock crowed all other cocks on earth and in heaven crowed too.

The Africans of the upper Nile sacrificed cocks to turn aside the winds that threatened damage to their crops. Two men caught a white cock in their hands and then tore it to pieces. Then each took that portion of the bird which remained in his hands, purified the vineyards, and then buried the bird "under the belief [he] would suffer no trouble during that year."

For the Jews, uniquely, the cock was associated with demons, as we noted earlier. Algerian Jews, when a person is sick, take a cock to a spring, kill it, and take its blood to put on the face of the stricken, proclaiming: "Hereby the demon of sickness is banished by blood and goes into the water." Again the Talmud gives a prescription for identifying demons: "Who wishes to perceive their footprints should take sifted ashes and sprinkle them around his bed. In the morning he will see something resembling the footprints of a cock." Yet at the same time, the crowing of the cock exorcises demons. Most striking of all, the crowing cock symbolized for the Jews "Israel and the redemption of the Messianic Age." The cock is Israel, who will crow, exult, to welcome the Messiah. In the same spirit, the faithful Jew, when he heard the cock crow, was enjoined to say a prayer, "Blessed be the God who has given to the cock the understanding to distinguish between day and night." By watching the color of the cock's comb, moreover, "one can determine the moment when God lays aside His mercy; this happens at some moment during the first three hours of the day, the color of the comb changing at that moment."

The symbolism of the cock remained powerful through Roman times, and Christians took over the bird as a symbol which had, as it had for the Greeks, a variety of meanings — the awakening to a new life of those converted to Christianity, the cock as a symbol of the resurrection, as the bird of Peter, who thrice betrayed Christ before the crowing of the cock. The cock, by the same token, announces Christ and is intimately connected with His crucifixion through the story of Peter. In a familiar passage in the New Testament Jesus says to His disciples, "Watch, therefore, since you know not when the master of the house comes, whether late in the evening, at midnight or at cockcrow, or at morning, lest when he comes he finds us sleeping." In the Christian symbolism, the lion was put first, then the cock, and finally the ram.

The Venerable Bede of Britain was, like St. Gregory, much taken with the cock as a Christian symbol. "I think," he wrote, "the cock is one of the saints who in the night and in the shadow of the world receive intelligence through faith and the constancy of the virtue of crying out to God that He should watch over them when the day arrives and that the shadows of their present life should be dispelled. . . ." Christ himself, according to the thirteenth-century cardinal Jacques de Vitry, is a cock who stirs up the sleepers and "pricks and stimulates them with the spurs of His admonishments."

In the Middle Ages there were numerous miracles associated with cocks. St. Germain, bishop of Auxerre, found that in the house of a humble man with whom he stayed, no cock crowed at dawn. When he inquired as to the reason he was told that the voices of the cocks had been taken from them as the price that the family must pay for the privilege of having a bishop spend the night with them. The bishop thereupon blessed some wheat, which was fed to the cocks and they soon "began to weary the ears of the people with frequent crowing."

Another famous cock crowed after he was dead and cooked and thereby disclosed a crime. As the story went, a man and his wife and son were on a pilgrimage to the great shrine of Compostela. On the way they stopped at an inn, where the daughter of the innkeeper took a fancy to the young man. When he piously rejected her, saying that his thoughts dwelt on higher things, she, to revenge herself, hid a silver plate in his knapsack and when he had left the inn with his parents raised a hue and cry, had the guards called to apprehend him; the plate was discovered and he was sentenced to the death "reserved for thieves, that is by crucifixion upon a two-pronged fork," and executed. The parents continued on to the shrine of St. James and prayed so ardently to the saint that when they returned to the inn they found that their son had come to life. When they went to tell the mayor of the town who had witnessed the execution that their son was alive, they found that dignitary just sitting down to dinner. He replied scornfully that their son was no more alive than the roasted cock on the platter before him. "At this moment," as Aldrovandi tells the story, "the cooked bird not only crowed but jumped up off the platter with his feathers grown back upon him." The wicked daughter then confessed and was fined for "the unspeakable sin by which she had ruined the innocent young man," and the cock was preserved and worshipped by the townspeople, "who, in his memory, with great reverence carry home a little feather pulled from his body."

In 1014 a similar miracle of resurrection occurred in Bologna. Two friends were eating a cock. One of them carved the bird up into small pieces and poured a sauce over it. At this his companion said: "Comrade, you have cut up the cock so thoroughly that even St. Peter, if he wished to do so, could not put him back together again." His friend answered, "Why not only St. Peter? If Christ himself should order it, the cock would never rise." At this the cock sprang up, flapped his wings, throwing sauce on the diners, and began to crow. Where the sauce landed the two men were inflicted with leprosy as punishment for their blasphemy, and of that dread disease they both died. But not before the leprosy was passed on to their progeny: "The cock who had once revealed Peter denying Christ upon earth now testified his approval of Peter reigning in heaven with Him whom he had denied."

St. Pachomius was changed into a cock by an evil demon and then tortured and tempted. But the saint struck a musical instrument and sang, "Lord, our refuge and strength, our great helper in afflictions. I shall not fear while the earth is shaken." As soon as the words had been sung, the demons disappeared. Later on the principal demon, taking the shape of a large cock, flew into the saint's cell "and howled at him, uttering long fierce cries, and at the same time flying at him and striking him sharply with its claws." But the saint simply blew on the demon and made the sign of the cross and once more his tormentor vanished.

Aldrovandi, who quoted the observations of the ancient writers on the powers of the cock at considerable length, shared their admiration of the noble bird, with "eyes shining and limpid."

Beside the martial qualities of the cock so celebrated by the classical authors, Aldrovandi placed the bird's domestic virtues. "He . . . is for us the example of the best and truest father of a family. For he not only presents himself as a vigilant guardian of his little ones, and in the morning, at the proper time, invites us to our daily labor; but he sallies forth as the first, not only with his crowing, by which he shows what must be done, but he sweeps everything, explores and spies out everything." When the cock has found some food, "he calls both hens and chicks together to eat it while he stands like a father and host at a banquet . . . inviting them to the feast, exercised by a single care, that they should have something to eat. Meanwhile he scurries about to find something nearby, and when he has found it, he calls his family again in a loud voice. They run to the spot. He stretches himself up, looks around for any danger that may be near, runs about the entire poultry yard, here and there plucking up a grain or two for himself without ceasing to invite the others to follow him. . . .

"To these characteristics add . . . the fact," Aldrovandi wrote, "that he fights for his dear wives and little pledges to fortune against serpents, kites, weasels, and other beasts of the sort and invites us to a similar combat whenever the occasion presents itself." Not only was he a good provider and guardian: "This fact is likewise worthy of admiration, that is, the cock falls silent and knows how to conceal that beautiful voice, I mean his crowing, when the hen, his wife, has died. Taking over her duties, he sits on the eggs which he understands is a woman's work and little befitting a male. . . ." Aldrovandi also informs us that if a cock crowed frequently during the night when a male child was born, the child was often named Galeazzo "as though the father wished to signify that his son was born under the happy auspices of this bird."

Among the remarkable accomplishments of the cock was the fact that he had medical skills. Thus "when they feel themselves burdened with an immoderate supply of blood, they scratch their crests with their nails until they produce a flow of blood from the wound and thus, as their own physician, deliver themselves from imminent ills."

If Aldrovandi was charmed by the crowing of the cock, by his beauty, his potency, his reliability as a timepiece, his "fatherly" concern for his wife and chicks, and his magical or religious powers, it is ultimately his bravery that impresses him the most.

Finally he writes: "The entire military discipline . . . of a camp can be denoted by the image of a cock. His crest stands for the soldier's helmet; he wears his spurs as a sword; he testifies the reveille with his crowing; he fights with open battle and attacks the enemy without ambush; he imitates the raised battle standard by his erect tail and indicates victory and triumph by his crowing."

While the cock was never again to stand so high as in classical times, he and his amiable consort, the hen, persisted in folklore, in art, in literature, and in religious symbolism (as well, of course, as in the barnyard). The opening lines of Shakespeare's *Hamlet* remind us of his power over the minds of seventeenth-century Christians.

Bernardo, Horatio, and Marcellus are discussing the appearance of the ghost of Hamlet's father:

BERNARDO [of the ghost]:
It was about to speak when the cock crew.

HORATIO:
And then it started like a guilty thing
Upon a fearful summons. I have heard,
The cock, that is the trumpet to the morn,
Doth with his lofty and shrill-sounding throat
Awake the god of day; and at his warning,
Whether in sea or fire, in earth or air,
The extravagant and erring spirit hies
To his confine; and of the truth herein
This present object made probation.

MARCELLUS:
It faded on the crowing of the cock.
Some say that ever 'gainst that season comes
Wherein our Savior's birth is celebrated,
The bird of dawning singeth all night long;
And then, they say, no spirit can walk abroad;
The nights are wholesome; then no planets strike,
No fairy takes, nor witch hath power to charm,
So hallow'd and so gracious is the time.

Greek, Roman, Jew, and Christian all used the symbol of the cock. But its symbolic significance certainly did not stop there. We have already noted its importance to many tribes of primitive peoples in Asia and Africa as well as in the high cultures of the Middle and Far East. In ritual and magic, in medicine, in folklore, the cock appears as a creature without rival unless it be the eagle, the hawk, and the lion. To be sure, he shares with the hen medicinal powers, but if the hen belongs more commonly to folklore, the cock is clearly identified with the most powerful forms of magic man can summon up or imagine. This fact should be kept in mind in the discussion that follows of cockfighting. While in much of the world cockfighting has no overt religious connotations, there are places such as Bali and the Philippines where it is far more than a sport, where, indeed, a great part of the cultural and social life of the community centers around the ritual of the cockfight.

The Cock

68

THE ORIGINS OF COCKFIGHTING, like the origins of
the chicken, are lost in those famous "mists of antiquity." As we have seen, some scholars (or speculators)
have argued that cockfighting was, in fact, the occasion for the domestication of the chicken: that the hen,
and her eggs, were, in other words, a consequence of
the fighting prowess of her spouse. It is certainly true
that cockfighting is the most universal sport known
to man. And it is also clear that it has been going on
for thousands of years, doubtless the oldest sport
known to man (if we exclude the sport of the hunt,
which had, after all, a highly practical objective).

The anthropologist Berthold Laufer believes that
cockfighting was in fact a by-product of divination
and began when tribes competed to see whose magic
was the more potent. However, it must be said that in
most primitive tribes where cocks are sacred, cockfighting is not practiced. Indeed, it is paradoxical
that the Hindus, who consider cows so sacred that
they allow them to roam the countryside and consume
precious food needed for humans, nonetheless engage
enthusiastically in cockfighting.

The problem might be stated in this fashion:
"Which came first: the fighting cock or the egg?"
Since the matter is beyond proving by the experts —
that is, by the anthropologists or archeologists — it

presents an inviting ground for the amateur whose guess is as good, in this question, as the experts'. Mine is that the employment of the fighting, or game, cock proceeded along lines more or less parallel to the domestication of the hen. Certainly, the Red Jungle Fowl of India and the Grey Jungle Fowl of Malaya were the progenitors of the modern fighting cock. The similarities are inescapable. It would take an experienced "chicken man" or cockfighter to distinguish the two birds today, so little do they vary in conformation and coloring. Moreover, the game hen is not a prolific layer even after several millennia of domestication.

Thus I am inclined to cast my vote with the Reverend Mr. Dixon for multiple origins, though on somewhat different grounds than the authority of the Bible. However that may be, the cock, fighting or otherwise, has been a potent symbol as well as a source of "entertainment" since the beginning of recorded history and, indeed, before. It is clear also that cockfighting has always had strong overtones of religious ritual.

The purpose of this chapter and that following is to trace the strange history of cockfighting from prehistory to modern times. The ancient Syrians, we are told by Diodorus Siculus, worshipped the fighting cock, and by the fourth century B.C., when cockfighting is first mentioned in Greek, it had certainly had a long history in India and southeast Asia. In Greece it was said to be Themistocles, the great Athenian general, who made cockfighting into a national sport, though it had certainly been practiced long before his time. It happened, so we are told, in this manner. When Themistocles was preparing to march against the Persians, he saw two cocks fighting, stopped his army, and made a speech to the soldiers: "Behold, these do not fight for their household gods, for the monuments of their ancestors, for glory, for liberty, or the safety of their children, but only because the one will not give way to the other." So exhorted, the Greeks defeated the Persians. A law was subsequently passed under the influence of the general Caelius, designating yearly cockfights for the citizens of Athens, and an amphitheater for cockfighting was built in the city of Pergamum. Young men were required to attend fights to learn the lesson of courage and fortitude even to death.

In another version of the story it is Miltiades who, when the Persians were invading Greece in the second expedition of the Persian War, called his allies together to witness a cockfight; when the Greeks saw "the endurance of the brutes . . . and their stubborn determination as they fought to the death," they took up their arms determined to fight with a similar spirit.

The Greeks called the irons that were attached to the legs of the cocks to equalize the battle "plucks" (Aldrovandi, who mentions this, calls them "goads"); they were made of steel and bronze. There was even an ancient adage: "Take off the spur if you are going to fight," a sentence which had reference to the lethal effect of the metal spur bound to the cock's legs.

The cocks were trained like gladiators, and before they fought they were given garlic, which was supposed to increase their courage. Garlic had, it was thought, the same effect on men, and Caelius notes that the joke in Greek comedy about a man fed with garlic referred to an especially belligerent character. "In the same way," Caelius adds, "those who go forth to camps and warfare take a little garlic because it makes them lively, increases their strength, and sharpens their courage. They also give it to their horses with bread and wine, so that when they go to battle they may sustain their labors more easily and become fiercer." Three plants that were also supposed to increase the ferocity of a fighting cock before battle were polytrichon (goldenhair), trichomanes (bristle fern), and adiantum (maidenhair).

As a fighter the cock was identified with both Ares, god of war, and Athena, goddess of wisdom and of the arts and peace, as well as with Dionysus, in whose theater the official cockfights were held. The association with Dionysus is especially interesting. Dionysus was the god of fertility, of wine, of song and drama. The cock as a phallic symbol, a representative of fertility and of the orgiastic, was a natural companion of the god, and the fights in his theater were undoubtedly very potent dramas for the faithful.

By Roman times a cock is often depicted in conjunction with Eros, the god of erotic love, and the cupids that are shown in scenes of cockfighting certainly perpetuate this theme. Goodenough gives us a reproduction of a funerary altar that shows the end of a cockfight in which, amid a number of Dionysian symbols, one cupid is carrying away the dead bird while another places his on an altar with palms and wreaths on it. The cock also is frequently identified through Hermes with wealth and the acquisition of money. Hermes, who was the god of commerce and trade, was also god of thieves, of gamblers, of athletic contests, and of eloquence. Since cockfights have apparently been bet upon since the earliest times, it was natural that the cock should have been identified with Hermes. And since gambling was an avenue to wealth, the identification was reinforced. The physical prowess of the bird and the "eloquence" of his crowing would have made the association a natural one. Hermes was represented by a herm, or phallus-shaped stone, and in some manifestations seen as a god of fertility and masculine potency. Hence also the cock.

Among many other elements of their culture the Romans inherited the Greek passion for cockfighting. The poet Oppian wrote that cockfights were held "on anniversaries . . . as a solemn rite" to remind men that they should be "perpetual imitators of the cock." Columella called those who trained cocks to fight "the gladiator-trainers of birds."

The story is told that when Severus, the emperor of Rome, decided to invade Britain, he ordered his sons, grown soft and self-indulgent, to witness cockfights daily as part of a program of physical and moral toughening, "not only to make them emulous of glory through the performance of great achievements, but also to be firm and unshaken in the midst of dangers, nay in death itself."

The fighting cock was also a symbol for the ancients of unwillingness to lead a servile life. Thus the tragic poet Ion wrote: "He falls to earth not yet crushed in body or both eyes by the blows, but with failing strength he groans and refuses to live a slave."

Aelian wrote of the posture of the defeated cock: "He ceases to sing, for his spirit is broken and he hides himself in shame. If he wins, however, he is proud, holds his head high, and appears exultant." Then he "crows" over his victim, and Lucilius writes that the cock victorious in a good fight, rises on his toes and stretches out the forepart of his nails.

Like the more generalized symbolic representations of the cock, cockfighting itself was translated in Christian ritual and metaphor. There are numerous Christian representations of cockfights, especially on sarcophagi, and one archeologist identifies them with the *agon* of Paul, "the 'struggle' with one's lower nature to conquer it so that one can inherit eternal life." An early Christian tomb shows cocks fighting, with a cross and a bunch of flowers between them.

St. Augustine wrote in *De ordine:* "One could see the cocks' heads thrust forward, their combs inflated; they were striking vigorously, very cautiously evading each other, and in every motion of these animals unendowed with reason there was nothing ungraceful, since, of course, another higher reason was guiding everything they did, finally the very law of the victor, a proud song and limbs gathered together like a ball as if in the proud scorn of domination."

Cockfighting could not be long contained, however, within a religious schema. The Belgian chronicler Johannes Goropius reported that in Brabant an elaborate cockfight, sponsored by the king, went on for eight days "amid huge enthusiasm." "In this combat," Aldrovandi noted, "their spirits burn up so greatly" that one master of fighting cocks challenged another to a duel on horseback and was killed in the fray.

By late medieval times cockfighting was endemic — so widespread, persistent, and "secular" that the Church made vigorous efforts to suppress it. In doing so, the bishops and authorities of the Church succeeded primarily in driving it underground or in forcing it to masquerade as a formal Christian ritual. In England (and perhaps elsewhere) cockfighting was, for the most part, limited to Shrove Tuesday preceding Lent. At this time, schoolboys who had paid their master a "cock fee" to keep cocks for them were allowed to fight their cocks in the school. In the words of a sixteenth-century historian: "Every yeare on Shrove-Tuesday the schoolboyes doe bring Gamecocks to their master, and in the forepart of the day, till dinner time, they are permitted to amuse themselves with seeing them fight." Chairs and benches were cleared and the schoolroom itself became a cockpit. The schoolmaster, for his trouble, received in addition to his cock-fee all the birds that were killed. The pupil whose cock survived the main, or series of battles, was excused from punishment during Lent. In addition he could save any schoolmate from the rod by placing his hat over the lad's posterior.

The pupils of the Cromarty Grammar School in Scotland enjoyed these battles from morning until evening on Shrove Tuesday. "For weeks after it had passed," an historian tells us, "the school-floor would continue to retain its deeply-stained blotches of blood, and the boys would be full of exciting narratives regarding the glories of gallant birds who had continued to fight until both of their eyes had been picked out, or who, in the moment of victory, had dropped dead in the middle of the cockpit. . . . Every pupil at school, without exception, had his name entered on the subscription-list, as a cockfighter, and was obliged to pay the master at the rate of twopence per head, ostensibly for leave to bring his birds to the pit. . . ."

We should note that from the Mediterranean basin cockfighting spread throughout ancient Gaul and among the Germanic tribes north to Scandinavia and south and west along the northern rim of Africa and the Malay Peninsula. From India it spread eastward to China, southeast to what is today Indochina-Laos, Thailand, Cambodia, and Viet Nam. The Phoenicians are reputed to have carried the sport to Britain; as we have already noted, when Julius Caesar arrived there he found the native Britons keeping birds for "pleasure and amusement" though not to eat.

Cockfighting is almost as central a social, cultural, and sporting event in the Indochina peninsula as it is in Malaya and the Celebes. It has flourished in China as long as any record has been preserved of that ancient civilization. A handsome Chinese scroll of the late eighteenth century that hangs on my study wall depicts the victor in a cockfight crowing triumphantly over his dying opponent and serves as a reminder that cockfighting in that country has continued into modern times. There is no information as to the fate of cockfighting in Red China but one would assume that the Communists with those "pretensions to Puritanism that radical nationalism tends to bring with it" have outlawed the sport. One also assumes that it will survive as it has done elsewhere despite governmental edicts.

The large-bodied, heavy chickens native to or developed in China — the Chittagongs and Shanghais — later Cochins and Brahmas — with their almost residual wings and heavy feathered legs, were not suited for fighting and it is clear that cocks were imported from India and Malaya. In no part of the world did cockfighting become a more deeply ingrained and ritualized activity than in the countries of Indochina and the Malay Peninsula. This infatuation has endured every vicissitude of history and survives, virtually undiminished, today, as we shall see.

One of the earliest accounts of cockfighting in China is by an English missionary, John Barrow, who visited China in 1805. "One of their favorite sports," Barrow wrote, "is cockfighting, and this cruel and unmanly *amusement*, as they are pleased to consider it, is fully as eagerly pursued by the upper classes in China, as, to their shame and disgrace be it spoken, it continues to be by those in a similar situation in some parts of Europe." Another traveler also mentioned that cockfighting, along with quail and cricket fighting, was a pastime of the mandarins. "Training," he added, "is a profession which gives occupation to numbers and the interest taken in these unworthy sports is so universal, that the gamester alone would credit their true history. The birds are furnished with steel spurs, as our Gamecocks in the pit, and the contest, therefore, seldom fails to prove fatal to one or both. The victor is put up for sale, or raffle, and the eagerness to become his master is demonstrated by the enormous sums staked, or paid down, for him."

When Magellan reached Borneo, he found that gamecocks were considered sacred and that eating them was forbidden. In Sumatra, which produced a famous breed of fighting cock, the bird was also worshipped. According to Nicolo di Conti, "They annex stately buildings to their Temples, where they keep

at public charge, divers fighting-cocks, which are
brought forth, as the people come to worship, and are
fought in a spacious court Eastward, on the right-
hand of the door of the House of their Gods: after
which a certain priest, skilled in cocking, and ap-
proved for his great ability in astronomy, and all natural philosophy, having a voluble ready way of speaking, first takes up the conquering cock after the battle
is over, and presents him to their deities, and then
comes and takes up the slain cock, and puts him in a
golden cauldron, where he bathes his bloody limbs in
Sankereen; and then, with gums and spices, burns his
body upon an altar made for that purpose; after
which his ashes are put carefully in a golden pot or
urn, there to remain for ever. And then the Brammen
or Priest makes a long speech to the people, showing
the excellency of cocking, and the great use and benefit of it to all such as know rightly to apply it, and
expatiates much upon the present combat, drawing
divers inferences from the various passages and trans-
actions made use of by the late foughten cocks, showing all the great magnanimity, courage, skill and constancy of these warriors. And lastly, he applies it so
pertinently to all that are present, in terms so fit and
suitable, that it conduces greatly to their edification,
grounding them in a firm and stable temper of mind,
with an unshaken valour, whereby they are now truly
said to be a people invincible; and verily I am of opinion that from hence at first came that saying so common among us still, viz. *He is gone to church to see a
cockfight.*"

When all is said and done, it is probably in England between the sixteenth and early nineteenth centuries that cockfighting was carried to its greatest
refinement. It was, apparently, Henry VIII with his
love of sport and his hostility to the Roman Church
who broke cockfighting loose from the religious in-

hibitions that had surrounded it for so many centuries and made it a popular pastime. While Shrove Tuesday cockfights continued in many English grammar schools down to the outlawing of the sport in 1835, secularized cockfighting became the premier sport in England, exceeding horseracing in popularity and celebrated in story, poem, and song;

> . . . Cocking is the Game I sing,
> Worthy of the greatest Captain, greatest King . . .
> This Pastime I above the rest prefer,
> In that it fits a Man for Peace or War.
> Cocking breeds Courage, where before was none.
>
> And makes men Stout and die that us'd to run,
> Cocking breeds cunning too, makes men contrive,
> And puts them in a way to live and thrive:
> And if the pious Indians say true,
> It makes men witty, Good, and Godly too.
>
> Who then would Hunt and Hawk their time away
> Or at the Cards, or Dice sit down to play:
> When they by Powerful Cocking, this may do,
> Gain Courage, Wit, and Wealth, and Heaven too.

Henry VIII built the first indoor pit near Whitehall Palace, and the first Stuart king, James of Scotland, went there several times a week during his reign. There was a royal pit at Birdcage Walk and other pits were built in Shoe Lane, Drury Lane, Pickled-Egg Walk, Jewin Street, Cripplegate, Old Gravel Lane, Gray's Inn Lane, and the New Vauxhall Gardens. The Whitehall pit was large enough to be converted into the Privy Council Office after the great fire of 1697. Beyond the more famous pits, we can only guess at the total number from the names given to various locations in London. In 1761 there were ten Cock Alleys, nine Cock Courts, four Cock Lanes, eight Cock Yards as well as Cock Hill, Cockpit Alley, Cockpit Buildings, Cockpit Street, Cocks Rents, and Cockspur Street. Cockfights were also put on in the theaters of the city. John Timbs, in his *Romance of London*, notes that the theater "pit" was in fact originally a cockpit. "One of our oldest London theatres," he wrote, "was called the Cockpit; this was the Phoenix, in Drury Lane, the site of which was Cockpit Alley, now corruptly written Pitt Place." The provincial cities followed suit. The Gwenap Pit, not far from the Cornish town of Redruth, is thought to have been the oldest open-air cockfighting pit in England, tracing its history back to Roman times and surviving in use at least until 1743, when John Wesley had to delay a sermon because of the noise of the fight.

We have a description of a lavish but by no means unusual cockpit which was built in Tufton Street, Westminster: "a large, lofty, circular building, with seats rising, as in an amphitheatre [one thinks of the amphitheater built in Pergamum at the direction of Themistocles]. In the middle of it is a round matted stage, of about eighteen or twenty feet diameter, . . . and rimmed with an edge eight or ten inches in height, to keep the cocks from falling over in their combats. . . . A large and rude branched candlestick is suspended low down, immediately over the mat, which is used at the night battles."

Cockfights were advertised daily: "At the Royal Cockpit on the south side of St. James Park on Tuesday the 11th of this instant February [1700] will begin a very great Cock-match; and will continue all week; wherein most of the considerablest Cockers of England are concerned. There will be a battle down upon the Pit every day precisely at three o'clock in order to have done by daylight."

Early on the practice developed of different shires, towns, and cities pitting their prize birds against each other. In 1546 Sir Henry Savile invited a cousin to visit him "and se all our good coxs fight, if it please you, and se the maner of our cocking. Ther will be

Lanckershire of one parte, Derbeshire of another parte, and Hallomshire of third parte. . . ."

A century or more later a London paper advertised "Monday the 9th instant March will begin a great match of Cockfighting betwixt the Gentlemen of the City of Westminister and the Gentlemen of the City of London for six guineas a battle, and one hundred guineas the odd battle, and the match continues all the week in Red Lions fields." A contest, or "main," consisted of an odd number of bouts, which might run from three to twenty-one or more. Each bout was bet on separately and then the "tie-breaker" decided, if necessary, who won the main — that is, whose birds had carried off the largest number of bouts. The same practice is followed in all the mains held today in the United States and in international matches.

While high entry fees prevented the poor from fighting cocks of their own in the great mains, they, in total, probably kept a greater number of birds than all the lords of the realm put together. Moreover they attended the fights in large numbers and wagered as avidly as their betters. Samuel Pepys noted: "To Shoe Lane to see a Cockfighting at a new pit there, a spot I was never at in my life: but Lord! to see the strange variety of people, from Parliamentman (by name Wildes . . .) to the poorest 'prentices, bakers, brewers, butchers, draymen, and what not; and all these fellows one with another cursing and betting. I soon had enough of it. It is strange to see how people of the poor rank, that look as if they had not bread to put in their mouths, shall bet three or four pounds at a time, and lose it, and yet bet as much the next battle, so that one of them will lose 10£ or 20£ at a meeting."

The poor man who had not the resources to compete with the leading keepers and breeders of cocks might make a comfortable living as a "feeder." Indeed, feeding and training were, next to breeding, the keys to successful fighting, at least in the opinion of cockers, and it is fascinating to read the diets prescribed for birds in training. Of all the ritual activities surrounding cockfighting none is stranger or more "magical" than the food fed to fighting cocks. Some of the recipes go back to Greek and Roman times. Others are universal. Cocks were kept in large airy pens or, later, staked by one leg so that they could move about in the grass and hunt for bugs and worms. The pens were arranged so that the birds could not see each other; otherwise they would injure themselves dashing at the slats or wire in an effort to fight.

Prior to a main feeding the cocks were given the closest attention by the birds' trainers. Some "feeders" were women, though when the birds entered the pit they were handled by male "settlers," the best of whom commanded as much as thirty guineas for a main.

One of the earliest English works on cockfighting prescribed a diet of stale white bread cut into squares and served "three times a daye, that is to say, at sunrise, at highest noon, and at sun-set; you shall let him have before him the finest, coldest, and sweetest spring water you can get."

Other diets were far more elaborate. One required a special bread made of the finest oatmeal flour with ale, the whites of a dozen eggs, and a half pound of butter kneaded together and made into flat thin cakes. Some feeders mixed in licorice, aniseed, "and other hot Spices," which it was thought would make the bird hot and fiery but in fact gave him indigestion. Another recipe called for brown sugar, "carroway seeds grossly bruised, with a lump of good sweet Butter as big as your fist at least, and a quarter of a Pint or more of the best White-wine that can be bought for the money with three or four spoonfuls of Syrup of Clove — gilliflowers put into it, and a Date or two, with some Candied Eringo Root cut very small." To this mixture was to be added "Wood-sorrel, Ground-ivy, Feath-erdew, Dandelion, and Burrage" with "four spoonfuls of the pure juice of lemons to every pint of distilled water," and all this made into "a good stiff paste."

A favorite food for many feeders was bread steeped in urine, a recipe as old as the Greeks and with an inescapable sexual connotation — a symbolic connect-ing of the male penis with the fighting cock.

In preparing a cock for a main, a period of special diet was followed by "sparring" exercises. Here the stumps of the spurs (which were cut off in order to fit the artificial spurs over them) were covered with soft leather. (The comb and wattles of a fighting cock are dubbed [cut off] when the bird is about six or eight months old — a ritual perhaps akin to circumcision, but in sparring the heads of the cocks were covered with a cloth hood which enabled the birds to see but gave some protection to their heads.)

In the early days of cocking these exercises were followed by "sweating" the bird, putting him in a close-covered basket of straw and placing him on a stove. It was a wholly deleterious practice, since chick-ens have no sweat glands and cannot perspire, and it was eventually abandoned (doubtless after having seriously weakened or even killed numberless birds). After taking "your Cock out of the stove," an early treatise stated, "and licking his head and eyes all over with your tongue put him in his Pen." Again it is an indication of the ritual activity (in this instance again with strong sexual overtones) surrounding cockfight-ing which usually had little to do with promoting the fighting qualities of the bird.

Another exercise that was faithfully followed in-volved, in effect, the feeder jogging with the cock. He was instructed to "take him into a fair even green Close, and setting him down, having some Dung-hill cock in your arms ["dung-hill cock" was the cockers' contemptuous term for run-of-the-mill barnyard cocks with no "game" in them], you shall shew it him, and so run from him and entice him to follow you, and so chase him up and down half an hour at least, suffering him now and then to have a stroke at the Dunghill cock." After such exercises — alternating between sparring and running — the cock was "scoured"; "for this will break and cleanse him from all grease, glut and filthiness, which lying in his body, makes him pursie, faint and not able to stand out the latter end of a battel." The "heating" (exercising), stoving, and scouring went on in a rigidly prescribed formula for a month at a time. What is surprising about this regimen is that the bird was able to survive and stagger into the ring at all.

The fights or mains were of three principal types. By far the most common was the classic main, where birds fought, as we have said, an uneven number of individual bouts, the grand prize going to the winner of the largest number of mains. There were also "Welsh mains," which were like tennis draws. Birds fought in a round of eight or sixteen and then advanced through the quarter- and semi-finals to the finals, which pitted the two survivors against each other. Since few birds could survive a series of such bouts and almost invariably arrived at the finals cruelly battered, the Welsh main was rarely fought. Another form of cockfighting as rare as the Welsh main was the Battle Royal, where, as the name suggests (indeed it is where the name came from), a pit full of birds was turned loose to see which one survived. This was a sport too cruel and capricious even for the British and it was largely abandoned by the end of the eighteenth century.

Sometimes there was no matching of cocks by weight. These might be called today an "unlimited" class. In eighteenth-century England they were called "Shakebags," because instead of being carefully weighed, the cocks were simply shaken out of their bags onto the ring.

Prior to a bout, spurs were tied to the legs of the contestants. They were fitted with leather and bound with strong twine. This was an operation requiring skill and experience. The spurs were originally of tempered silver (the process of silver tempering has been lost), gradually replaced by steel. As distinguished from Eastern spurs (which have knifelike blades), the spur most commonly used in Western cockfighting is sharply pointed. Spurs varied in length (the same length, of course, was used on both birds in a bout) and in the cant or angle of the iron itself, with infinite variations designed to give a bird an advantage over his adversary. The oldest extant English spurs are apparently those given by Charles II to his mistress, Nell Gwynn, in the 1660's.

Before the silver spur had established itself as the required spur in all proper mains, an advertisement from the time of Queen Anne indicates that other types were used: "Note that on Wednesday there will be a single battle fought with Sickles, after the East India manner. And on Thursday there will be a Battle Royal, one Cock with a Sickle, and 4 Cocks with fair Spurs. On Friday there will be a pair of Shakebags fight for 5£. And on Saturday there will be a Battle Royal, between a Shakebag with fair Spurs, and 4 Matchable Cocks which are to fight with Sickles, Launcet Spurs and Penknife Spurs, the like never yet seen. For the Entertainment of foreign Ambassadors and Gentlemen." It is clear that at this stage in English history, cockfighting was often more of a public spectacle than a sport. But such eccentricities were, increasingly, frowned upon by the true lovers of cockfighting.

Long before the introduction of bronze (and later silver and even gold) spurs — and long after — cocks fought what came to be called "naked-heel," that is with their own natural spurs.*

The problem with the cock's own spurs is that they grow slowly and it is not until most birds are two years old that their spurs are fully developed. Moreover, some birds have longer spurs than others and thus a decided advantage. Or some birds have spurs that are too long and equally disadvantageous. In naked-heel fighting the spurs are, to be sure, usually filed to a sharp point if they are immature or have grown dull. In some countries, on the other hand, spurs are deliberately dulled so that the bouts will last longer. But binding metal spurs on the legs of cocks had the obvious benefit of equaling the contests. Birds in their second year with spurs not fully developed could be fought against older birds without regard to the length of the bird's natural spurs. From early times the artificial spurs seem to have been of two types predominately: those that were sharp-pointed like the bird's own spur and those that had a swordlike blade — slashers, as they came to be called. Within these two main types there are infinitely subtle variations; whether and how much the shaft or blade is curved; the point at which it is attached; and even the method by which it is affixed to the bird's leg.†

The advocates of the pointed spur argue that it requires far more skill on the part of the combatants.

* The final scraping of the spur was usually done in sight of the spectators to prevent poisoning the spur; sometimes the trainers were required to lick the spurs before the battle to prove that no poison had been applied. Naked-heel fighting still predominates in some countries — Spain is one (and in Spain the spurs of dead cocks are sometimes fixed to the legs of cocks whose own spurs have not grown to their mature length). The arguments between the naked-heel advocates and those who prefer metal spurs are more than two thousand years old.
† The makers of spurs are skilled craftsmen, and these murderous but simple-looking weapons sell for twenty to fifty dollars the pair; although cockfighting is illegal in most of the United States one today can find advertisements in cockers' journals such as *Grit and Steel*.

They look down on those cockfighters and cultures —
primarily southeast Asia, the Philippines, and Latin
America — where "slashers" are used. With the
slasher, its opponents state, the element of skill is minimized and that of chance increased. A single glancing
blow of these deadly swords can dispatch a cock.

Under the codified rules that were finally established, the birds were to set against each other "until
one cock has refused ten times." The democratic spirit
of the cockpit is indicated by the provision that "all
disputes about bets, or the battle being won or lost,
ought to be decided by the spectators." Actually, it
was probably less democracy than expediency that
dictated this provision. Cockfights were notoriously
rowdy affairs. Drinking was invariably an accompani-
ment, and any individual, master or judge, who tried
to pass judgment in some of the rougher districts of
London would have been in danger of life and limb.

During the course of a bout, the setters-to, or handlers of the birds in the ring, had an elaborate set of
rituals used to encourage and revive wounded birds.
Perhaps most striking of these is what might be called
beak-to-mouth resuscitation. Here the bird's handler
puts the bird's whole head into his mouth, sucks out
any blood or mucus in the cock's mouth and lungs,
and presumably breathes new life into it. This method
is still used in mains all over the world, but the more
modern and enlightened cockers have abandoned it, referring to it caustically as "showboating," an exercise
done more for the satisfaction of the handler and the
spectators than the good of the bird himself.

However that may be, sucking the wounds of an injured cock is one of the oldest prescriptions for healing a bird. Markham's *Country Contentments* directed: "When the battail is ended, the first thing you
do, you shall search his wounds, and as many as you
can find, you shall with your mouth suck the blood out
of them, then wash them very well with warm urine,

to keep them from rankling, and then presently give him a roll or two or your best scouring, and so stove him hot as you can . . . then, in the morning take him forth, and if his head be much swell'd, you shall suck his wounds again, and bath them with warm urine." If the cock's eyes were injured the feeder was instructed to chew up some ivy and "spit it in the eye of the Cock." The cock thus cared for was put out to his walk. After a month the feeder should check him again and if he found any swollen bunches, hard and blackish, he "should open them with a knife, crush out the cores with your thumbs, then with your mouth suck out all Corruption, and then fill the holes full of fresh Butter, and it will cure [him]."

Henry VIII's endorsement of cockfighting was followed by that of a number of other monarchs. Besides James I and Charles II, William III and George IV were avid cockers. Kings of Denmark and Sweden were also enthusiasts, and many members of the British aristocracy indulged — the Duke of Northumberland, Lord Vere, the Duke of Hamilton, Lord Chesterfield, the Earl of Berkeley, Lord Lonsdale, and Lord Clive, the conqueror of India. The greatest cocker of all England was the Earl of Derby, of whom it was reported that he raised no less than three thousand cocks a year. He did much to refine the breed of the Old English Game Fowl — a strain known originally as the Knowsley Black-breasted Reds — and though newer breeds appeared to dispute its hegemony, the earl remained faithful to the Old English. A few hours before his death a fight was reputed to have been staged in his bedroom to divert him.

Among the devoted cockers in eighteenth-century England were a number of naval officers, Admiral Boscawen for one, and fighting cocks were often taken aboard warships of the British navy. Henry Aiken tells the story that during a battle, engaged in by

Admiral Lord Howe's fleet on June 1, 1794, ". . . a gamecock on board one of the ships chanced to have his house beaten to pieces by a shot . . . which accidentally set him at liberty; the feathered hero, now perched on the stump of the mainmast, which had been carried away, continued crowing and clapping his wings during the remainder of the engagement, enjoying, to all appearances the thundering horrors of the scene."

Breeders such as the Earl of Derby paid high prices for prize birds, especially for hens, which were thought, for several centuries, to be far more important in producing champion birds than their mates. When one breeder was offered fifty pounds for a setting hen, he sold her and then smashed the eggs with his foot. When the buyer protested that her eggs should be his also, he was told that if the eggs had been included the price would have been a thousand pounds.

At the other end of the scale were the sporting poor, street people, stableboys, runaway apprentices, rogues, and vagrants who lived by their wits and acquired gamecocks by various dubious expedients. Here cockfights were far more modest affairs, but a winning bird was a winning bird and a poor man might breed as shrewd as a rich one. Riots, fights, and brawls were notorious at such contests, especially where cocks from one community were matched with those from another. Wednesbury in Staffordshire was a town so noted for its birds and its toughs that it figured in a popular song:

> At Wednesbury there was a cocking,
> A Match between Newton and Skrogging;
> The colliers and nailers left work,
> And all to Spittles' went jogging
> To see this noble sport.
> Many noted men there resorted,
> And though they'd but little money,

Yet that they freely sported.
Raddle tum rum tum ta,
Rol de rol la la la,
Raddle tum rum tum ra
Fol de rol la la la.

There was Jeff'ry and Boburn from Hampton,
And Dusty, from Bilstone, was there,
Frumity he came from Darlston,
He was as rude as a bear:
And there was old Will from Walsal,
And Smacker from West Bromwich came;
Blind Dobbin, he came from Rowley,
And staggering he went home.
Raddle tum, etc.

A fight ensues between the owners of two cocks fighting in the pit:

Ruff Mory bit off a man's nose,
It's a wonder no one was slain,
They trampled both cocks to death,
And so they made a draw main. . . .
Peter Hadley peep'd through the goss,
In order to see them fight;
Spittle jobb'd his eye out with a fork
And cried, "B——st thee, it served thee right."
Raddle tum, etc.

Newcastle and Liverpool rivaled London as cockfighting centers. In Liverpool the Devil's Acre contained many cockpits, and one writer noted: "These cockpits were the resort of all the low ruffians of the neighborhood. In consequence of the fights and disturbances which continually took place, the 'Watch' had no alternative but to suppress cockfighting in this district. Later, the promoters moved to Lovelane, which was another 'hot spot' for this type of sport."

In the individual bouts that made up a "main," the rituals were as elaborately set as they were for the period of preparation. Birds, their feathers carefully trimmed, were commonly carried to the pit in a sack, since darkness kept them in a quiescent state. They were then weighed and carefully matched by weights. Betting, as we have seen, has been associated with cockfighting from its inception, and indeed it is impossible to imagine the sport surviving without betting. There was, in every bout, a price which might range from a few pence or shillings among farm boys and the urban poor to ten guineas (perhaps two hundred and fifty dollars in modern currency) ; the greatest purse ever fought for in England had a thousand pounds on each bout and five thousand on the main. In modern times, the largest purse for a main that these writers know of was thirty thousand dollars at an international main held in the Philippines in 1970.

It was in the *Virginia Gazette* of July 2, 1772, that one finds a particularly colorful account of a famous English cocker, Sir John Astley, a member of Parliament from Shropshire. Sir John fought one battle for a thousand guineas, "during which," according to the *Gazette*, "his Cock received a Blow which staggered, and was supposed by everyone present to have done for him; but the Feeder immediately handled the Cock, and set him against his Antagonist, whom with one Blow he killed, and which Nichols, the Feeder, took up the Conquerer and kissed his Rump. Sir John preserved him as long as he lived, and when he died erected a Monument to him, on which, in Bass Relief, is to be seen Nichols, the Feeder, kissing his Rump, on whom he also settled an Annuity of fifty Pounds a Year. The Monument is of Marble, at his Seat in the Country, and cost above five Hundred Pounds."

The size of the purses for the individual bouts and for the main itself was controlled by the entry fees. These were (and still are, for the most part) distributed among the winners of individual bouts, with by far the largest portion reserved for the winner of the main. But the purses were only the beginning of the money that changed hands. The real action took place among the spectators, who bet on favored cocks, often with complicated odds, and on the owners themselves, who frequently bet large sums on particular birds in which they had confidence. Hogarth's famous etching of a London cockfight depicts a definitely lower-class scene with the spectators and cockers betting, collecting, and paying bets. So it is with every cockfight. Someone calls out a bet and it is taken by a shout or a gesture. No money is exchanged and no record kept, but a cocker is jealous of his honor and few bets are welshed on.

The eighteenth century saw the development of a definite code of rules governing cockfights. The most important rules had to do with the circumstances under which a bout was won or forfeited. It is an article of faith with cockers that virtually all gamecocks will fight to the death. That this is far from the case is clear from the rules governing cocks who refuse to fight at all. The "masters of the match" are to count out loud to forty or so; then, if one or both birds refuse to fight, they are removed from the ring by their "setters-to." It is often the case that one bird will refuse to fight, run, or by raising his hackles in a particular fashion "show the white feather," a white hackle that signals his refusal to continue the fight.*

In the eighteenth century, when the British began their exploitation of the Indian subcontinent, they discovered that chickens and more especially cocks were very much in evidence. Cockfighting was one of

* St. Augustine was one of the first to comment on this trait: "The signal of the conquered," he wrote, "is the ruffled feathers of the neck, an unsightliness of voice and movement; everything I know not how in this is fitting and proper according to the laws of his nature." An ordinary cock will run when he is bested, showing, as Augustine says, the white feather by raising the hackles at the top of his neck. This gesture of defeat by the cock is markedly different from "raising his hackles" as he begins to fight. Then all his neck feathers stand out in an angry ruff as he prepares for battle.

the most popular pastimes of Indian peasant and
maharajah alike. Of course, though the British were
not at first aware of the fact, it was from the ancient
cultures of India and Iran that the gamecock had
spread to the British Isles when Britons were not far
advanced from the level of savages. So there was more
than a little irony in the fact that the conquering
British, one of the great powers — soon indeed to be
the greatest power of the modern world — arrived in
India to find that one of the few passions (or cultural
artifacts) they shared with the peoples they so ruth-
lessly conquered and exploited was cockfighting.

Warren Hastings, whose name, more than that of
any other man, was associated with the establishment
of British rule in India, was a devotee of cockfighting
and when he was not subduing Indian princes, he was
often pitting his cocks against theirs. The fashionable
portrait painter Zoffany came to India to seek com
missions from the British nabobs, many of whom had
grown fabulously rich by pillage and corruption.
There he painted a famous picture of an Anglo-
Indian cockfight at Lucknow in the Oudh. The two
most prominent figures in the painting are Colonel
Mordaunt, the English commander at Lucknow, and
the Nawab-Wazir, or native ruler of the Oudh, Asaf-
ud-Daula. A contemporary wrote of Asaf-ud-Daula:
"He is mild in manners, generous to extravagance,
affably polite and engaging in his conduct; but he
has not great mental powers, though his heart is
good." He was infatuated, Mary Webster writes, with
everything English and spent vast sums "on gardens,
palaces, horses, elephants, and, above all, on fine
European gems, lustres, mirrors and all sorts of European manufactures, more especially English . . .
from a little dirty paper lantern to mirrors and
lustres which cost up to £3000 each."

This was the man who commissioned Zoffany to
paint what must certainly be the most elaborate and

"Colonel Mordaunt's Cock Match"

magnificent cockfighting scene ever placed on canvas.

On the left of the picture as one faces it are the dignitaries of the Oudh, including the slim, commanding figure of Asaf-ud-Daula. On the right are the figures of the English participants, including Colonel Mordaunt in his uniform, seated on an ottoman in right center. While the cocks fought from the English side are apparently English-bred, the handlers of two birds that are fighting are both clearly Indian. Two Englishmen, one a rather uncouth fellow with a broad-brimmed hat on the back of his head, the other an aristocratic-looking young gentleman, are both holding cocks as though they were preparing to fight them. On the left (or Indian) side two men and a boy hold birds as though they, too, were awaiting their turn. Again the Indians seem to be of distinctly contrasting castes. What these figures suggest is that Indian cocks fought only other Indian cocks while the English-bred birds, in turn, fought only each other.

One is puzzled that the Indian and English birds were not matched against each other. The reason, almost certainly, is that the styles of fighting of the two breeds and, above all, the spurs used, were so different that an even match was not possible. The British used, as we have noted, pointed spurs — rather like the rapiers used by fencers — while the Indians, in common with the cockfighters of every Eastern and Pacific island people, used spurs with razor-sharp edges, very much like the classic sword or the épée of the human fencer. Thus the anomaly. At the point at which the two cultures perhaps approached most closely — their devotion to cockfighting — a barrier still remained. The picture does make clear, however, that even though the twain were not to meet in ultimate engagement, both Indian nobles and their British overlords, who, it must be said, not infrequently joined hands to pillage the native peasantry, "gave" cockfights to which they invited each other. In this case it was apparently Colonel Mordaunt's party, although it was Asaf-ud-Daula who commissioned the painting.

When Zoffany returned to England, where Warren Hastings was fighting for his life and reputation against Burke's charges of maladministration, Hastings commissioned him to paint a copy of Colonel Mordaunt's cockfight for him.

The only legal interruption to cockfighting prior to 1834 was the act passed during the reign of Cromwell, the so-called Statute of 1654, which forbade cockfighting. Doubtless, Puritan zeal and political expediency were both behind the act — certainly the Puritans had long denounced the sport. Apparently cockfights had been used as occasions for covert meetings of Cromwell's enemies, most of whom were concentrated in that class most addicted to cockfighting.

From the early days of cockfighting there had been those who denounced it as a cruel and barbarous practice. In 1770, Richard King in *The Frauds of London Detected* wrote of cockfighting as "of all games . . . surely one of the most barbarous, and a scandal to the practioners who follow it, both high and low; for, not withstanding its antiquity as a diversion in England, it is now become a disgrace to humanity. . . . At the scenes of cruelty the greatest depredations are committed by the attendants thereon, the most prophane and wicked expressions are made use of, the most horrid and blasphemous oaths and curses denounced against Fortune . . . with a jargon of disconsonant tongues as hard to be understood and in as great confusion, as that at Babel . . . among whom are to be found my Lord in dispute with a butcher, and his Grace with a farrier, all hail fellow well met. From these, and other meetings of the like nature, let me dissuade my readers, where nothing is to be

obtained but at the expense of humanity, and to the
discredit of Christianity."

While ministers and prelates of the Church of England were often enthusiastic cockers, the Puritans
and later the members of the various Dissenting sects,
the Chapel men and Covenanters, spoke out vigorously against cockfighting as a sinful and ungodly
pastime. For more than two centuries, they spoke in
vain until finally the Dissenters, joined by the hu-
manitarian reformers and then by the respectable
middle classes, prevailed on the members of Parliament to declare cockfighting illegal in 1834.

Cockfighting was one of the first and most notable
victims of the new spirit of reform and, as much as
any other measure, its prohibition marked the polit-

ical downfall of the country gentry. Many a squire
withdrew to his study and to the solace of his port to
curse the spirit of modernity and the sentimentality
of the modern age which, while it condemned hundreds
of thousands of human beings to miserable lives in
noisome factories, did not scruple to deprive the aristocrat and the honest working man alike of their ancient pleasures. No one was harmed by cockfighting
except the reckless in their pocketbooks. Could the
Birmingham mill owner or the coalmine tycoon say
as much? There was indeed more than a little of the
priggish and censorious in the spirit of the reformers,
more than a little envy of lords and gentlemen with
their high and mighty airs, and more than a little
hostility toward the rough pleasures of the often desperate poor.

So the cockers were done in. Victorian prudishness
and self-righteousness put them down — lord and
laborer alike. Cockfighting was, to be sure, a brutal
sport, but this is a rather brutal world and it perhaps
is not too much to suggest that the passion to reform
it might have been directed at worthier targets. In
the long run it made little difference. The world did

not seem to improve very much and cockfighting went on rather as before. In England, as elsewhere, it was to prove ineradicable. If there were certain awkwardnesses in the clandestine pursuit, they were doubtless more than compensated for by the added zest of savoring a forbidden pleasure and by the cunning required in the continuing game of wits with the representatives of the law, men often aware that they were hardly dealing with a criminal element.

Cockfighting

I F COCKFIGHTING was seriously inhibited in England after 1835 by being forbidden by law, it continued to flourish in America. The ships that had carried settlers to the British colonies along the Atlantic Coast had carried chickens and game birds. Cockfighting was frowned upon by the Puritans of New England, but wherever the colonists tried to imitate the ways of the landed gentry of Old England, cockers bred their birds and cockfighting flourished. Hence from New York to South Carolina and, later, Georgia, cockfighting was one of the most popular forms of entertainment. There are even indications that the Puritans indulged. An historian of the founding of Stamford, Connecticut, tells us that it was originally given an Indian name, "Rippowam." The settlers decided a few years later to change the name of the town to a British name. Some backed the name "Ayrshire," because that had been their home, and others preferred "Stamford." The decision was made to let two gamecocks fight it out. One was named "Ayrshire" and one "Stamford"; a cockpit was constructed in front of the meetinghouse, the birds were pitted, and Stamford won. The story may well be apocryphal; it certainly seems an incongruous way for a Puritan town to choose a name.

As in rural England, so in America: cockfighting

was most often associated with a tavern, and this was particularly true in the South, where towns and centers of population were few and far between. In the English colonies as in the mother country, cocking was a sport participated in by the upper class and the common man alike, the difference perhaps being that in America it was the common man's sport, a sport to which the rich and aristocratic were usually admitted on the poor man's terms. In the middle colonies and the South, favored household slaves were most commonly the "feeders" and "setters-to." Wherever there were substantial numbers of Irish immigrants cockfighting also flourished.

M. L. E. Moreau de St. Méry, the French exile who lived in Philadelphia in the 1790's, noted in his journal, "The commonest form of betting is on cock fights, which take place every day. Some men devote all their time and efforts to the training of fighting cocks. In order to make them pugnacious, nothing is neglected. They are subjected to a diet which excites them, and even to the use of strong drinks. They are armed with iron spurs, their combs are cut to offer less of a hold to the enemy; they are urged on by cries and placed in an enclosure from which they cannot escape. The fight rages amidst a crowd that seems to be made up wholly of Englishmen, but which is composed of their descendants, and the unfortunate cocks tear each other to pieces and die in order to decide their bets. The public houses [taverns] benefit, too, by making sure that the atrocious winners — the men, that is — drink up their winnings in the company of the vanquished — men again." It is worth noting that Moreau de St. Méry was thoroughly aware of the identification of the cockers with their birds, hence "the atrocious winners — the men, that is." Anyone who has seen a cockfight or even talked to cockfighters, as we noted earlier, can hardly escape this intermingling of the cock with his master.

Jane Carson, in *Colonial Virginians at Play*, writes
that "colonial Virginia sporting tastes placed cockfighting immediately after hunting and horse racing."
While there was apparently little if any cockfighting
in the southern colonies in the seventeenth century,
by the early decades of the next century it was well
established. Hugh Jones, the historian of Virginia,
wrote in 1724: "The common planters [ordinary
farmers] leading easy lives don't much admire labor,
or any manly exercise, except horse-racing, nor diversion, except cock-fighting, in which some greatly
delight."

By the 1750's the Virginia newspapers carried
frequent announcements of cockfights, often between
cocks from different counties. Thus a match at the
New Kent county courthouse on Tuesday, May 20,
1755, was between birds from that county and those
from their neighboring county of Gloucester with ten
pistoles a battle and a hundred for the main. Gentlemen of Brunswick and Sussex counties matched cocks
in a widely publicized match on Easter Monday, 1768,
thirty cocks to fight at five pounds a battle and fifty
pounds the main. These were fights involving gentlemen, and they were often followed by balls. Indeed,
by the time of the Revolution, cockfights rivaled horse
races and often lasted for several days. Philip Fithian
noted that the slaves on his plantation had a two-day
holiday "at Cock Fights through the County." Fithian, tutor to the children, stayed home and read Plato.
One of his charges was of less scholarly inclination.
"Harry's genius," Fithian wrote of young Harry
Willis, "seems towards Cocks, low Betts, much in
company with the waiting Boys, &, against my strongest Remonstrances & frequent severe corrections, he
will curse, at times, horribly, & swear fearfully!"
Harry obviously mixed with the blacks whom his
tutor observed in "a Ring . . . at the Stable, fighting Cocks." As in England great lord and the low-

class sporting chap met on the cock walk and at the pit, so did master and slave share a common delight in keeping and fighting cocks.

Toward the end of the war, when Baron Ludwig von Closen was with Rochambeau in Virginia, he wrote of a cockfight as "something to see out of curiosity, but the spectacle is a little too cruel for you to enjoy; you see these poor things knocked about, pricked, blinded, and finally killed with their steel spurs. . . . I will bring back with me some of these spurs to satisfy the curiosity of those who would like to see a cockfight. Those in North America are pointed like the awl of shoemakers; those of Spain are like penknives with a double edge. . . . I have seen some very dexterous [cocks]," he wrote, "who played with this instrument with the greatest daring and skill; thus they often win a reputation for fifty miles or more."

The Marquis de Chastellux tells, in his *Travels*, of stopping at a tavern in the woods when he was traversing Virginia and finding a large crowd gathered to watch a cockfight. "When the principal promoters of this diversion, propose to [match] their champions, they take great care to announce it to the public; and although there are neither posts, nor regular conveyances, this important news spreads with such facility, that the planters for thirty or forty miles around, attend, some with cocks, but all with some money for betting, which is sometimes very considerable. . . .

"Whilst our horses were feeding, we had an opportunity of seeing a battle. The preparations took up a great deal of time. . . . The stakes were very considerable; the money of the parties was deposited in the hands of one of the principal persons, and I felt a secret pleasure in observing that it was chiefly French. I know not which is the most astonishing, the insipidity of such diversion or the stupid interest with which it animates the parties. . . . Whilst the interested parties animated the cocks to battle, a child of fifteen, who was near me, kept leaping for joy, and crying, 'Oh! It is a *charming diversion.*' "

In 1787 Elkanah Watson, a New Englander living in the South for a time, visited a cockfight in Hampton, Virginia. As he approached the appointed spot, the roads, he noted, "were alive with carriages, horses, and pedestrians, black and white, hastening to the point of attraction. Several houses formed a spacious square, in the center of which was arranged a large cockpit; surrounded by many genteel people, promiscuously mingled with the vulgar and debased. Exceedingly beautiful cocks were produced, armed with long, steel-pointed gaffs, which were firmly attached to their natural spurs.

"The moment the birds were dropped, bets ran high. The little heroes appeared trained to the business, and were not the least discountenanced by the crowd or shouting. They stepped about with great apparent pride and dignity; advancing nearer and nearer, they flew upon each other at the same instant with a rude shock, the cruel and fatal gaffs being driven into their bodies, and, at times, directly through their heads. Frequently one, or both, were struck dead at the first blow, but they often fought after being repeatedly pierced, as long as they were able to crawl, and in the agonies of death would often make abortive efforts to raise their heads and strike their antagonists. I soon sickened at this barbarous sport, and retired under the shade of a wide-spread willow tree. . . ."

The American cockers, like their British counterparts from whom they indeed derived, had an elaborate mythology which dealt with such matters as breeding, feeding, and training, all embellished with accounts of legendary birds who had won Homeric battles. The Colonial Americans used many of the same techniques that had been passed on among cockers from Greek times (or earlier, perhaps) ; they cited the same justifications against the critics of the sport; they bet in the same reckless and improvident fashion, and they added a justification that it had not occurred to the British to make — the democracy of the sport. They never tired of repeating that it was a sport where wealth and social standing counted for nothing.

New York was a center for cockers and cockfighting, both before and after the American Revolution, and the memories of such famous figures as Uncle Billy Rodgers and Uncle Pete, men who dominated the sport in the middle years of the nineteenth century, are still preserved by the cockfighting fraternity. Uncle Billy was probably a black man and Uncle Pete owned the most popular gambling house in New York City. At the other end of the social scale was Cornelius Van Sickles, scion of an aristocratic Dutch family, whose fame rested primarily on the fact that he would never bet less than a hundred dollars on a fight.

In Brooklyn, an Irish stronghold, Patrick Duff produced a strain of cockers, part Irish and part Old English, known as "Connecticut Strawberries," who were virtually invincible. "The Hump" (as Duff was called because of a congenital deformity) won a thousand dollars — a very large sum in 1847 — from a gambler named Johnny Crapeau. In an effort to "fix" the fight, the Hump's spurs were put on upside down. The cock was badly wounded in the beginning of the fight but finally won in a battle long celebrated in song and story in the cockfighting circles of New York. Free Negroes were very prominent in the sport, and Nigger Jackson's strain of fighting cocks was as famous as Patrick Duff's "Connecticut Strawberries." It is also worth noting that in America, as opposed to England, while rich and poor met in the cockpit on equal terms, it was the poor rather than the rich — the Irish immigrant and the free black most characteristically — who dominated the sport. The wealthy sportsman who wished to participate did so on the terms of the common man, the small hardscrabble farmer, the rancher of modest means, the cowboy or hired hand, the drifter, the mechanic.

In addition, there were minor variations in the rules and rituals governing cockfights in America. The pit was originally circular with padded sides between 16 and 24 inches high, the diameter of the pit 16 or 18 feet. Sometimes the floor was covered by carpet. In the center there was a chalk-drawn circle with two opposing lines, each a foot from the center mark. The birds were "brought up to the mark" at the beginning of the fight. There were usually two judges, one chosen by each contestant, and a referee appointed by the judges. Once in the ring, the birds could not be taken up by their handlers. If a wounded bird fell, he could be assisted to his feet but not lifted completely off the ground. A cock which refused or was unable to fight was counted out — a count of three tens and a twenty. The only trimming allowed by American rules was the longer feathers of the tail, the wing feathers, and the fluff surrounding the bird's vent.

Cockfighting in America spread west with the frontier and was especially popular in those areas settled by Southerners and by the Irish. A famous West Coast cocker was Captain Anthony Greene, an Irishman, whose family had crossed the Great Plains in 1850 and made their home in Sacramento, California, where at the age of seven young Anthony acquired his first cock and a mentor, George Lloyd, from the town of Limerick. In a biographical sketch he wrote on July 27, 1914, he noted, "In the late fifties and during the early sixties Calif. was a hot bed of cockers, and the Southern States were represented by many noted cockers. . . ."

The reformers who made cockfighting illegal in

England had their American counterparts, but the latter had much slower going than their English cousins. For one thing, there was no sentiment for national legislation on the matter; thus it was left to the states, where the cockers fought resourceful and determined delaying actions. States where there was little cockfighting (and where it was confined largely to the rougher elements) led the way in banning cockfighting, but there was little anticocking legislation even on the state level until the early decades of the twentieth century, a hundred years or so after the parliamentary statute which ended public cockfighting in England. When legislation was passed it varied greatly in its provisions and effectiveness. In some states the possession of game cocks was *prima facie* evidence of illegal intent; in others the fact that birds were dubbed — their combs and wattles trimmed — was accepted as proof that fighting was intended. Some states made the seizure of artificial spurs a requirement for arrest and conviction. Still others were content to outlaw the fights themselves. No one could be arrested unless he had been caught in the act of pitting birds at a main.

No matter how the laws were drawn, tightly or loosely, they were evaded. Some cockfighting has remained legal in spite of the constantly renewed efforts of reformers to have it banned. Oregon, Arizona, and Florida are among the few states left in the Union where cockfighting has not been made illegal; it is forbidden in forty-one out of the fifty states. In Oregon the opposers of cruelty to animals have tried to have it banned by the courts under a general state law forbidding cruelty to animals, but in a court decision in 1972 Judge James Main declared, reasonably enough, that if the Oregon legislature had intended to make cockfighting illegal they would have passed a law to that effect. The decision was, in effect, a victory for cockfighters all over the United States.

While cockfighting continues in virtually every state where it is prohibited by law, it does so under obvious handicaps. The large mains attracting cockers from all over a state and, indeed, from a number of states, colorful events with large purses and big crowds, are usually too risky to attempt. Even sympathetic sheriffs can hardly avoid enforcing the law when breaches are forced on their attention. Thus, the few states like Arizona and Oregon in the Far West, Arkansas in the Middle West, and Florida in the South are precious refuges for those cockers who, believing that they belong to a great national fraternity, are unwilling to confine their activities to their own locales.

Of all the states, California, where illegal cockfighting flourishes, is considered to have the strictest law against the sport. (The law makes it risky even to own game birds.) And California cockfighters, who, as we have seen, have an extraordinarily rich trove of stories, legends, and tall and short tales, believe that the newspaper baron William Randolph Hearst was their nemesis, or at least aspired to be. As the story goes, many of the movie stars of Hollywood were caught up in a cockfighting craze in the twenties. Will Rogers is supposed to have introduced the sport to the film set, and Hearst, who was at the beginning of his long romance with Marion Davies and much involved in promoting her career as an actress, was drawn into the cockfighting mania. There are two versions of why he became the bitter enemy of the whole fraternity. One is that as a rich and arrogant man he offended some code of cockfighters. He was, in consequence, denied the right to pit his birds and decided in revenge to use his vast influence in the state legislature to have the sport banned. His knowledge of the customs of cockfighting was employed to see that the law was drawn so tightly that no one could evade it.

The other version goes that Marion Davies went to a main on her own, was persuaded to drink too much, made reckless bets, and was, in consequence, taken to the cleaners, arousing Hearst's anger. Whether the story is apocryphal or not, the fact remains that the California law is stringent and clearly the work of one who knew — or was advised about — the ins and outs of cockfighting. The possession of spurs or of a dubbed cock or of a cock whose natural spurs have been cut in order to fit steel spurs over the stumps are all evidence of the intent to fight and thus chargeable.

California cockfighters have, in the face of the toughest state laws in the Union, risen magnificently to the test. They have been as cunning, as determined, and as invincible as their prized birds. Several years ago they won a court case which has given them considerably more latitude. A cocker in Santa Cruz County caught with dubbed birds argued that he kept the birds to show them in poultry shows for their coloring and conformation and pointed to rules governing the showing of gamecocks which specified that their combs and wattles must be dubbed. The court upheld him, and cockers throughout the state profited from the decision.

In Kansas cockfighting is forbidden only on Saturday or Sunday — a strange combination of residual Puritanism and tolerance for a long-established rural sport. In Kentucky only cockfighting "for profit" (whatever that means) is prohibited, and in Alabama cockfighting is legal so long as it is conducted with strict regard to privacy so as not to outrage public morals. Vermont and Maryland, like Oregon, extended a general statute against cruelty to animals to cover cockfights by defining as animals any living creature other than man. Particularly in the southeastern United States cockfighting has a quasipublic status in that mains are frequently advertised in magazines such as *Grit and Steel* that are edited exclusively for *aficionados* of the sport. The state of affairs today is, in fact, much as it was described in the November, 1952, issue of the *National Humane Review:* "There is hardly a sizeable community in the whole of the United States in which cockfights are not being conducted more or less regularly. And where this condition exists it is very often the fact that local law enforcement authorities know about it — or don't want to know about it. Cockfights are always fairly widely publicized. They have to be to attract the necessary crowd of 'fanciers' and spectators. They are staged over and over at the same pits. They are often announced weeks and months in advance in national magazines. Any law-enforcement officer who wants to prevent the cockfights will have little difficulty in locating most of them. . . . Tens of thousands of birds are maimed, mangled, and killed in agony every year in illegal pits. The sport's devotees boast openly of corrupting public officials. In commercial terms, it is at least a $10,000,000-a-year business."

Several comments are in order. The vast majority of mains are small local affairs that are not publicized except through personal communication among the local members of the fraternity. Often the site for fights is shifted regularly. Cockers are secretive and reluctant to admit any outsider to a main unless he is personally vouched for by a trusted cocker. I also doubt that many, if any, public officials are "corrupted," as the magazine charged. Many certainly are sympathetic and some law-enforcement officers in small communities are themselves involved in raising and fighting cocks. What is meant by a ten-million-dollar-a-year business is also uncertain. Fighting cocks are certainly expensive. A bird of a well-known strain will bring from fifty to several hundred dollars. (A local construction worker in Santa Cruz not long ago paid a thousand dollars for ten gamecocks.) The prizes for the victors in local bouts are usually modest and are made up out of the entry fees. Substantial sums of money change hands in betting on particular bouts or the outcomes of mains. But few people make large sums of money out of the sport. In this sense, I suspect, it could be said to be the least commercialized sport in the country, and this in a time when most other sports are big business. Certainly cockfights do not depend on a "necessary crowd of 'fanciers' and spectators." An adequate number of "fanciers" is two, each with one or more birds.

Scarcely a week passes without a more or less ritual raid on cockfighters. In Santa Cruz County, over a hundred birds were recently confiscated in two separate raids. One raid was prompted by a vengeful neighbor and was made on a cocker whose birds were plainly dubbed and ready for fighting. The birds were seized by several patrol cars full of police and carried off to the Humane Society to be held pending court hearings. Since the Humane Society had no proper accommodations for fifty fighting cocks they were put in cages intended for domestic animals, primarily dogs and cats, and there, of course, they fell to fighting and maiming and destroying each other, an outcome which brought the furious owner to court to get an order requiring the county to take proper care of the birds while the case was pending. Some three or four thousand dollars' worth of fighting cocks were involved. When the case came to court a week or so later, the charges were dismissed on the grounds, established in an earlier case, that the birds might have been intended merely for exhibition purposes. The second raid took place during a Mexican-American cockfight, and in this instance it was impossible to evade the charge. Some seventy birds were confiscated.

A recent raid in Los Angeles on a major main netted over a thousand birds, worth nearly a hundred thousand dollars; and a story datelined New York, February, 1972, read: "The cockfighting score yesterday stood at 60 birds impounded, five birds dead and 96 men arrested. In apparently unrelated actions early yesterday, police in Manhattan hauled in 68 men surprised in a fight in the Soho districts of warehouses and artists' lofts, and police on Long Island pulled in 28 men nabbed watching a cockfight in a house at Central Islip." In cities with large Spanish-speaking populations such raids are frequent. They come when word of a large illegal main circulates so widely that the police feel compelled to act. The thousands of small mains that take place every year around the country proceed undisturbed, for the most part, and it would be hard to convince overworked law officers, or indeed any large segment of the public, that it was a major dereliction of duty not to spend more time playing hide-and-seek with ingenious cockers.

Besides *Grit and Steel*, several other magazines serve the large fraternity of American cockers. They contain advertisements for various breeds for sale, announcements of major mains, articles on breeding, and a constant stream of stories, usually nostalgic, about famous birds and famous breeders. An article in one issue defends the fighting qualities of the Aseel, or Oriental cross, which was imported in the United States in the late nineteenth century, against the charge that they are less courageous fighters than other strains. The author has seen Orientals fight every bit as fiercely as the "hatch, Claret, Round-head, Redquill, Warhorse, Brown Reds," and other birds known for courage. "Anthony Green," the author writes, "some years back bred an Oriental Jap cross that won wherever fought. . . . I never did hear of anyone getting wealthy whipping those Jap [sic] crosses."

For verification the author calls on "any cock

fighter fighting at Baxter Springs, Kansas, Roy Gray's Pit, Paris, Arkansas, and several in the Islands who report very good results." Any breed or strain will have its portion of "runners" — birds refusing to fight.

Another article "proudly" presented in the same issue of *Grit and Steel* is entitled "Highlights of William J. Vizzard's Career in Cocking," by his son, James.

James recalls such moments of high drama as "a seventeen cock main" in Los Angeles, won fourteen to three. The senior Vizzard lost with "a Dom cross of Payt Jordan's but won with a Payton Jordan–Red and a Payt Jordan Dom–Aseel cross as well as with twelve greys. . . . These Grey cocks," the author continues, confident of the fascinated attention of his readers, "were ³⁄₁₆th Aseel and were bred jointly by Peter McKinley of Neb. and by my father. . . . The original matings were one-fourth Aseel on each side mixed with Georgia-Shawl and the Old New York Mahoney. Later more Mahoney fowl was bred in, and they were set as a family with ³⁄₁₆th Aseel one-eighth Shawl and the rest Gull and Mahoney Commodore." This is the way cockfighters, at least American cockfighters, talk to each other. Vizzard, one of the most renowned cockers of the 1930's and 1940's, fought, according to his son, two to four mains a year for twenty-one years, "winning every one of them. In his entire career he lost three mains," generally fighting two hundred to two hundred and fifty separate fights a year and winning eighty to eighty-five percent of them.

The elder Vizzard's favorite cock was Asa, "one-half of Asa Camp's Morgan or Gilkerson White-hackle," who "fought in Troy, New York, in short heels, winning seven times." His brother won a fight in a Los Angeles main, "being rattle blinked and his leg broken near the leather, and died before he could be put in the box." Asa was "a combination fighter; he could side-step, break high and in a close fight could turn loose a terrific shuffle." The cock lived for ten years, full of honors, and the progenitor of many younger warriors almost as formidable. "He was a highly intelligent cock; he talked all the time in the cockhouse, and every time my father would bend over to do something in a lower set of coops, Asa would reach out and pluck his hat off his head." In his last year of life Asa had two heart attacks but was saved with nitroglycerin pills. The third attack was fatal and Asa entered into history.

In the same issue of *Grit and Steel*, Clarence Boles reminisced about his father's line of Orientals — "Daddy Boles' Japs" — and their fighting prowess. "Old Cap," born around 1897, was the ancestor of a notable family of fighting cocks, including "Silver Bell," winner of five fights in one season "without getting a feather broken." According to Clarence Boles the "high light" of Daddy Boles's "life in the world of cocking" came when his father was invited to a meet on the West Coast soon after moving from Denver. When he arrived at the site of the main, there was only one other cocker prepared to fight birds. This was a millionaire "copper king" named Sullivan, with his fancy automobile and liveried chauffeur. The Boleses had a rented wagon drawn by a white mule.

When Sullivan asked Daddy Boles how much he wanted to fight for, Daddy replied, "Ten dollars a battle."

"Hell," Sullivan replied, "I wouldn't get the feathers mussed on my birds for ten dollars."

"Well, just take your damned cocks and head for home with them," Boles said.

At this point Sullivan turned to his handler and said, "Go ahead and match him; from the look of those grey dubs we won't get a feather broken anyway."

The result was that Daddy Boles won six straight fights and then pitted his sixth bird, "Spike Bill," against another of Sullivan's fowls and won a seventh, thereby vindicating the common man as well as winning seventy dollars.

Among the advertisements carried by *Grit and Steel* is the notice of a "School for Cockers" run by the Bishop brothers of Seagoville, Texas. Ten students would be enrolled at a tuition of one hundred fifty dollars for the two-week course. "Each student," the ad reads, "will bring two cocks. . . . We will teach how to feed cocks, to come off the score line fighting and cutting. How to properly heel a cock, and how to pit from long and center line under Wortham's Rules. . . . We have been successful winning with our method of feeding. All students will be expected to apply themselves 100%. There will be NO DRINKING during school hours." From which it seems fair to assume that cockfighting still flourishes in Texas.

Cockfighting, dogfighting — the fighting of pit terriers — and quarter-horse racing were also imported from England and were very much to the Southern sporting taste and to those ideals of honor and chivalry which were so much a part of the Southerner's temperament. The South has certainly remained the center of the most intense cockfighting, matched only by the Southwest, where Mexican-Americans and, in a few scattered areas, Philippine farm laborers are avid cockers. In the Puerto Rican population of New York City, cockfighting also flourishes under the most uncongenial conditions possible. Cockfighting is not only illegal in New York State, but even the keeping of chickens is forbidden by city ordinance. Yet despite such handicaps it is undoubtedly the case that a night seldom passes without a clandestine main or at least a furtive engagement between a few hastily pitted birds.

We have noted earlier that cockfighting is as close to a universal sport as history records. We might thus take some account of cockfighting in various parts of the world.

In France and Belgium, cockfighting has a long history. The most famous cocker of France — whose national symbol, of course, is a cock — was Henri Cliquennous, who in the mid-nineteenth century developed a French strain of cock that was known as "one of the largest, most powerful, and most courageous fighting-cocks in the world." In the last decade of the century, a renowned American breeder, one Dr. Clarke, sent over a group of birds that were matched against Cliquennous's fowls. Armed with the more lethal American spurs, they routed the French birds. The Frenchmen immediately adopted the American irons, and the French birds thereafter more than held their own in mains with British and American cocks. As recently as 1939 there was an account in the London *Daily Express* (March 14, 1939) of a match at Calais "in a covered courtyard behind a cafe. . . ." Some two hundred men, women, and children paid to watch the bouts. At the end of one fight, the reporter noted, "both birds [were] torn, bleeding, barely breathing. . . . The crowd shouted insults, then roared applause as one slowly lifted himself, pecked at his opponent's eyes, leaped in the air and struck one steel spur clean through the other bird's head."

Before it was outlawed in Belgium, the sport claimed over one hundred thousand enthusiasts who belonged to the National Federation of Cockfighters. Cockfights go on in rural Belgium, doubtless as frequently as in England or America. Much the same can be said of other European countries, especially those which, like Spain and Italy, have an ancient tradition of cockfighting.

Among the Hindus, naked-heel fighting has long been preferred, since the time of each bout is thereby extended. Naked-heel fighting has led, in turn, to a strong emphasis on endurance rather than speed and agility and has put Hindu-owned birds at a serious disadvantage in fights where artificial spurs are used. Many cocks could fight a whole day, and some famous bouts lasted two or three days before a bird was killed or was too exhausted to fight. Since the relationship between cockfighting and masculine sexuality should by now be well established, one is tempted to conjecture that the same sexual attitudes which in Hindu culture prized in the human male the capacity to prolong intercourse were manifest in efforts to prolong individual cockfights. Moreover, the English and Western emphasis on short fights, swift kills, and thus numerous contests in a relatively brief period of time, as contrasted with the extended Indian bouts, clearly demonstrates the profound difference in attitude of these two cultures toward time. The Western spirit is to crowd as much sensation into as short a period of time as possible, while the Eastern mode is to savor the moment and to draw it out in a way that is intolerable to the Western consciousness.

In much of present-day India, cockfighting has passed from the sport of princes and rajahs to the ordinary people of the country, who engage in it avidly, following formulas for diet and training several thousand years old and sometimes pitting their birds in the open streets.

In southeast Asia — the Celebes, the Malay Peninsula, Bali, and Borneo — cockfighting is a way of life surrounded by a remarkable variety of religious and cultural rituals. An English visitor to Malacca in the nineteenth century wrote, "The cocks, which at the present day represent specimens of the finest class, are trained much in the same way as in Europe, but are armed, in place of a spur, with a broad, flat blade, resembling their own favorite weapon — the kris; with which they are able to inflict frightful wounds, without being of so deadly a nature as with the more pointed instrument in use in our country. . . ."

Walter Kaudern, in his *Ethnographical Studies in Celebes*, describes the passion for cockfighting on that island. "The Organ [Orang] Bugis as well as Orang Macassar most carefully attend their Gamecocks, even more than to their horses. A gamecock is kept in a basket some time before a fight. Every night he has his bath and his shampoo to harden his muscles." The value of a cock was also related to whether or not he had been born in a holy place, and the local variations in rules governing cockfights are almost infinite.

In Borneo, like the Philippines, cockfighting is legal, and here the dominant categories are those of the natives of North Borneo, who use spurs, and the Mohammedans of the coast, who practice naked-heel fighting. In the native fights of North Borneo, bouts are divided into three rounds: "Each side has the right to stop the fight three times during its course at any stage. This break is termed a 'purut' (corresponding to the end of a boxing round) and occupies an interval of no fixed duration, but it gives the owners an opportunity to revive their birds by fanning them, staunching their wounds, and washing off the congealed blood adhering to eyes and comb." After the third "purut" the fight must continue until one bird is the victor. In the Philippines — the Islands, as cockfighters say — the cockfights have the symbolic importance that they have in other parts of the "East" but without the restrictions encountered in most countries. Consequently the Philippines are the cockfighting center of the world, and large international mains are held there from time to time. The Philippine natives fight with slashers and bet with a recklessness that is proverbial.

Many California cockers use the pretense of breeding birds for sale in "the Islands" as a cover for their own cockfighting activities. It is doubtless true that they do export fighting cocks for high prices because natives of the Philippines will pay extravagant prices for prize birds.

In the Hawaiian Islands cockfighting is illegal. Although conducted clandestinely it nonetheless has the character of an official sport. The police are engaged in a constant if sporadic battle against the cockers. A recent newspaper item recounted the arrest of nine men for cockfighting in the towns of Waianae and Waialau and charged them with 148 counts of gambling and cockfighting. Some three hundred spectators had been present at the respective fights. Law enforcement is a dilemma for the Hawaiian authorities because tourists, most of them other Americans on the lookout for forbidden pleasures, often make up a large portion of the spectators at the illegal fights.

According to the March 29, 1972, issue of the *Honolulu Star-Bulletin*, the Hawaiians may have found a delightfully ambiguous solution. The council of the isle of Maui took the cock by the comb in declaring that cockfighting should be recognized as a "cultural heritage" in Hawaii. This lead was followed by the legislative committee of the Council of Hilo, which voted five to one "to support the principle of the Maui resolution after assurances that it did not mean that the council was advocating legalized cockfighting." Presumably it was recognizing illegal cockfighting, or perhaps cockfighting to be conducted only in museums devoted to the "cultural heritage" of the islands.

In Latin America and South America cockfighting flourishes. Again in the Spanish and Eastern tradition, there is a good deal of naked-heel fighting and where spurs are used, slashers are much preferred. It is a common sight in Mexican villages to see fighting cocks staked: that is, tied to stakes with a short piece of rope so that they can range without getting within reach of each other. This practice is, in fact, quite widely used in America, especially by California cockers, where the toughest nylon is used.

Cuba is the center of cockfighting in the Caribbean, although it is endemic on all the West Indies. In the nineteenth century there were cockpits (if they could be called that) which held a thousand spectators, and a traveler named Samuel Hazard has left us a description of the "shouting, bawling, vociferating, and motioning to each other in the making of their bets, until the place is a very Babel." The bets are made, the birds are pitted, and excitement grows wildly. "At last," Hazard wrote, "the combatants are both seriously hurt, and perhaps blinded by the blood and dust; and then there is a lull in the fighting, while the backers doctor up their birds, wiping the blood from their heads, blow through a quill a little alum to heal their eyes, or spit a mouthful of *aguardiente* [a native liquor] over their heads; the audience, meanwhile, keeping up the racket until the chickens commence it over again, with just the same fury, clawing, nipping, and dodging, until one or the other is dead or so disabled he can no longer fight, when the play is up, and a roaring cheer breaks from the lucky betters."

In South America, Peru prides itself on having a tradition of superior birds and cockfighting that goes back to the Spanish *conquistadores*. "At Lima," we are told by another traveler, "the diversion of cockfighting is followed with great avidity . . . the duties of society were not only neglected by many individuals, but there were continual disputes among the amateurs [the lovers of the sport]." The cockpit in Lima was an amphitheater with twenty-nine ascending galleries. Cockfighting was permitted here two days a week and on saints' days and Sundays. "The seats in the corridors are let at different prices," we are told, "but the spectators who stand in the nine open spaces between the area and the galleries are admitted gratis. Notwithstanding the crowd is often immense, no disorder occurs, and the judge who decrees the prizes has always a guard with him to enforce his authority."

Undoubtedly the most detailed and extensive study of a cockfight is that of an anthropologist named Clifford Geertz, who wrote an essay entitled "Deep Play: Notes on the Balinese Cockfight," in an issue of *Daedalus*, the journal of the American Academy of Arts and Sciences (Winter, 1972), devoted to "Myth, Symbol and Culture." Geertz and his wife established themselves in a Balinese village and through the happy misfortune of being present during a police "raid" — cockfighting, although a combination of national sport and religion for the Balinese, is nonetheless illegal (the result, as Geertz puts it, "of the pretensions of Puritanism radical nationalism tends to bring with it") — they gained the trust of the inhabitants of the village and an insight into the complex ritual of a Balinese cockfight.

The fight had been held (rather recklessly, since it was an illegal activity)* in the village square, perhaps because it was intended to raise money for a school. Geertz, who has a most engaging style, describes the raid: "In the midst of the third match . . . a truck full of policemen armed with machine guns roared up. Amid great screeching cries of 'pulisi! pulisi!' from the crowd the policemen jumped out and, springing into the center of the ring, began to swing their guns around like gangsters in a motion picture, though not going so far as to actually fire

* Prior to the arrival of the Dutch in 1908 it was the duty of an adult male to bring a cock to a fight and the "taxation of fights, which were usually held on market day, was a major source of public revenue; patronage of the art was a stated responsibility of princes; and the cock ring . . . stood in the center of the village near those other monuments of Balinese civility — the council house, the origin temple, the marketplace, the signal tower, and the banyan tree." Now cockfighting was far less open but nonetheless ubiquitous.

them. . . . People raced down the road, disappeared head first over walls, scrambled under platforms, folded themselves behind wicker screens, scuttled up coconut trees. Cocks armed with steel spurs [blades] sharp enough to cut off a finger or run a hole through a foot were running wildly around. Everything was dust and panic."

The fact that the American professors ran with everyone else amused and pleased the villagers, and they were taken into the family, so to speak. The Geertzes discovered that "as much of America surfaces in a ball park, on a golf links, at a race track, or around a poker table, much of Bali surfaces in a cock ring. . . . To anyone who has been in Bali any length of time, the deep psychological identification of Balinese men with their cocks is unmistakable. The double entendre here is deliberate. It works in exactly the same way in Balinese as it does in English, even producing the same tired jokes, strained puns, and uninventive obscenities."

Gregory Bateson and Margaret Mead, who made one of the most striking studies of Balinese society, have suggested that for the Balinese their cocks are seen, in Geertz's paraphrase, "as detachable, self-operating penises, ambulant genitals with a life of their own." In Balinese the word for "cock" also means "hero," "warrior," "political candidate," "bachelor," "dandy," and "lady-killer." The cockfight provides a metaphor for almost every aspect of Balinese life from lovemaking and politics to court trials and personal quarrels. "I am cock crazy," the Geertzes' landlord told them; "we are all cock crazy."

The Geertzes noted that Balinese men spent "an enormous amount of time with their favorites, grooming them, feeding them, discussing them . . . or just gazing at them with a mixture of rapt admiration and dreamy self-absorption." Whenever they saw "a group of Balinese men squatting idly in the council shed or along the road in their hips down, shoulders forward, knees up fashion, half or more of them will have a rooster in his hands, holding it between his thighs, bouncing it gently up and down to strengthen its legs, ruffling its feathers with abstract sensuality. . . ."

Geertz noted that the cocks in classic fashion were fed a special diet by the Balinese. Red pepper was forced down their throats and up their vents "to give them spirit." Moreover, they were "bathed in the same ceremonial preparation of tepid water, medicinal herbs, flowers and onions in which infants are bathed, and for a prize cock just as often. Their combs are cropped, their plumage dressed, their spurs trimmed, their legs massaged. . . ."

It is not just sexuality that the Balinese identifies with in the gamecock, "not just his ideal self, or even his penis, but also, and at the same time, with what he most fears, hates, and ambivalence being what it is, is fascinated by — The Powers of Darkness." The cockfight itself was thus "a blood sacrifice offered, with the appropriate chants and oblations, to the demons in order to pacify their ravenous, cannibal hunger. . . . In the cockfight, man and beast, good and evil, ego and id, the creative power of aroused masculinity and the destructive power of loosened animality fuse in a bloody drama of hatred, cruelty, violence, and death." Balinese describe heaven and hell as the states of the man whose cock has just won or lost a fight.

Professor Geertz goes on to relate in great detail the fight itself, with special emphasis on the ritual nature of the betting. He mentions that spurs are sharpened only at eclipses and the dark of the moon. Time is counted by the time it takes a pierced coconut to sink in a pail of water and the handler of a wounded bird "blows in its mouth, putting the whole chicken head in his own mouth and sucking and blow ing . . . ," a ritual which, as we have seen, is almost universal and doubtless as old as cockfighting.

The rules of the Balinese fights are written in palm-leaf manuscripts passed on from generation to generation as part of the general legal and cultural tradition of the villages.

For Professor Geertz the ultimate importance of the cockfight for the Balinese is as a social ritual which dramatizes and confirms the essential nature of the group and which helps to define the relationships of families and castes within the larger group. It is as formal, as precise, and as highly organized as the most elaborate religious rites of whose character it so clearly partakes. Beyond this it appears to him as ritualized violence, that violence which the Balinese, perhaps even more than Westerners, are expected to sublimate. In Geertz's view the explosion of violence in the cockfight is a highly potent form of catharsis for the Balinese. It has thus a fourfold function: it serves as a sex symbol (very different from a Hollywood starlet, to be sure) which strengthens and confirms the male in his sexuality and his masculine aggressiveness; it reinforces the whole structure of village life; it represents animality — all the dark forces of nature — as opposed to civility; and, very close to that, it provides a ritual release of violent impulses and angers that the remarkably restrained and formal Balinese must somehow rid themselves of.

Professor Geertz's analysis of the Balinese cockfight is highly suggestive — in more ways than one. What it suggests most specifically is that the "modern spirit," the spirit of improvement and reform, of psychotherapy and group dynamics, of social manipulation designed to rid us of our aggressions, may be going at things from the wrong end. It is the most modern and progressive societies that have found cockfights intolerable and that have outlawed them, or tried to, and it is the older, more traditional societies that have followed suit, afraid, in many instances that their failure to do so will mark them as "backward," "primitive," and "uncivilized" in the eyes of the progressive nations.

Banning public cockfights in the more "advanced" countries failed signally to diminish violence. Nor would I wish to suggest that legalizing cockfighting would at all reduce it. The opposition to cockfighting is a rather revealing quality of mind. One suspects that it has something to do with the notion — common to enlightened societies — that evil can be legislated out of existence. Devoted civil libertarians who are horrified at the thought of forbidding liquor or pornography see nothing contradictory in trying to legislate out of existence a sport that quite clearly reaches to the deepest levels of the human psyche. Perhaps this is the very point. The spectacle of public cockfighting is a reminder of those dark forces of nature that the Balinese — painfully aware of them as elements of their world — seek to exorcise; whereas we — members, as many of us feel, of a more advanced society — prefer to pretend that they do not exist.

Clifford Geertz expresses the point well. "Every people . . . loves its own form of violence. The cockfight is the Balinese reflection on theirs; on its look, its uses, its force, its fascination. Drawing on almost every level of Balinese experience, it brings together themes — animal savagery, male narcissism, opponent gambling, status rivalry, mass excitement, blood sacrifice — whose main connection is their involvement with rage and the fear of rage, and, binding them into a set of rules which at once contains them and allows them play, builds a symbolic structure in which, over and over again, the reality of their inner affiliation can be intelligently felt."

When Geertz goes on to compare the drama of the cockfight for the Balinese to the drama of *Macbeth* for a Western audience, the reader may feel a twinge of uneasiness. The notion that *Macbeth* is a curative relief for that impulse to violence common to the human species which in Bali finds its outlet in cockfighting is a notion perhaps a little too glib and "literary." There is an abundance of evidence that Western man's rages and lusts, however sublimated their forms, are fully as cruel as those to be found in other cultures. Perhaps Professor Geertz would have been on more solid ground if he had taken as an example of the potential for violence in that subdivision of Western man called Americans the case of the Viet Nam War rather than the play *Macbeth*. The Balinese, a notably gentle and graceful people, have a symbolic enactment of violence which horrifies liberal opinion; American violence has resulted in the deaths of enormous numbers of Asians.

In any event, we must be grateful to Professor Geertz for bringing the strange history of cockfighting up to date. Perhaps he has done so with a rather heavy load of sociological and psychological interpretation. But whether or not we wish to travel the whole way with him, we must certainly be aware by now of the fact that history contains no form of behavior relating to humans and their animal companions which is richer in symbolic meanings, or which penetrates more profoundly into the inner recesses of the masculine psychic life than the cockfight, almost everywhere forbidden and almost everywhere practiced.

From Roman times to Aldrovandi's monumental work on chickens little was apparently written (or thought) about chickens. There were, as we have seen, no learned treatises on the chicken, no philosophical works, no illuminated manuscripts painstakingly inscribed by monks detailing the habits and the uses of the chicken. Yet everywhere the chicken lived and flourished in happy anonymity, the hen providing her master or mistress with that perpetual bounty of eggs that, more than anything else, assured her survival, while her mate by his irrepressible ferocity remained similarly an object of human interest and attention. Together hen and cock constituted a walking *materia medica,* a whole medicine cabinet of remedies. Before doctors had appeared as a professional class (which was really not until the eighteenth century), every man was his own doctor with some assistance from witches, magicians, and itinerant practitioners of the most dubious qualifications. In such times virtually the only medicine was folk medicine, which is not necessarily to say it was bad medicine. In folk medicine the chicken thus remained the most efficacious creature. A person suffering almost any conceivable malady of the body or even the spirit was inclined to reach first for a chicken. Not until the end of the nineteenth century was that ubiquitous bird replaced as the average man's apothecary.

In ancient Greece, as we have seen, hens were sacrificed to Aesculapius, the god of medicine, for the benefits they were supposed to bring to mankind. Fever, dysentery, melancholy, epilepsy, cough, colic were all treated by applications of various parts of the chicken. Oil of eggs was guaranteed to make hair grow and other potions were used against "poison, corns on the toes, the bites of mad dogs and vipers, and frenzy."

Hippocrates, the father of medicine, favored the whites of four eggs beaten up in three quarts of water as a laxative. Galen, another famous Greek physician, recommended eggs as an excellent diet for the sick. Eggs were especially recommended for the patient suffering from fever, since they were easy to digest. Along with eggs the patient might take the tender white meat of capons. Galen's remedy for the chronic bed-wetter is a kind of classic. One took the gizzard of a cock and dried it in the sun and then added a dram of juniper juice, dry acorn, flower of wild pomegranate, and oak apple "all crushed together with rose, honey." Or a spoonful of fried windpipe of a cock taken with wine or water. Or one testicle of a cock. In the use of eggshells, it was often important to use shells out of which chickens had been hatched. Gattinaria recommended for those who could not pass urine the shell of such an egg; he gave it to "a certain noblewoman," he reported, "and she passed twelve glasses full of urine."

The testicles of cocks were recommended in the sixth century A.D. by Alexander of Tralles to give strength to a weak patient. Similarly an old cock who had just had a severe fight with another bird might be cooked with barley and raisins, pennyroyal, hyssop, thyme, violets, vinegar, and honey. "Offer the patient as much of it as he can swallow at one draught," the physician directed.

As hens' eggs and cocks' testicles stimulated "lust," so they were effective as cures for various ailments of the human genitals. For loss of virility, Pliny prescribed "a mixture of eggs with three *cyathi* [about four ounces] of raisin wine and a half-ounce of starch." For inflammation of the penis Galen recommended a mixture of cumin and eggshells cooked together: "This should be applied to the affected part, and . . . promises a remarkable effect." A cock's testicles ground up in water were prescribed for epilepsy. In the absence of sleeping pills ancient physicians recommended the white of an egg applied to the forehead on a linen bandage. Eating cock feet also was considered a soporific, as was a chicken feather dipped in vinegar.

The ancients apparently had their share of headaches, for there are numerous headache remedies that involve chickens. The white of an egg was taken much as aspirin is today for a headache or pain in any part of the body. Pliny wrote that when a man suffered from chronic headaches a cock should be shut up and forced to abstain from food and water for several days, then its feathers should be plucked from its neck and bound around the patient's head along with the cock's comb.

Pliny wrote that chicken broth stopped dysentery, and Galen prescribed the blood of a cock for stopping cerebral bleeding; roasted eggs were an antidote to the vomiting of blood from mouth and nose. Pliny also recommended unborn chicks cooked in the egg, mixed with half a pint of sour wine and flour with an equal amount of oil, for dysentery. Broth made of a young cock was also good for dysentery, while that of an old bird was recommended as a laxative. Chicken dung with vinegar and warm water induced vomiting and was thus an excellent antidote against poisonous mushrooms; mixed with oil and soda it healed corns.

"The ashes of an egg soaked in wine will heal an

eruption of blood," Pliny wrote. Eggshells were thought to make an excellent coagulant if they were ground up and placed in vinegar until they were soft. Then they should be dried in the sun and dusted over the wound. They were even more efficacious, it was said, if mixed with horse dung. Sucking an egg was recommended for those with sore throats, since the egg white "clings tenaciously to the affected parts and stays there like a poultice."

Avicenna wrote: "Sucking eggs is good for the cough, pleurisy, consumption, and for hoarse throat because of their warmth, as well as for compressed breathing and the spitting of blood, especially when the yolk is swallowed warm." The yolks of five raw eggs in a quarter pint of wine were recommended for consumption — "those who spit blood." Hoarhound juice poured into an eggshell and mixed with honey was guaranteed to "break up boils in a marvelous manner and lead a sick stomach back to health." Chicken fat was also an essential element in many medications.

There was general agreement among ancient physicians that whenever a warm egg was called for as a remedy it was better to have one warm from its mother than artificially warmed. As with egg whites for eyes so with chicken fat for ears. Marcellus Empiricus of Bordeaux wrote that "chicken fat melted and dropped in [the ear] while warm can heal whatsoever disease of the ears." Egg whites were also useful in treating ailments of the auditory meatus, and Galen recommended a mixture of opium and mother's milk with egg whites for the earache. Pliny also suggested chicken fat to heal a rough tongue. Oil of eggs with goose fat helped relieve toothache. The ash of eggshells was useful for a wide variety of things. Mixed with wine it made an excellent toothpaste.

Pliny wrote that the ash of eggshells mixed with myrrh would stimulate a woman's menstruation. On the other hand, if a woman failed to menstruate at the proper time a popular remedy was to hard-boil three eggs; peel them, slice them crosswise, put them over a fire, and pass the vapor into the uterus by means of a pipe or funnel. To bring forth a dead fetus, Hippocrates recommended soda cooked with resin and shaped into the form of a penis, smeared with cock fat, and place upon the opening of the uterus. Kiranides wrote that the still-throbbing heart of a cock bound to the pelvis of a woman in labor would hasten birth. (Pliny's preference was for an entire egg with rue, anise, and cumin taken in wine.)

The physician Marcellus Empiricus had the following remedy for inflammation of the breast as well as for worms. "Take a raw egg open at the top, fill it with green oil and pour it out; then fill it with the urine of a virgin boy and pour this out. Then add a little honey, mix with the inner parts of the egg itself, and give the result of all these operations to the fasting patient. It will drive out the oldest feces and noxious worms and relieve the most acute fever."

For arthritis a four-year-old hen was "stuffed with wormwood and boiled in three buckets of water until the liquid is reduced two thirds. . . . Then a vapor is created with the remaining fluid and the patient's limbs warmed with it twice a day." Another popular remedy for arthritis was the wing bone of a hen bored through with a spoon, tied with thread in seven knots, and held over the swollen portion of the body; it "produces a remarkable healing result." The brain of a hen was useful in stopping nosebleeds.

Not only was the chicken, and its by-product the egg, an essential element in the cure of most internal ills; it was almost equally efficacious for external wounds and lesions. "The scab of Persian fire," a painful skin ailment, could be cured by a poultice of chicken dung mixed with honey. For burns the body should be smeared with raw egg and a beet leaf placed over the burn itself. Galen was satisfied with the white

The Chicken Apothecary

129

of an egg applied directly to the burn. It cooled and healed. The ideal applicator was a feather. An alternative was a combination of lard and chicken fat. Oil extracted from eggs cured the itch, especially if a little hen's blood was mixed with it.

Boils, according to Sextus Empiricus, could be burst by applying the dung of a red cock to them. Other experts preferred the dung of a white cock. For ulcer on the leg a combination of burned eggshells and old shoe soles mixed with cow dung collected in the month of May — the whole dried and crushed and sprinkled on the wound — was recommended. Avicenna prescribed the use of eggs for ulcers or abscesses "near the anus and the pubis," applied with rose oil and a lint bandage. Whites of eggs were an excellent coagulant for bleeding wounds, and Aldrovandi adds that they are "beneficial for cleansing and drawing wounds together which have opened. Pliny recommends fresh hen's dung smeared on the head as an antidote to baldness. If one was troubled by head lice a hen's egg washed off with the juice of the cyclamen herb was guaranteed to bring relief.

Chicken gall strengthened the eyes. The Greek physician Dioscorides wrote: "The white of an egg applied to the forehead with incense drives off and averts discharges from the eyes." Another remedy for running eyes, recommended by Pliny, was a woman's milk mixed with the white of eggs and applied with a piece of wool. The eyes must have given the ancients a good deal of discomfort; there are literally dozens of remedies for sore and inflamed eyes. Galen has a particularly engaging one: the blood of a mouse, a woman's milk, and a cock's gall, "shake well before using." Hen's fat was good for sties.

Averroes, the great twelfth-century Spanish-Arabic philosopher, prescribed the broth "of a young fat hen" as "the best medicine for leprosy." A careful distinction was made by most writers between the broth of a young hen or pullet and that of an old hen. Their medicinal qualities were quite different. The broth of an old cock also had a different effect. "It bathes, washes away, opens, dissipates windiness, provokes and loosens the bowels, and purges black bile." Mixed with senna it was good for arthritic pain. Old cock broth was also of use against "long fevers . . . torpid limbs . . . illnesses of trembling joints, for headaches . . . for nausea, for the liver, kidneys and bladder, against indigestion and asthma." The brains of cocks were useful in treating cerebral palsy.

The feathers and brains of a cock were excellent antidotes for snakebites. "The most celebrated physicians unanimously declare," Aldrovandi wrote, "that the cock's brain is of value against the state of shock or convulsion produced by the bite of a poisoning animal." Another remedy for snakebite was to split a live hen and bind it over the bite, "for by its heat it draws the poison into itself." For those too fastidious to employ such a bloody remedy, a hen's anus, plucked clean of feathers, would serve as well.

Such remedies, prescribed by the physicians Avicenna and Galen, and by Pliny, dominated medical thinking century after century. Aldrovandi endorsed them and added a few of his own. Of them all chicken broth was perhaps the most ubiquitous. The French, by Aldrovandi's time, favored chicken jelly made from young pullets and a chicken broth. Aldrovandi's recipe for chicken jelly called for cooking a pullet and a calf's foot until the meat of the chicken began to dissolve. "Then strain and press out the juice. A bit of sugar and cinnamon should be added. The liquid should be purified with egg whites and shells, strained again and colored as one wishes with saffron, or with green or red dyes."

Almost fifty pages of Aldrovandi's own treatise on the chicken is devoted to its medicinal uses. The Italian naturalist opens this section by stating, "The genus of chicken offers so great an advantage to men in its use in medicine that there is almost no illness of the body, both internal and external, which does not draw its remedy from these birds, in addition to the fact that . . . there is no other food which nourishes us in illness without burdening us except the food which is made from these creatures." Indeed, there was almost "no particle of the chicken . . . which does not have its usefulness recognized by the physician." Aldrovandi excepted the excrement of the chicken, but even he gives a recipe for the white portion of a cock's dung to be used for "an ulcerated artery of the lung."

In Aldrovandi's day the chicken gizzard, whose efficacy had been derided by Galen, had came back into favor. The current view was that it should be soaked in warm lye for an hour, then washed three times, steeped three times in wine, and washed three more times; the whole performance repeated and the gizzard then dried and given to the patient suffering from stomach trouble. For vomiting, Aldrovandi recommended that "one bedbud crushed in a sucking egg" would cure vomiting.

Lest we imagine that "modern" times were more enlightened than old days it might be well to note that the Reverend Mr. Dixon, writing less than one hundred fifty years ago, quoted (from the seventeenth-century writer Francis Willughby) in his work on chickens many of the remedies which had first appeared in Galen some two thousand years earlier, to wit: "The Jelly of an old Hen" made of a hen mixed "with calves' feet, and sheep's feet, or beef, boiled six or seven hours" in a closed pot to which were added spices or "cordial waters," was reputed "a great strengthener and nourisher." Similarly, cock ale was made of a hen boiled until the flesh fell off the bones; "then it is beaten with the bones, and strained for wine or ale with spices. . . . The flesh of a black Hen, that hath not laid, is accounted better and lighter." Cock broth, "famous for easing the pains of the Colic" and "good against a Cough," was made by running an old cock "till he fall with weariness, then kill and pluck him, and gut him, and stuff him with proper physic, and boil him until all the flesh falls off, then strain it. This broth mollifies . . . and moves the belly. . . ." The brain of the chicken, Dixon quoted, would cause blood to coagulate and (taken in wine) stop internal bleeding. Women anointed the gums of infants with chicken brains to make them "breed teeth." Another remedy of Willughby's was "the inward tunicle of the Stomach, dried in the sun, and powdered," which "binds and strengthens the stomach," stops vomiting and diarrhea, and melts gallstones. The gall of the hen removed spots from the skin and was good for the eyes, while the grease or fat of hen cured chapped lips, "pains in the ears, and pustules in the eyes." Dixon quoted Willughby to the effect that chicken manure was as efficacious as a pigeon's, but weaker. Taken morning and evening for four or five days it cured colic, pain in the womb, jaundice, the stone, urinary tract infections. The ashes of dung sprinkled on the flesh dried running sores and scabs.

Amid much in the chicken apothecary that seems plainly absurd today there are some that still make good sense — such as a cream of chicken soup for those suffering from stomach ulcers. The simple fact is that the combinations of egg and chicken remedies were almost endless. Each ancient writer had his favorite cure for a particular disorder and many of these were passed on from generation to generation, down, quite literally, to the beginnings of modern medicine. What one learns from a reading of these various remedies, some so bizarre, others so practical, is a good deal about the state of medicine throughout by far the greater part of human history and something about the most common ailments of mankind.

Clearly disorders of the stomach and bowels were the most common complaint of ancient, medieval, and renaissance man, followed by respiratory diseases. In treating both constipation and various forms of dysentery the chicken (and the egg) were highly favored by ancient authors and indeed by writers of medical treatises as late as the nineteenth century. The impression one comes away with from reading these almost inexhaustible remedies (one of my favorites requires the boiling of eggs in donkey's urine for kidney pains) is of the poignance of human disease, pain, and suffering, and the enormous ingenuity that devoted men expended, century after century, in trying to discover ways of curing the sick or relieving their suffering. Many of the remedies are more poetry than medicine, to be sure: camomile flowers, violets, the washed leaves of senna, oil, safflower seed, an ounce and a half of fresh oak polypody (a fern), washed raisins, honey, milk, hyssop seed, carrot seed, anise, and always, always the ubiquitous egg. But one thing is certain. If the egg was not as efficacious as the physicians of earlier times thought it to be, it was more wholesome by far than many of the remedies with which men have in modern times solaced or benumbed if not cured themselves.

THE RELATION between people and chickens is perhaps most engagingly traced in folklore. The religious and magical properties of hens and, more particularly, cocks have been dealt with elsewhere. The emphasis here is on the remarkable accumulation of folk sayings and stories featuring chickens. The origins of most of the aphorisms are ancient and obscure. Many, we know, are at least as old as Greece and Rome, for a number are first encountered there.

We have two categories of folklore concerning the chicken: the first proverbs, the second folk tales or fables. Both, almost invariably, appear in a number of versions in different cultures and different historical eras. A familiar proverb of the ancients to describe a futile task was "You're gluing an egg together," which calls to mind the nursery rhyme of Humpty Dumpty and the modern aphorism "You can't unscramble an egg." That Roman meals often began with eggs is suggested by the sentence in Horace, "from eggs to apples," indicating a lavish banquet. "He came forth from an egg" was said of those who were strikingly handsome. The phrase also had reference to the birth of Castor and Pollux who, according to one legend, were hatched out of eggs. After Jove in the guise of a swan had made love to Leda, she produced two eggs. From one came Castor and Pollux and from the other Helen of Troy. These were, to be sure, swan eggs, not hen eggs, but they gave fame to the egg and it was, after all, the hen who was the paramount producer of that sphere.

When, in the ancient world, two people seemed remarkably similar in appearance or talent it would be said that they appeared to have been hatched out of the same egg. And of things much alike it was said "as similar as an egg to another egg."

The Greeks had already compared poor handwriting to chicken scratches. In Plautus's *Pseudolus* one of the characters, holding up a poorly written love letter, declares, "By Hercules, do hens also have hands? For a chicken wrote this." The later Dutch word for bad handwriting was *Henneschrapsel*, or hen-scratching.

Since for the ancients auguries were often to be found in dreams, there were interpretations of chickens in dreams. If a man dreamed that chickens were entering his house it meant that he would be enriched with wealth and honors. But if the hens were small ones it meant that the riches and honors would be modest. The ancients also held that the sirens who lured men to their ruin had the feet of cocks although "in intellect are not dissimilar from a higher being." Cocks fighting in one's dreams not unnaturally signified wrangles and quarrels.

Cock's milk was taken to indicate either a bountiful supply of this world's goods or that which was rare or unique, as "the rarest of things are cock's milk and a well-plucked pheasant."

Not long after the invention of printing, folklorists began gathering anthologies of country proverbs and sayings. One such collection, published in 1579, contained the sentence: "I would not have him to counte his chickens so soone before they be hatcht." The word "chicken" to describe a coward is at least as old as Shakespeare: "Forthwith they flye Chickens, the way which they stopt Eagles." One of the characters in Farquhar's *Beaux' Stratagem*, written in 1707, says to another: "You assure me the Scrub is a Coward." To which the other answers: "A chicken as the saying is." And Dryden wrote in the Prologue of *The Spanish Friar*, published in 1681: "Where 'tis agreed by bullies chicken-hearted/ To fright the ladies first and then be parted." Whoever said it first, it is a base canard against the chicken. The cock is, after all, a symbol of bravery while the mother hen, if anything, exceeds him in courage when she defends her chicks.

"Children and chickens would ever be eating" undoubtedly antedates Thomas Tusser's *Five Hundred Points of Good Husbandry*, published in 1580.

"If you would have a hen lay, you must bear with her cackling" appears in Thomas Fuller's *Gnomologia*, 1732, and from the same collection: "It is no good hen that cackles in your house and lays in another's," or, in the same spirit, a Danish proverb: "It's a bad hen that lays away from the farm."

"An egg of one hour old, bread of one day, a goat of one month, wine of six months, flesh of a year, fish of ten years, a wife of twenty years, a friend among a hundred, are the best of all number" appeared in a collection of aphorisms published in 1623. Certainly one of the most poignant chicken proverbs is that of George Herbert: "The chicken is the country's, but the city eats it."

If it is difficult and often indeed impossible to trace the provenance of most proverbs, we can guess at the age and origin of some. "Spunky as a Dominicker rooster" is almost certainly nineteenth-century, since the Dominique breed only came to prominence in that era and it was not until the nineteenth century that "rooster" replaced "cock" in general usage. By the same token we can be sure that "A good cock crows on any dung-heap" antedates "A good rooster crows in any henhouse," although one must, of course, allow for the substitution of the modern "rooster" for the older "cock" in many sayings that go back to much earlier times. These, you might say, had been bowdlerized in order to make them fit comfortably in the mouths of Victorians. "Polite as a rooster" is surely modern, since it was the nineteenth-century poultry fanciers who celebrated the "politeness" of roosters on the analogy of the English country gentleman. By the same token, "Cock of the walk" is no older than the "walks" that English cock breeders and fighters put their birds on to train and toughen them. Nineteenth-century America converted "brave as a gamecock" to "game as a rooster." (One could hardly have said "brave as a gamerooster"; that would have been too patent an evasion.) Yet a common phrase was "crowed like a gamerooster," which surely was originally "crowed like a cock" or "gamecock." "Red as a cock's comb" is of older vintage. "Cocky as a Bantam rooster" and "crazy as a mad rooster" are modern and it is interesting to note that "cocky" remains in the language while "cock" virtually disappears.

The aphorisms relating to the hen are almost endless and since the name of the hen undergoes no such transformation as that of the cock they are harder to place in time. One of the most common — "Don't put all your eggs in one basket" — doubtless goes back to the beginnings of eggs and the beginnings of baskets, although its prudential nature strongly suggests the Puritan Reformation. Another: "The man who puts all his eggs in one basket should watch that basket." "Better an egg today than a hen tomorrow" has a fatalistic tone — a bird in the hand is worth two in the bush; get what you can today without waiting for an added increment tomorrow. There is certainly nothing Puritan about that sentiment.

"Big as hen's eggs" must measure something that is by nature much smaller (since an egg is not as big as a mountain): strawberries or diamonds, for instance, or any precious stone.

"To have both the hen and the egg" is a variation on having one's cake and eating it too.* "Eggs and oaths are easily broken" bespeaks a somewhat cynical and disillusioned age. The same might be said of the sentence: "He that buys eggs buys many shells" — life is fragile and uncertain; the good and nourishing also alarmingly perishable.

"Children and chickens must be always pecking" might be interpreted in several ways: that both are in restless and continual motion, or, with a more contemporary gloss, that "the pecking" or picking of children at their elders is like the pecking of a chicken.

"Send not for a hatchet to break open an egg" refers, as we would say today, to overkill. Have the means appropriate to the ends. "I have other eggs to fry" — other tasks more pressing or important. "So hard up they have to fry the nest eggs when company comes" is echoed by other sayings which emphasize the relationship of the poor to their chickens. The nest egg is notoriously of dubious quality, having been left in the nest for a long period of time as an incentive to the hens, or, to give the passage an even more ironic twist, it is made of wood or glass (in this day and age, of plastics, of course). It reminds one of: "When a poor Jew kills a chicken, one of them is sick." For "poor Jew" other groups often substitute "poor Pole," or "poor Irishman," etc.

"Full as an egg is of meat" speaks for itself, a plenitude, a fullness. "Better half an egg than an empty shell" is, as are so many of these sayings, a peasant's

The "Folk" Chicken

139

---

* It is a characteristic of our society that we have lived under the illusion that we could indeed "have both hen and the egg"; that we could have the egg, in short, without the cackling hen; the hen without the crowing cock; the flesh of the chicken without the unpleasant task of killing, plucking, and cleaning it. But it is one of the arguments of this work that such an idea is illusory: in short, that we must still pay the piper.

wisdom. One takes what one can get in a hard world; half a loaf is better than none.

But there are mysteries of course. Why, for instance, is "to lay an egg" a synonym for failure when an egg is also a symbol of nature's bounty and certainty (that is, "sure as eggs" — inevitable)?

"They quarrel about an egg and let the hen fly," and one walks as carefully as if one were "walking on eggs." "Scarce as hen's teeth" is scarce indeed. The unborn chick has, to be sure, an egg tooth with which to saw his way out of his shell, but that is promptly absorbed.

The person who finds an egg with two yolks should make a wish while eating it. Eating a chicken gizzard will make a man beautiful in one superstition, while another declares: "Swallow a gizzard whole and you will become handsome." Another country superstition is that if a housewife burned the shells of the eggs she had used to make a cake before the cake was baked, it would fall. The aphorism that chickens crowing before sunset means death is rather a puzzle since cocks often crow all day long. Beside it one must place the superstition that cocks crowing after sunset means news will soon arrive of some important event. Another puzzler is the saying that if one dreams of finding eggs, he or she will be in a fight the next day. The belief that if a hen crows there will be sickness in the family is of ancient vintage.

Another strange belief was that a farmer's chickens would be like the first person that came to his house on New Year's morning — if a stout, prosperous person, plump chickens; if a poor, meager person, scrawny chickens. A variation in the southern United States was that if a Negro came on New Year's Day, the chickens born that year would be black. Another axiom held: If a woman enters your house on New Year's Day, you cannot raise chickens that year. And a more startling axiom held that if a person was bitten by another person and put chicken manure on the bite, the biter's teeth would rot away. An ancient saying was that treasure could be found by plowing with a cock and harrowing with a hen. It was doubtless a wry comment on the odds of a farmer growing rich, that is, "as hard for a farmer to grow rich as to plow with a cock and harrow with a hen."

The hen as mother has a particularly large inventory of sayings: "fussy as a hen with one biddy" (or chick) or "proud as a hen with one chick" (it is certainly true that a hen with one chick often seems far more anxious and possessive than a hen with a dozen). Also, "It's a poor hen that can't scratch for one chick."

"Sociable as chickens in a coop" obviously derives from the eighteenth or nineteenth century before modern researchers had discovered the pecking order. And yet, of course, once the pecking order is established, hens in a coop *are* sociable.

In America "blue hen" was a nickname for the State of Delaware — blue hens were reputed to be especially peppery and combative. Thus, "She's one of the blue hen's chicks" described a high-spirited and high-tempered young woman.

"Cross as a setting hen" is another ancient proverb, as is "A setting hen is never fat," which indeed is true since a setting hen's temperature rises, she burns off her fat and eats very little during her cycle. "Setting hens don't want fresh eggs" speaks, I suppose, for itself and has an appealing intricacy. But why one should "never sell a hen on a wet day" I can't really imagine, except that a wet hen is hardly at her best: i.e., "madder'n a wet hen." Nothing is more futile than "seeking a hare in a hen's nest," or a more ignominious fate than being "pecked to death by a hen," or more dejected than a plucked chicken in a rainstorm.

Eggs (and chickens) and the weather have long

been assumed to have a close relationship. Thunderstorms were thought to spoil eggs, and an old English proverb spoke of folks "as quare as a chicken hatched in a thunderstorm."

The onset of cold weather was thought to be signaled by the thickening of the feathers on a cock's legs. When chickens' feathers droop it is supposed to be a sign of rain and conversely when they sing during a rain it foretells clear weather, as also when they sit on a fence in the rain and pick their feathers. But chickens dusting in the sand give warning of bad weather.

To throw an egg backward over a house was thought, in certain rural communities, to bring good luck to a thrower. To see two hens with their heads together as though they were talking was a sure sign that people were talking about you.

When a hen cries between the hours of eight and twelve at night, it is announcing that a bachelor has made off with a spinster. If a cock crows in the front yard, it is a sign that its owner will swap horses that day; if it comes to the front door and faces the house, a stranger is coming to visit. In the same vein, if two hens start fighting, it again means a stranger is coming to visit; if two cocks fight, two men are coming. Country folk in many parts of the British Isles thought it dangerous to keep eggshells because witches went to sea in them and it made little sense to provide transportation for witches.

Every proper farmer goes to bed with the chickens and gets up with the crowing of the cocks. And careless deeds and wicked acts come home to roost like chickens, perhaps when the day of life is ending and night (and Final Judgment) approaches.

If "chick," "chicken," "spring chicken," and "pullet" have all been used to describe young women, "hen" (except for "mothering hen") has generally been used in an uncomplimentary sense with reference to older women — "She's no chicken; she's on the wrong side of thirty. . . ." (Jonathan Swift) — and often to aggressive and meddling women. Thus "henhouse" was once widely used to describe a house controlled by a woman; in the same spirit "hen-party" summons up the picture of gossiping females; a "hen-pen" was, most typically, a private girls' school. "Henpecked" is perhaps the most widely used term applied to a wife-dominated husband, while a "henhussy" was a man who poked into affairs of the opposite sex.

One proverb in three variations is in the same spirit. The Irish version goes: "A whistling girl and a cackling hen come to no good end." A variant reads, "A whistling woman and a crowing hen/ Are fit for neither God nor men." A Scottish form declares, "A crooning cow, a crowing hen, and a whistling maid boded never luck to a house."

A much more cheerful version is the following: "Whistling girls and hens that crow/ Make mirth wherever they go." There may be some of the same feeling in the adage that it is bad luck to sell a crowing hen.

John Florio in his *First Frutes*, published in 1578, sounded the same note with: "They are sorry houses where the hens crow and the cock holds his peace." All of these sayings were plainly based on the fact, already commented on by Aldrovandi, that certain hens dominated the cocks in the barnyard and, even, occasionally, tried to mount other hens.

A modern expression of the theme is D. H. Lawrence's essay "Cocksure Women and Hensure Men." Proverbs and essays all reflect classic masculine anxieties and resentments in the "war between the sexes."

"Cockeyed" comes from "cockeye," a squinting eye. "Cockily," "cocksure," and "cockiness" certainly have reference to the proverbial pride and arrogance of the cock. On the other hand a "cock's egg" is a small egg without a yolk, and the phrase goes back to those ancient times when people believed that cocks on occasion laid eggs.

A number of plants, weeds, and grasses contain "cock" in their name as "cock's eggs," "cock's foot," "cockshead," "cock sorrel," and "cockweed." Similarly with "hens" (as in "henbane" — poisonous nightshade), "henbit," "hen pepper," and "hens and chickens," an herb.

"Capon's feather" is a folk name for common columbine and "capon's-grass" is rattail fescue. "Chanticleer" or "Chantecler" means a loud crower and it was certainly a common name for a cock as far back as Chaucer's day. A "chickenberry" is an egg (also "henfruit" or "chickenfruit") and of course, "cackleberry." "Chicken-breasted" is a malformation of the chest referring to narrowness in the rib cage and the projecting of the breastbone. "Chicken" as a prefix usually means small as in "chicken lobster" or "chicken halibut," and of course it means picayune when followed by "shit." "Chicken-livered" goes with "chickenhearted" and is even harder to understand. Chicken livers are certainly a delicacy and even if the chicken were the coward that the phrase implies, it is hard to see just where the liver comes in.

A "chicken-pull" refers to the game played with a chicken's dried wishbone when two children pull and the one who gets the larger portion of the bone when it breaks gets his or her wish. I fear many children today grow up in the era of packaged chickens without ever seeing a wishbone, let alone having the substantial pleasure of pulling one.

"Chicken-toed," like "pigeon-toed," described the person whose toes turn in, though it is somewhat of a canard. A good sound chicken stands straight and squared-away. "Cock" is the main element in dozens of words and phrases from "cockade" to "cockyolly-bird" (a small bird of any species). There is "cock-a-hoop" referring to loud and assertive talk, to exultance, to specifically setting a cock on a hoop and drinking without stint, and there is "Cockaigne" from coquaigne, referring to a mythical medieval country, "an abode of luxury and idleness." It came also to refer to the lazy and self-indulgent city-dweller — a cockney — and, finally, to the lower-class Londoner with his distinctive drawl as with Liza Doolittle in *Pygmalion*. A "cockalorum" was a kind of bantam man, small and self-important, a strutter. A "cocka-trice" was a fabulous creature hatched, it was thought, from a cock's egg by a serpent whose glance would kill, and thus it follows that a "cockatrice" is a wicked person. "Cock-brained" means foolish or lightheaded, and a story of a "cock-and-bull" is per-haps based on a mythical encounter in which a cock killed a bull. All that the *Oxford English Dictionary* tells us is "a long, rambling, idle story, 1621." "Cockyleeky" is a soup made of a cock boiled with leeks, which is probably about the best one can do with a tough cock.

An old English oath was to swear "by cock or pye or mousefoot." The phrase was so common that the sign of a "cock and pie" (or magpie) often appeared as the sign for alehouses in the sixteenth century and this despite the fact that pious Christians considered it sinful "to swear by creatures." (In *Henry IV*, Shallow declares, "By cock and Pye, sir, you shall not away tonight.")

Finally there is the ubiquitous "cocktail," beloved by so many Americans. I forbear to say more about the cocktail — as opposed to honest-to-God real drink-ing liquor — than that it dishonors the noble bird after whose tail it is named. Its origins seem to be in litera-ture and its meaning originally much like that of "cocky" or "cocksure," as in the rather insolent or spirited angle of the cock's erect tailfeathers. Thack-eray at least speaks of one of his characters as "such a . . . coxcomb as that, such a cocktail. . . ."

"Hard as sneaking past an eager cock" has reference to that licentious bird's insatiable sexual appetites. "Cock-penny" was the penny paid by a schoolboy to the master at Shrove Tuesday for the keeping of his cock.

"Cock's comb" (later "coxcomb") was a conceited fool, a show-off and flashy dresser, while "cock's-shut" was a country word for twilight, the time when poultry went to roost and were shut up for the night.

In Joel Chandler Harris's *Uncle Remus: Plantation Proverbs*, Uncle Remus remarks, "Hongry rooster don't cackle w'en he finds a wum." A West African proverb goes: "The hen never forgets him who has stolen her chicks." A Dutch proverb reads: "Hens like to lay where they see an egg," and a Scottish proverb states: "Fat hens are ill layers."

Friday has, I suppose because of Christian fasting on that day, a special significance in regard to chickens. If it is bad luck to eat a crowing hen except on Friday, eggs laid on Friday will cure colic and one should not sell a hen on Friday.

For anyone who has ever cut the head off a chicken the phrase "running around like a chicken with its head cut off" will have a special vividness.

The egg comes in for its share of common or folk expressions. First off, there is the "egg and dart" architectural motif. Then the famous "egghead," a word which gained currency in the early fifties, primarily to describe the liberal intellectuals who flocked to the support of Adlai Stevenson. The implication was that the skull of such an intellectual was thin and the brain soft like the inside of an egg. An "eggsucker" is like an "ass-kisser," one who seeks favor, a sycophant; but telling a person to go suck eggs is to tell them to begone and not waste your time. An "egg trot" by a horse is the kind of easy trot on a gentle old horse that a "henwife" taking her eggs to market would find comfortable and that, more important, wouldn't break the eggs.

Just where "to egg someone on" came from I can't presume to say (perhaps from throwing eggs at an adversary) and "eggy" for irritated or excited is just as obscure. There is also the expression: "As innocent as a new-laid egg."

The list could, I suspect, be extended indefinitely in literally dozens of languages. But the point is surely clear enough — the closeness in which man and chicken have lived for centuries is attested to in a rich store of proverbs, sayings, figures of speech, and axioms.

Fables concerning hens and cocks appear in the folk literature of every civilized country. From Aesop on, their story has been featured in poems, in songs, and in traditional children's stories and rhymes. Like many of the proverbs, the fables repeat certain basic themes.

A classic fable tells of the vanity of the cock in believing that it is his crowing which makes the sun rise. Then there is Aesop's prototypical fable of the cock persuaded by the fox to crow with such vigor that he closes his eyes and the fox makes away with him — another story of vanity. Still another tale tells of the fox who pretends to be sick, is admitted to the henhouse by sympathetic hens, and then eats them all. In fact, the chicken and the fox are, from the earliest days, the central figures in many folk tales dealing with animals and, invariably, making a moral point. (One such tale tells how a cock teaches a browbeaten husband how to rule his wife.)

A fable from classical times tells of a hen who, having found some serpent eggs, set on them and prepared to hatch them. A swallow who observed her said, "You mad thing, why do you cherish those eggs? When they hatch out, you will receive the first injury from them," meaning "that wickedness is implacable even though it may be showered with the greatest kindness."

And there was not only the goose that laid the golden egg but a hen with priority as in the verse of the Greek poet Gabria: "Once a hen laid a golden egg, and a certain miser, deceived in his mind, killed the hen to obtain her gold. But his hope destroyed the greater gift of fortune."

A cat who had caught a cock wished to eat him but not without reasonable cause. He therefore accused the cock of being a nuisance and not allowing people to sleep at night. The cock replied that he did this as a service to men to arouse them to their labors. The cat then charged that the cock was impious and unnatural because he had intercourse with his mother and sisters. Again the cock argued that this was done for the benefit of man, for the hens in consequence laid eggs. At this the cat, now thoroughly irritated, declared that if the cock was so ingenious in his replies he, the cat, would never get his meal and with that devoured the cock. "This fable indicates a depraved nature that wishes to sin will do so openly if it cannot do so with a plausible pretext."

Two cocks fought over hens. The defeated bird fled and hid himself, but the victor, full of vanity, stood on the fence and crowed at the top of his voice. At this an eagle seized him and the defeated bird came forth "and boldly thereafter trod the hens." This was a good Christian parable: the proud are humbled and the humble are shown favor.

A dog and a cock became friends and went traveling together. At sunset the cock flew up into a tree to roost and the dog lay down in a hollow log. When the cock crowed, a fox came to the tree and implored the cock to descend so that he could embrace "the creature who gave forth such admirable song." The cock told the fox to wake up the doorkeeper who slept at the foot of the tree and ask him to open the door.

When the fox asked the cock to wake the doorkeeper, the cock readily complied and the dog finished off the fox, the moral of the story being, according to Aldrovandi, "that prudent men use cunning against stronger men who insult them. . . ." The Aesopian cock who disregarded a gem for simpler food was taken to represent the man who "ignorantly spurns the most sweet fruit of virtue, immersing himself in and nourishing himself upon vices!"

In one ancient fable, the hen and her chicks were overtaken by winter, and the hen to save her chicks stripped off her feathers and made them a nest while she, naked, died of the cold. This tale was told as a rebuke to unnatural mothers who abandoned their offspring. In another, a mouse warns her baby to fear quiet cats but not noisy cocks. Still another tells of a city greenhorn who tries to wash a black hen white. Other fables deal with cocks that crow to announce their mistresses' adultery and are usually killed for their pains.

In an Italian fable an evil fairy disguised as a cloud forced the inhabitants of a city to give her a young woman every year as tribute. Otherwise she threw objects from the cloud and killed people. After years of sacrificing girls to the evil fairy-cloud, a young man disguised himself as an eagle and flew to the fairy's castle, where he found all the young women. From them he learned that the only way to free them was to kill a seven-headed tiger with an egg inside it, extract the egg, and hit the witch in the forehead with it and thus kill her. Turning himself into a cock, the young man killed the tiger, extracted the egg, and freed the girls.

While Chaucer's *Canterbury Tales* transcend folk literature, the tales themselves are full of the commonplace stories of Chaucer's England. The "Nun's Priest's Tale" is based on Aesop's fable about the fox and the cock that we have already noted but the story

of Chanticleer and Pertelote, as Chaucer tells it, takes
on quite a new dimension.

A poor widow had a cock, Chanticleer,

> In al the land of crowing nas his peer.
> His vois was merier than the mery orgon
> On messe-dayes that in the chirche gon;
> Wel sikerer was his crowing in his logge,
> Than is a clokke, or an abbey orlogge.
> By nature knew he ech ascencioun
> Of equinoxial in thilke toun.

This handsome, boisterous bird had "sevene hennes
for to doon al his plesaunce,/ Whiche were his sustres
and his paramours. . . ."

The fairest of these was his wife, "faire damoysele
Pertelote." Chanticleer tells Pertelote that he has had
a dream in which a strange doglike creature (a fox)
kills him. Pertelote chides him for being a coward and
offers to prepare medicine that will cure him of his
fears. Chanticleer protests, and a learned discussion
follows on the nature of dreams and their ability to
give forewarnings of danger. Chanticleer quotes ancient authors and tells Pertelote of several occasions
on which dreams predicted accurately the future. But
he is distracted by her charms and declares:

> "I am so ful of joye and of solas
> That I defye bothe sweven and dreem."
> And with that word he fley doun fro the beem,
> For it was day, and eek his hennes alle;
> And with a chuk he gan hem for to calle
> For he had founde a corn, lay in the yerd.
> Royal he was, he was namore aferd;
> He fethered Pertelote twenty tyme,
> And trad as ofte, er that it was pryme.
> He loketh as it were a grim leoun;
> And on his toos he rometh up and doun,
> Him deyned not to sette his foot to grounde.
> He chukketh, whan he hath a corn y-founde,
> And to him rennen thanne his wyves alle.

In March, the month "when God first maked man," Chanticleer, his dream forgotten, was persuaded by "a col-fox, ful of sly iniquitee," to try to emulate the masterful crowing of his father. "So was he ravisshed with his flatterye" that Chanticleer "stood hye up-on his toes/ Strecching his nekke, and heeld his eyen cloos,/ and gan to crowe loude. . . ." The fox thereupon seized Chanticleer by the neck and made off with him. Pertelote and the other hens raised such a clamor that soon the widow, her daughters, the hands, and even the farm animals were in hot pursuit of "Russel Fox."

At this point Chanticleer, grasped by the neck as he was, managed to gasp out advice to his captor to cry out, "Turneth agayn, ye proude cherles alle! . . . Maugree your heed, the cok shal heer abyde;/ I wol him ete in feith. . . ." As the fox opened his mouth to denounce his pursuers, Chanticleer flew off to the top of a nearby tree. The moral of the tale is plain enough:

> But ye that holden this tale a folye
> As of a fox, or of a cok and hen,
> Taketh the moralitee, good men.
> For seint Paul seith, that al that writen is,
> To our doctryne it is y-write, y-wis.

In this case beware of flattery.

Chickens and stories about them seem to be especially ubiquitous in wartime. Joseph Plumb Martin in his narratives of the suffering of a Revolutionary soldier tells of coming, half-starved, onto a flock of chickens in a barnyard, an experience shared by many soldiers in many wars. He found some corn, enticed a few within reach, caught one, "wrung off its head, dressed and washed it in the stream, seasoned it with some of my salt, and stalked into the first house that fell in my way, invited myself into the kitchen, took down the gridiron and put my fowl to cooking upon the coals. The women of the house were all the time going and coming to and from the room. They looked at me but said nothing. 'They asked me no questions and I told them no lies.' When my game was sufficiently broiled, I took it by the *hind* leg and made my exit from the house with as little ceremony as I had made my entrance. When I got to the street I devoured it after a *very* short grace and felt as refreshed as the old Indian did when he had eaten his crow roasted in the ashes with the feathers and entrails."

Many wartime tales involving chickens deal with the other side of the story from Private Martin's — the efforts of farmers to preserve their chickens against marauding soldiers. Timothy Read's grandmother, Charlotte Lovell, told of sitting on the porch with her skirts spread out and her chickens hidden under them and singing so that Yankee soldiers prowling the premises for loot and food would not hear their chuckling and rustling.

In *A Stillness at Appomattox* Bruce Catton gives a vivid account of the early stages of encounter that marked the end of the Civil War. A brigade of Federals came under Rebel fire near a farm, "a shell blew the end out of the farmer's chicken house, and the air was abruptly full of demoralized chickens, squawking indignantly, fluttering off in frantic disorganized flight. And here was the last battle of the war, and the men were marching up to the moment of apotheosis and glory — but they were men who had not eaten for twenty-four hours or more, and they knew Virginia poultry from of old, and what had begun as an attack on a Rebel battle line turned into an hilarious chase after fugitive chickens. The battle smoke rolled down over the crest, and shells were exploding and the farm buildings were ablaze, and Federal officers were waving swords and barking orders in scandalized indignation. But the soldiers whooped and laughed and

scrambled after their prey, and as the main battle
line swept on most of this brigade was still continuing
to hunt chickens or was building a little fire and preparing to cook the ones that had been caught."

It is doubtless in children's literature, in nursery
stories and rhymes so closely related to folklore, that
the chicken, or at least the hen, comes into its own.
One of the most famous German children's stories is
Clemens von Brentano's "Göckel, Hinkel und Gacke-
leia." There are cocks and hens scattered, of course,
all through Mother Goose, and then there are those
immortal fowl, the Little Red Hen, Henny-Penny,
and Chicken Little. The Little Red Hen is the most
quintessentially Protestant of these birds. Whenever
she asks the other lazy barnyard animals to help sow
the wheat or reap, thresh, mill, or bake it into bread,
they all quack, squeak, and grunt their refusals, "Not
I," "Not I," "Not I." "Then I will do it myself," says
the hard-working, cheerful, thoroughly responsible
Little Red Hen.

At the end when the bread is baked "so light and
sweet" and the Little Red Hen asks who will come
and eat it, all the lazy animals cry, "I will." But they
will not get any. It is reserved for the Little Red
Hen's chicks. She admonishes the slothful animals:

Lazy folk must hungry go,
For they would not help me sow,
Neither would they help me reap, —
They had rather rest and sleep.
  All alone I baked the bread,
  Lazy folk shall not be fed.
  Eat it all, my chickies, do, —
  Mother made it all for you.

Chicken Little is, of course, the flighty bird who
mistakes a pebble falling off the roof for a piece of the
sky. "Oh, dear me!" she cries. "The sky is falling. I

must go and tell the King." And off she dashes, spreading the rumor as she goes. After various adventures Chicken Little and her friends arrive at the palace, where the wise old king lifts the pebble from Chicken Little's head and assures her that the sky is not really falling in. The moral here is perhaps more universal: Don't believe rumors.

And then, of course, there is in many stanzas and many versions:

> Higgledy, Piggledy, my black hen,
> She lays eggs for gentlemen;
> Gentlemen come every day
> To see what my hen doth lay.

Many of the children's songs about chickens are sung to accompany dancing and games. "Cluck, Old Hen" is an American folk song with numerous variations under the title "Cackling Hen."

"Chickama, Chickama–Craney Crow" is a Southern playsong that goes:

> Chickama, Chickama–Craney Crow
> Went to the well to wash his toe.
> When he got there
> His chicken was gone
> What time, Old Witch?

As the song is sung the child playing the witch hides behind a tree or bush and the other children — the chickens — line up behind their leader Chickama–Craney Crow. The chickens march around in front of the witch's hiding place, singing, and when they get to "What time, Old Witch," the witch runs out, grabs a chicken, takes it to her hiding place, and calls out "One." So the game goes until half of Chickama–Craney Crow's chickens are stolen. Then the witch draws a line on the ground with a stick and the witch's chickens and Chickama–Craney Crow's have a tug-of-war. The first child pulled across the line becomes the new witch.

A black folk song to accompany the "Chickenfoot" goes:

If ya cain't chicken foot, ya' cain't dance nothin.
Ya' chicken foot, neck and gizzard,
My black gal is slick as a buzzard.

From the Ozarks the "Chicken Reel":

Chicken run fast, chicken run slow,
Chicken run by the Methodist preacher
Chicken never run no mo.

In the Appalachians Alan Lomax found a number of songs whose subjects were chickens and that in most instances went back to old English folk songs. A typical one was "Chickens They Are Crowin' ":

The chickens are crowin', a-crowin', a-crowin'
The chickens are crowin' for 'tis almost daylight
My mother she will scold me, will scold me,
My mother she will scold me for stayin' away all
    night.
My father he'll uphold me, uphold me, uphold me,
My father he'll uphold me and say I done just right.
I won't go home 'till mornin', 'till mornin', 'till
    mornin'
I won't go home 'till mornin' and I'll stay with the
    girls all night.

A group of young black girls at the Kirby Industrial School in Almore, Alabama, danced and sang a song for the Lomaxes that began:

All around the kitchen, cocky doodle, doodledoo.
All around the kitchen, cocky doodle, doodledoo
Now stop right still, cocky doodle, doodledoo. . . .

Other children's songs and stories tell of the hen who hatched ducklings and her anxiety when they plopped themselves into a pond. One tells of baby chicks who try to follow their duckling friends into the pond and expire in a diminuendo of peeps.

And last, and one of the most engaging of all:

Chick, chick, chick, chick, chicken,
   Lay a little egg for me
Chick, chick, chick, chick, chicken,
   I want one for my tea
I haven't had an egg since Easter
   And now it's half past three
Oh, chick, chick, chick, chick, chicken,
   Lay a little egg for me.

The "Folk"
Chicken

156

PART TWO

I f the cock has preempted the center of the stage to this point in our narrative it is primarily because of his potency as a symbol. It is not the first time in history, to be sure, that the more practical, useful, and less colorful and dramatic female has existed in the shadow of the more strident and assertive male. The hen will, in the chapters that follow, appear quite clearly as the tragic heroine of this history. Meanwhile, we might take some particular note of her role and that of her marvelous product, the egg.

Both hen and egg had, as we have already seen, powerful symbolic and magical properties. Of course, the hen was supreme as a symbol of motherhood. The poet Oppian wrote in the second century B.C.: "With how much love the playful hen nourishes her tender young ones! If she sees a hawk descending, cackling in a loud voice, her feathers raised high, her neck curved back, [she] spreads her swelling wings over the clucking chicks. Then the frightened chick chirps and hides himself under these high walls, and the fearful mother gathers the long line of young chicks under her plumage; careful mother that she is, she attacks the bold attacker and frees her dear chicks from the mouth of the rapacious bird and sings to her featherless young; deprived of hair they leave their festive nests in shining brightness."

Plutarch in *De amore parentis* writes of the mother hen: "What of the hens whom we observe each day at home, with what care and assiduity they govern and guard their chicks? Some let down their wings for the chicks to come under; others arch their backs for them to climb upon; there is no part of their bodies with which they do not wish to cherish their chicks if they can, nor do they do this without a joy and alacrity which they seem to exhibit by the sound of their voices." Plutarch uses the example of the mother hen to chide humans for their infidelity. "It is no wonder," he wrote, "that when we think over these facts which are examples for those who follow nature, she alone reproves the inhumanity of man because he does not bear a love without reward toward others nor know how to love except for the sake of gain."

Harbaugh offers a translation of a Greek epigram on the devotion of the hen for her chicks:

Beneath her fostering wing, the hen defends
Her darling offspring, while the snow descends;
And through the winter's day unmoved defies
The chilling fleeces and inclement skies;
Till vanquished by the cold and piercing blast,
True to her charge she perishes at last.

We have already had a good deal to say about the magical qualities of hens. The theme is echoed in Juvenal's recording of the popular saying that a fortunate man was spoken of as "the son of a white hen."

Hens performed an important service in the opinion of the ancients, giving notice of a change in the weather by singing at night more than usual. Moreover, if hens with chicks refused to leave their houses in the morning, the farmer should look for a heavy rain. Festus Avienus, the translator of the Asia Minor poet Aratus, wrote that one could expect rain "when the little hen cleans her breast with curved beak." It was also thought that rain was in the offing when chickens took especially heavy dust baths or when they gathered together in one place. If a cock crowed at the time when the rain began to fall it was taken as a sign that the rain would soon stop. The hen's molt was warning to the farmer that it was time to sow his winter seed. If they molted first from the head, he should sow rather earlier; if from their posteriors, he should sow late.

In Christian theology and especially in the writings of St. Augustine (whose own mother was such a crucial figure in his conversion to Christianity), the image of Christ and the Church as mothering hen is frequently referred to, most notably perhaps in Christ's lament: "Jerusalem, Jerusalem, how often have I wished to gather your children together, as a hen gathers her chicks, and you did not wish it?" St. John Chrysostom, like Augustine, was attracted to the metaphor of the Church as the mothering hen: "As a hen with chicks not only keeps them warm," he wrote in his commentaries on Matthew, "but also loves as her own the chicks of whatever other bird she may have hatched, so the church yearns to call not only her Christians but others, whether Gentiles or Jews; if they have been placed under her she vivifies them all with the warmth of her faith and regenerates them in baptism, nourishes them with her sermons, and loves them in maternal charity." In Chrysostom's metaphor the two Testaments — that of the prophets and that of the apostles — are like the ways of a hen. "The virtue and omnipotence of the Lord are a great marvel not clearly understood," said Peter Gregory, "because the chick while shut up in the eggshell and before he breaks it is made to peep after the nineteenth day of the hen's incubation of the eggs."

We see the hen again as a Christian symbol in the writings of Nicolaus Reusner, who wrote under the

title "Nothing Sad When Christ Has Been Accepted":
"The hen gathers her chicks together and covers them
under her faithful wings; by her clucking she testifies
that she is a loyal mother. Terrible Satan afflicts and
torments the saints and harms them by whatever
means he can. You protect them, Christ, under the
powerful shade of your wings and you alone keep them
from the savage enemy."

With the Reformation, the hen and the egg took on
a new symbolic significance. John Bunyan, in his *Book
for Boys and Girls,* published in 1686, wrote: "The
egg's no chick by falling from the hen/ Nor man's a
Christian till he's born again."

*The Hen
and Her Egg*

162

A few years earlier, Samuel Sewall, the New England witchcraft judge and diarist, wrote on January
13, 1677: "Giving my chickens meat, it came to my
mind that I gave them nothing save Indian corn and
water, and yet they eat it and thrived very well, and
that that food was necessary for them, and how mean
soever, which much affected me and convinced me
what need I stood in of spiritual food and that I should
not nauseat [avoid] daily duties of Prayer, etc."

The Reformation produced what I call "The Protestant Hen"; I shall have more to say about her later.

Aldrovandi, of course, had his own observations of
hens as mothers: "They follow their chicks with such
great love that, if they see or spy at a distance any
harmful animal, such as a kite or a weasel or someone
even larger stalking their little ones, the hens first
gather them under the shadow of their wings, and
with this covering they put up such a very fierce defense — striking fear into their opponent in the midst
of a frightful clamor, using both wings and beak —
they would rather die for their chicks than seek safety
in flight. . . . Thus they present a noble example in
love of their offspring, as also when they feed them,
offering the food they have collected and neglecting
their own hunger."

Aldrovandi also observed what modern researchers have noted — that some hens were dominant and had masculine characteristics, even to small spurs. He compared such hens to women who tyrannized their husbands, who did "not blush to perform the functions of a male," or who practiced "lewdness with women." In Aldrovandi's words such a hen "entices other hens as if she were really able to perform as a male and wearies them by leaping on top of them; she raises her crest and tail and walks about in such a fashion that it is difficult to tell whether she is a female or a male." There were unnatural hens as well as unnatural women.

It might be appropriate at this point in our narrative to mention an auxiliary use of the hen. Hens have been almost as popular as rats with experimental psychologists. The problems of innate versus learned behavior are dramatically demonstrated with chickens and, of course, the famous peck-order — applied to every living social group, including humans — was first demonstrated with chickens.

The official discoverer of the peck-order among chickens was T. Schjelderup-Ebbe, a Norwegian psychologist. To put the manner simply, he found that in flocks of hens put together promiscuously, a certain hen dominated all the rest (by pecking) and that all birds lower in the order similarly dominated those beneath them, down to the last "hapless hen which was pecked by all and could peck no one." (Experimenters found also that hens injected with male hormones became more aggressive and usually dominated the other hens.)

Numerous other experiments with the peck-order have explored refinements. In one such experiment two separate flocks were kept. In one flock the birds were allowed to develop their peck-order and then left undisturbed once it had been worked out. In the other new birds were constantly introduced, which resulted in endless fights and squabbles as the order was re-worked. As a result, not surprisingly (most work with laboratory animals produces results that common sense would have predicted), "birds in the unstable flock fought more, ate less food, gained less weight and suffered many more wounds." Eureka!

One ingenious experimenter, in order to determine how cocks and hens might sort things out, castrated a number of cocks which, when placed with the hens, were dominated, just like other hens, by the more aggressive females. They then fed the castrated cocks on sex hormones, "which restored their sex drive without increasing their aggressiveness. Hens that ranked below these males in the peck-order mated readily with them. But hens that outranked them repelled their advances and drove them wildly about the pen," leading to the conclusion that "among chickens dominance by the male is a prerequisite for sexual acceptance by the female. However, we also noted that females fled from males which were too aggressive sexually." Leaving us, alas, in some uncertainty about the whole issue.

The point worth noting here is that, as with rats, the study of chickens under laboratory conditions by psychologists has been, for the most part, intended to reveal patterns of behavior relevant to the understanding of human reactions, individual and social. Wherever this presumption has existed it has resulted in research of little validity. Chickens are not people; therefore experiments — such as that on the pecking order — which suggest or intimate some connection are for the most part quite meaningless, and it is interesting to note that the science of ethology, or observing animal behavior in the natural surroundings of the animal itself, has largely superseded the older laboratory-style studies.

Indeed, looking back on the thousands of such experiments it is hard to escape the feeling that it represents one of the greatest wastelands of modern science or social science or pseudoscience. When the history of laboratory experiments on animal behavior is written it will be a story of almost unparalleled stupidities and horrors which have, *in toto*, contributed little or nothing to man's knowledge of himself as an individual or as a social creature and very little to our knowledge of the animals that have been the objects of these experiments. (An inspired newspaper headline some years ago announced, "Mice Hint Man May Be Wilder Than Psychologists Suspect." The "hint" came when it was discovered that laboratory mice, on the basis of whose behavior some generalizations about humans had been ventured, behaved very differently from wild mice.)

The peck-order among chickens has received a disproportionate amount of attention from researchers in animal behavior because of obvious but superficial analogies to what might be considered dominance and subordination in human societies. The famous peck-order really comes to no more than this: groups or societies of living creatures can exist only in some kind of order. If we were to propose a universal law to describe this phenomenon (and I am sure many have been proposed) it would go something like this: "All higher living organisms move from disorder to order." For humans, of course, we would have to add, "and back again to disorder." Human beings seem less able to tolerate a fixed order than other animals. If chickens are allowed to grow up in successive generations unconfined, as they have for much the greater part of the time they have been domesticated, there is very little evidence of a pecking order. The older birds dominate the younger (as one is tempted to say they should). Young birds of a particular generation may contend among themselves for supremacy, but they seldom contest the issue with their seniors. Since they find their own food and do not have to compete at a common "feeder," there is little fighting and unpleasantness. What fighting there is is usually playful and of a ritual character rather than a serious struggle for domination.

In the laboratory of the biologist the hen is now as often used as the rat and the mouse, largely because of the utility of the bird in cancer research. The Rous carcinoma, a cancer discovered in chickens some thirty years ago, marked an important advance in cancer research and is still utilized in laboratory experiments directed toward finding a cure for cancer in humans. Indeed it seems safe to say that if a cure or antidote to cancer is finally discovered, chickens, and more particularly hens, will have played a vital role in the process. And thus bestowed a blessing on the human race almost as notable as the egg.

And the egg! What is one to say of that marvelous and incomparable object praised by poets and depicted by painters, perhaps the most enchanting form in nature?

We will deal in a separate chapter with the egg as food. Here we are concerned only with its religious, magical, and medicinal uses. As a symbol of fertility it was used in the orgies of Bacchus and the Orphic mysteries. On a more practical level the whites were used as glue. In Aldrovandi's words: "Eggs were believed to reproduce all nature and to have a greater power for placation in religion and for prevailing upon the powers of heaven." The Roman poet Juvenal reports that eggs were commonly used in rituals of expiation: "Unless she purifies herself with a hundred eggs," and Ovid wrote: "Let the old woman come to purify both bed and place, bearing in her trembling hand both sulfur and eggs." An egg was carried in the procession of Ceres and one was borne off to mark the end of the first lap at the chariot races in Rome.

From very early days the finding of eggs has been identified with riches. The relationship is readily apparent. Eggs are a treasure, a bounty of nature, and when hens are unconfined they deposit these treasures in unexpected places. To find such a hidden nest before a hen has started to set and incubate the eggs is a perfect analogy to finding hidden treasure.

Chrysippus of Cnidos wrote of a dream he had of eggs hanging from his bed. When he consulted an interpreter of dreams he was told he would find a treasure wherever he would dig. He dug and found a vase full of gold and silver and took some silver to the interpreter as payment. To which the interpreter said, "But will you give me nothing of the yolk?"

As for glue, Pliny wrote that "egg white mixed with quicklime glues together fragments of glass." "Its strength is so great," the Roman author added, "that wood soaked in egg white does not burn nor does clothing which has been treated with it." Egg white was also an ingredient in paint, especially in the silver and lead gilt used to decorate marble. Aldrovandi wrote that painters "broke" the egg white with a sponge until it was thin and watery. Then they mixed it with their colors, "as our Italian painters do." "Once," Aldrovandi added, "egg white was used for adorning and curling the hair by young men; now it is so used only by the girls."

In Jonathan Swift's *Gulliver's Travels* the discussion over which end of an egg to break is taken as a symbol of futile and bloody wrangles of dogma. "It is computed," one of the characters declares of the dispute between the Big-Endians and the Small-Endians, "that eleven thousand persons have, at several times, suffered death, rather than submit to break their eggs at the smaller end."

A priest's rule that is true:
Those eggs are best are long and white and new.

An apple, an egg and a nut
You may eat after a slut.

Which is to say in their skins and shell they remain uncontaminated by a dirty cooking wench and thus may be eaten with confidence.

And then a riddle:

When I was going over a field of wheat
I picked up something good to eat,
Whether fish, flesh, fowl or bone,
I kept it till it ran alone.

ANSWER: an egg.

One of the most famous aphorisms on the egg is Samuel Butler's remark that a hen is only an egg's way of making another egg. The remark has about it that kind of perversity which suddenly forces us to look at life in a new perspective. What is particularly intriguing about the sentence is that it anticipated the distinction first made by biologists in the late nineteenth century between somatic cells and germ cells. A long argument had raged, after the discovery that the body was composed of cells, around the question of whether the cells were the same as those male reproductive cells which fertilized new life in a mother's body. The experiment which first proved that two kinds of cell were involved was made with chicken egg embryos. From the cock's sperm in the fertile egg, a portion suspected of containing reproductive cells, as opposed to those which formed the living tissue of the developing chick, was removed. The embryo was allowed to develop into a chick, hatch, and grow to a mature bird which was normal in every respect except that it could not reproduce — was sterile. Thus it appeared that all living bodies, man and animal alike, were made up of two kinds of cell — somatic cells, which constituted the tissue of the developed body, and germ cells, which carried on the reproductive function. Thus it was possible to say, in an extension of Samuel Butler's aphorism, that the human being was only the germ cell's way of perpetuating itself. Men and women, from the perspective of nature, are only an incident — a method of transmission, so to speak — in the immortal life of the germ cell.

While this way of putting the case carries echoes of the old argument of which came first — the chicken or the egg — it also gives us a perspective on nature as separate from humanity and thus seems to me to be a useful antidote to the recurring impulse on the part of certain philosophers, psychologists, and pantheists to absorb man into nature. Whether we wish to see man as over and above nature or inferior to her, we must, I think, beware of a radical difference of intention between nature and humanity.

We have already taken note of the theological implications of that persistent question "which came first, the chicken or the egg?" For many of us this was the first time when, as children, we were confronted with a question which appeared to be a simple exercise in logic, but which developed into a series of circular, frustrating contradictions ultimately more puzzling than the knottiest theorem. Even the ancients had difficulty dealing with this paradox. Macrobius, writing around A.D. 400, reports a conversation where the same question was put, with the reply "You jest about what you suppose to be a triviality, in asking whether the hen came first from an egg or the egg from a hen, but the point should be regarded as one of importance, one worthy of discussion, and careful discussion at that."

The most probable answer is that there is no answer, and in fact neither came first. The chicken and the egg evolved together, and through countless centuries of gradual change the ancestral chicken and the ancestral egg must have been, in the Darwinian sense, at all times biologically successful. The question simply falls away when one considers the chicken and the egg as processes as well as objects. Each represents not a separate unit, but transitional stages in a cycle of life, all parts of which are molded by evolutionary pressures.

Whether or not one feels satisfied by such an explanation depends upon personal perspective, but it is clear that to anyone concerned with biological phenomena there is much to be gained by considering creatures as moments in a life cycle. The egg, representing the female component of the germline, is the bridge between individual cycles and is present in some form at all stages. Thus even when the chick is in the egg there are eggs within the chick, microscopically small but full of potential. A discussion of the biological relationship between the hen and the egg could logically begin at any point, and it is therefore somewhat arbitrary that we take as an origin the early development of the egg within the young hen, who is just reaching sexual maturity.

The hen's ovary differs very little in basic design from those of mammals and other vertebrates. However, the large size of the organ in chickens, large because of the relatively enormous eggs it produces, is such that the hen can accommodate only one within her body cavity. This is actually a secondary adaptation, for during development of the embryo, as in other vertebrates, the ovaries arise as paired structures. In chickens the right ovary fails to develop, for reasons that are not understood, and in the adult only the left is functional. Interestingly, if the left ovary is removed within thirty days of hatching, an operation not much more difficult than caponizing a cock, the vestigial right ovary will in some mysterious fashion recognize the loss and resume development, often resulting in a normally fertile hen.

For the most part the ovary consists of a rather unstructured mass of fibrous connective tissues, blood vessels, and nerves. This is surrounded by a thin cortex of small epithelial cells, and the entire structure is connected to the body wall by a stalk through which the ovary communicates with other organ systems. Just beneath the outer layer of epithelial cells is found, with the microscope, a scattering of cells that can be distinguished from all others by the general appearance of their nucleus and by their size, which while still microscopic, is somewhat larger than tissue cells. These are the germ cells, which have been reserved, since the earliest stages of embryonic life, for the single and only purpose of propagating the species. They have contributed nothing to the hen during her entire development, not a single feather, not a muscle, not a nerve. Their number is not accurately known, and has been estimated at from several thousand to more than a million. Presumably each is potentially capable of developing into a mature egg, and the left ovary therefore has an enormous reproductive potential that can be only partially realized during an ordinary lifetime. At sexual maturation, which is usually eighteen to twenty weeks (but which may vary considerably depending on day length), it becomes apparent that a small fraction of these minute germ cells has begun its long journey toward eggdom. Most remain quiescent, however, and the nature of the mechanism that awakens particular germ cells individually and sequentially from their long slumber is not known. Current thinking has it that these earliest events in egg development are governed by the ovary itself and not by hormones released from distant endocrine organs. This is a matter of considerable economic significance because, if the initiation of egg maturation could be controlled and manipulated by hormone administration, the number of eggs laid in a year could theoretically be increased, and it is not at all impossible that the reproductive life span could be substantially lengthened.

Perhaps the earliest observable event in egg development is the association of the germ cell with follicle cells. These small cells, derived from the epithelial cortex, surround the germ cell and cling intimately to it. The entire structure is termed a follicle,* and for the remainder of development as the germ cell grows in size, the follicle cells grow in number and continue to cover it.

The intimate physical relationship between the ovum † and the follicle cells suggests, as is so often the case in biology, an important functional relationship. This is certainly the case, for in recent years it has been demonstrated that the ovum itself is incapable of accumulating yolk without assistance. Yolk materials are initially synthesized in the liver, where they are released into the blood in soluble form. In the ovary the follicle cells, but not the ovum itself, are able to capture molecules of yolk. It is likely that follicle cells perform some initial chemical processing, after which they transport the yolk into the interior of the ovum, where it is rendered insoluble. It is interesting that in so many creatures, from insects through the entire spectrum of the vertebrates, developing eggs universally require the service of these cellular handmaidens.

Another probable function of the follicle, perhaps in cooperation with ovarian cells of other types, is synthesis of the sex hormones — the ovarian steroids. Of particular interest and importance is the female hormone estrogen. This hormone is necessary for the maintenance and function of the entire reproductive

---

* It is frustrating that in biology there are often several names for nearly identical structures. In humans the egg is contained within a "Graafian follicle," and the structure which transports the egg following ovulation is not an "oviduct," but a "fallopian tube."
† "Egg" as popularly used refers to the shell, white, and yolk, and generates some confusion. Technically the word *egg* should refer only to the generative cell, which is what the cook refers to as the yolk; the white and the shell are secondary coverings. For purposes of this discussion the generative cell will be termed the "ovum," and "yolk" is intended to mean a particular class of materials accumulated within the ovum.

system. Estrogen acts by affecting the brain, which in turn regulates those pituitary functions that are critical for egg formation.

In addition estrogen affects the brain in a quite direct fashion by modifying the hen's behavior. It has been shown in a series of simple experiments that many of the most characteristic behavioral patterns of the laying hen are estrogen-induced. These include the prelaying call and nest inspection, when the hen fussily pokes her head into several nests before singling out her own. This prelaying behavior is often observed in hens kept in battery cages as well. There may be a call followed by a period of considerable agitation, in which she clearly attempts to escape. It is sad commentary that hens deprived of the ancient ritual of nest examination and selection may instead pace the limited confines of their cage at a rate of up to two thousand paces per hour.

The success of the mating act is also related to this hormone. In many animals the maturation of the egg is perfectly synchronized with sexual activity because estrogen induces "heat," a complex and profound set of behavioral changes which permits normally shy, aloof, or fierce animals to be mounted and penetrated. Hens do not clearly demonstrate heat, and we have pointed out elsewhere that copulation in chickens more nearly resembles rape than it does the mutually fulfilling experience that other creatures enjoy. Nevertheless, there is a degree of submissiveness in the laying hen. Usually she will flee, but when apprehended she often becomes submissive, and in fact assumes a characteristic and quite unnatural position which makes insertion of the penis possible. Some hens, whether because of unusual amounts of estrogen or because of a philosophical acceptance of the inevitable, will take the mating position immediately when approached by the cock.

The ovary is responsible for the production of

other steroid hormones, notably progesterone and, surprisingly, detectable amounts of testosterone, the male hormone. In cocks, secondary sex characteristics — feather coloration, spurs, the comb, crowing, among others — are directly related to testosterone. The hen is not without certain of these traits, though never are they so gloriously developed. All hens have combs, for exam.ple, and in some they are quite prominent. Certain low levels of testosterone are required for this, and other characteristics such as coloration may also depend upon this masculinizing activity of the ovary.

Accumulation of yolk is very gradual initially, and occurs so slowly that it is not known with accuracy how much time passes between formation of the minute primary follicle and the time at which the follicle is apparent to the naked eye. By some two weeks before ovulation the developing follicle can be located by inspecting the outside of the ovary, where it appears as a small bump. At about seven days before ovulation the rate of yolk accumulation increases enormously, and the follicle soon protrudes conspicuously beneath the overlying cortex. The value of this accelerating pattern of yolk formation is that at any given time only a handful of very large follicles can be accommodated in the available space within the body cavity. Examination of the ovary from a hen in the midst of a laying cycle displays, then, a large number of very small follicles, and five or six which are rapidly enlarging. These will be of unequal size, and close examination will reveal a hierarchical succession of follicles which clearly anticipates the sequence in which they will be ovulated and laid.

It has been known for many years that egg production is controlled by pituitary hormones. The principal hormones involved are FSH (follicle stimulating hormone) and LH (luteinizing hormone). The role of FSH is mainly to encourage growth and maturation of the follicle. LH is also important for follicular development, but in addition it has another critically important function, that of inducing ovulation. The interactions of these substances with other hormones, and with environmental factors, constitute an enormously complicated web of integrated physiological mechanisms, and in many cases the details of these interactions are poorly understood. For the purposes of this discussion there is one aspect of all this that calls for brief consideration, because it may lead to an intuitive, if not an analytical, grasp of the hen's reproductive processes and cycles.

"The master gland" is a phrase often used to describe pituitary function and is found in nearly every biology textbook published before 1950. This terminology indicates quite correctly that pituitary secretions affect all functions, and directly control other endocrine organs which, in turn, have physiological consequences throughout the body. However, the "master gland" image also suggests that the pituitary has functional autonomy, and in this respect the words mislead. In the past quarter century a quite different image of this gland has gradually emerged and the pituitary is now seen by biologists as a functional extension of the central nervous system. The anatomical relationship of the pituitary to the base of the brain, with which it is connected by a stalk, is not just a developmental coincidence but represents an obligatory relationship; if the stalk is cut the gland either fails to function, or it functions in an uncontrolled manner.

The pituitary, then, is more a slave than a master. This does not in any way demean its importance, for it is a very important slave indeed; the pituitary is the point at which, in the hen as in us, nervous information is translated into those chemical signals which synchronize and regulate other physiological events. This arrangement seems eminently sensible, for certainly there must be some mechanism by which the environment, as perceived with sense organs, can influence internal chemistry. The fact that this essential role of the pituitary would have seemed quite foreign to an endocrinologist a generation ago is a measure of how young, indeed, our study of biology really is.

The hen perceives her world, to a great extent, through her eyes, as we perceive ours. Most of this visual information is translated into short-term motor responses, perhaps a scratch here, a peck there, or the retreat to the security of the roost when light begins to fail. But other much more long-term responses to light are also available, and in particular it is the ability of the hen to sense the length of the day, and to respond to apparently imperceptible changes in its length as the seasons move, that allows her periods of laying to be synchronized with the great cycles of nature. During the winter, when chicks would have least chance of survival, the brain instructs the pituitary not to make available sufficient quantities of FSH and LH for egg maturation, and only when the period of light becomes sufficiently long, and conditions are otherwise tolerable, does pituitary function resume and laying commence. To those who are lucky enough to own a flock of chickens, the appearance of large numbers of eggs in the nests is, as surely as buds swelling on trees, a sure and welcome signal that winter will not endure.

Not all hens begin to lay at the same time, and the length of laying is likewise unpredictable. This is particularly true of chickens raised in an open and natural environment. Part of the reason for this variability is certainly genetic, but it is also true that factors other than sunlight influence laying. Through her sense organs the hen responds to heat, cold, sound, touch, pain, and others — even the sensation of a crop full of grain. This mass of sensory information probably has a permissive rather than a directly regulatory function; if the environment is reasonably sat-

The Hen
and Her Egg

176

isfactory the hen will respond to day length, and reproduction may proceed. It is difficult, at this time
impossible, to sort out these functions. The brain of
the hen may be small by some standards, but it is
nevertheless an integrative organ of great capacity,
and represents to even the most capable and sanguine
neurophysiologist a structure of almost unimaginable
complexity.

Ovulation — release of the ovum from the follicle
— is a precisely timed event in the hen and occurs
usually at about twenty-five-hour intervals. The mechanisms responsible for triggering ovulation are, of
course, of great interest to any concerned with egg
production schedules, but they remain poorly understood in spite of the most intense efforts by legions of
researchers. There appears to be a brief but intense
release of LH (or a similar hormone — there is some
dispute) from the pituitary, and the egg is released
in six to eight hours following. The physical, mechanical events occurring between LH secretion and release
of the egg remain mysterious; it is likely that contractions of muscular elements within the follicle and
deterioration of overlying follicular tissues are both
involved.

In any case, ovulation is spectacular, occurring in
moments; the egg literally erupts from the torn tissues which formerly surrounded and constrained it. At
the same time another process begins, and illustrates
again the remarkable synchrony of all these events.
The ostium, the funnel-shaped opening to the oviduct
which partially surrounds the ovary, becomes extremely active. Fleshy projections from the oviduct
become engorged with blood, and muscle within the
tissue causes the structure to writhe and contract. At
the moment of ovulation the ovum is grasped and en-
gulfed, and begins its long passage down the oviduct,
where it will acquire its investments, the white, the

membranes, the shell, and from which it will emerge completed a day later.

It is here in the infundibulum that fertilization occurs. Sperm may be available as a result of a recent mating, or they may have been stored in short, tubular projections in lower portions of the oviduct. Sperm may remain viable in these storage areas for, it has been variously estimated, from twelve days to several weeks. Certainly the breeder who wishes to obtain specific pairings must have means of isolating hens for long periods from the attentions of unwanted cocks. If no sperm are present the egg will remain forever infertile, for once the outer layers of white and shell surround the yolk, sperm entrance becomes mechanically impossible.

Fertilization, momentous occurrence that it is, is accomplished very quickly, and the fertilized ovum remains in the infundibulum only some fifteen minutes. Rhythmic, peristaltic contractions of the muscles of the oviductal walls move it into the magnum, where it receives the white, or albumin. The structure of the magnum tells a good deal about the way in which it functions. The inner surface consists of a series of longitudinal folds which spiral, rather like the rifling of a gun barrel. The egg is therefore slowly rotating as it moves, and the first layer of egg white, which is particularly dense, becomes twisted. These twisted ends, called the chalazae, give polarity to the egg and define its long axis — the first indication of its eventual shape. The whitish, rather opaque chalaza, which reminds one of the way bubble gum is wrapped, is easily seen in an opened egg. Passage through the magnum requires two or three hours, during which the remaining albumin is deposited in concentric layers.

Transit through the next portion of the oviduct is more rapid, requiring slightly more than an hour. Here in the isthmus the two shell membranes are formed — very thin, tough, transparent layers that are familiar to any cook, or to anyone who has gathered an unshelled egg. The two membranes are in contact with each other at all but one point, the blunt end of the egg, and the space between them forms the air sac.

The longest period in the egg's journey is spent in the shell gland, or uterus, so called because of its homology to the mammalian womb. Here the egg remains relatively stationary for eighteen to twenty hours. It is in contact with the spongy secretory tissues of the shell gland on every surface, and gentle, rhythmic kneading movements of the uterine musculature give final shape to the egg as the calcium salts are gradually deposited.

The eggshell is a remarkably complex structure, consisting of several layers. The outer mineral layer, which is of course formed last, contains the familiar brown color if any is to be present. The coloring, which is often speckled, is due to a type of molecule known as the porphyrins, and is closely related to hemoglobin, the pigment of the red blood cell.

The egg may be completed some time prior to laying, and during this period the uterus acts as a simple storage organ. Exactly what triggers the event of egg laying is not known. It is however established that the actual expulsion of the egg, as a result of muscular contractions, depends on the interaction of nervous signals to the muscles of the uterus and the vagina, and the influence of hormones released from the posterior region of the pituitary. These hormones, one of which is oxytocin, strongly stimulate muscular contractions also, and it is fascinating to consider that these are the identical substances which in mammals stimulate uterine contractions leading to birth, and which after birth cause milk to be ejected from the breast in response to suckling. Nature is enterprising in making use of her resources.

After expulsion from the uterus only a few seconds are spent in passage through the vagina and, in what is so obviously for the hen a moment full of pride and satisfaction, the egg, magnificently completed, is laid.

The temporal pattern of egg laying, which greatly influences total production, results from a complex interaction between genetics and the environment. In a homogeneous flock kept under conditions of optimal lighting, usually twelve to fourteen hours per day, eggs are laid in sequences. There is disagreement as to whether these are homologous to "clutches" of wild species. The length of each sequence is highly variable, even under the most carefully controlled conditions, but in modern varieties a single sequence may yield thirty or forty eggs, or occasionally, even more.

Under these controlled conditions the first egg of a sequence is generally laid in the morning. The time between eggs is slightly more than twenty-four hours, and as a result subsequent eggs are laid progressively later, with the last egg of a sequence usually laid in the afternoon. The time interval between layings minus twenty-four hours is the "lag." It seems rather peculiar that the laying cycle is slightly longer than the length of the natural day, for it is not explained by the length of time required for egg maturation. It appears that the laying cycle is governed by a counting mechanism, the so-called internal clock. The hen's clock may well be homologous to those circadian rhythms which appear to be nearly ubiquitous in animals, which in addition to producing jet lag provide for such varied activities as stellar navigation by migrating birds and regulation of nocturnal foraging in mice. The nature of these internal physiological rhythms is no better understood in the hen than in other creatures, but at least one point can be made, which is that the rate at which the clock runs is a heritable trait. It is possible to select for breeds with various laying patterns, and in some there may even be a negative lag at certain points in a sequence.

In hens kept under natural conditions, particularly those allowed to forage, this pattern of sequential laying is often somewhat irregular and may be completely obscured by demands of the environment. Nevertheless, in my own flock of Bantams, I have repeatedly observed that the first eggs are laid early, and in general an egg laid in the late afternoon signals the end of a sequence. One is always curious as to the adaptive value of such a phenomenon as lag, and although I have not seen it discussed, one interpretation comes to mind. Chickens belong to the group of birds known as "indeterminate layers," in which there is no fixed number of eggs in a sequence. It would seem reasonable that by the hen's laying at progressively later times, the approach of twilight gradually begins to coincide with laying, and becomes the signal to end a sequence before excessive numbers of eggs crowd the nest and make incubation difficult.

The onset of broodiness is a fascinating process to observe. Like nesting behavior in other animals, the brooding hen displays a radically altered set of behavioral patterns. How many children sent to collect the eggs have printed forever on their memory the awful experience of reaching under a laying hen, only to have the outraged beast erupt from the nest, flapping and squawking in the most terrifying way, and quite often setting off similar alarm reactions in other chickens in the vicinity. Yet this same hen when broody will, as we have noted, usually refuse to budge.

This maternal behavior, this almost universal symbol of motherhood, is also regulated by hormones, and some knowledge concerning them is available. By far the most important secretion is prolactin,* a protein

* Alas, other terms are also used. With almost equal frequency this hormone is referred to as luteotropic hormone (LTH) and as mammotropin (MH).

hormone which is elaborated by the pituitary, and like other activities of the pituitary this is a brain-mediated event. Prolactin can, with rather heroic biochemical techniques, be purified from isolated pituitary glands. When this purified material is injected into a non-broody hen, radical behavioral changes occur and broodiness results within hours. More remarkable is the finding that injections of prolactin will cause the cock, even the most masculine, arrogant, splendidly endowed cock, to behave like a mother hen and brood the eggs or care for the chicks.

It is at this point that the reader might lose patience with the scientist. "For God's sake, explain away nature if you must, but leave us the mystery of the cock and the hen — we need that." But the mystery is still very much with us, and no biologist is foolish enough to think that much is truly explained by injecting a hormone and observing an effect some time later. Prolactin and other hormones act as biological triggers in the central nervous system. Between the initial action of the hormone and the behavioral changes which eventually result lies a nightmarishly complex series of neural, physiological, and chemical events. The detailed operation of a brain, particularly a brain which displays intelligence, is very nearly as mysterious to a modern biologist as an electronic computer might be to *Homo neanderthalis*.

This is not in any way to diminish the importance of the discovery of prolactin, because since it is a triggering substance, and one concerned with reproduction, it has enormous biological significance. A measure of this is the finding that prolactin is found not just in chickens but throughout the vertebrates, and perhaps in certain of the invertebrates. In other birds prolactin also triggers nesting and care of the young. In the case of pigeons it has another interesting effect in that it causes the production of "crop mild," a white, cheesy substance secreted in the crop and re-gurgitated into the mouths of the nestlings.

In man, the isolating of prolactin was accomplished only recently, in 1970. Its function is, in concert with other hormones, to stimulate the breast to produce milk. This is true of all mammals, but in lower crea-tures it also produces behavioral changes associated with motherhood. Prolactin stimulates the house mouse to gather bits of yarn and paper to make its nest, and it is likely that prolactin is responsible for maternal behavior in even the most fierce and solitary mammals.

Even in creatures which do not care for the young prolactin is essential for reproduction. In central Cal-ifornia, where this is written, salamanders abound in the redwood forests. During the rainless months of summer when the creeks are dry, they find shelter under fallen logs or in damp crevices. Salamanders, being amphibians, must return to water to lay their eggs, and when the rains begin they leave their sum-mer home and migrate toward the streams, often in enormous numbers. Mountain roads occasionally be-come dangerously slick because so many are killed by cars as they cross in search of water. Thus prolactin, the same substance that causes the hen to call her chicks to the nest at dusk, is responsible for trigger-ing the annual migration of salamanders, and for that reason is sometimes given yet another name — the "water drive hormone."

Given the bewildering variety of life (who would think that a chicken and a salamander could be re-lated, though they shared a common ancestor just a few million years ago?), there is need to identify those features that remain constant. With the force of adap-tive pressures, as skin develops scales, scales become feathers, and fingers lengthen into wings, a few sub-stances such as prolactin resist the pressure of evo-lution, and represent a kind of biochemical signal in-dicating again that chickens, and ourselves, are still members of a family, and a single family at that, of living creatures.

Considering the strange biological history of the egg, it is not surprising that its symbolic power is rivaled only by that of the cock. In Egypt eggs were hung in the temples to encourage fertility, and everywhere, of course, they have been associated with birth and renewal. The Hindu description of the beginning of the world saw it as a cosmic egg. First there was nonbeing and then that nonbeing became existent and turned into an enormous egg, which incubated for a year and then split open, with one part silver and the other gold. The silver half became the earth; the gold, the sky; the outer membrane, mountains; the inner, mist and clouds; the veins were rivers, and the fluid part of the egg was the ocean, and from all of these came in turn the sun.

In certain other religions the egg was equated with the sun and the yolk was seen as a kind of mixture of earth and water. Thus the egg was featured in many pagan "rites of spring." The word "Easter" comes, in fact, from the name of the Anglo-Saxon goddess of spring, Eoestre, whose festival was on the first Sunday after the full moon following the vernal equinox. The goddess Eoestre is depicted in an ancient Anglo-Saxon statue as holding an egg, the symbol of life, in her hand.

Apparently eggs were colored red to represent the life force as early as 5000 B.C. and given as emblems of friendship during the festivals of the spring equinox. No one knows how long ago the custom began in China of giving red eggs to children on their birthdays; red for the Chinese symbolizes long life and happiness. The Persians have also exchanged elaborately gilded and painted eggs for thousands of years.

Christianity readily adopted eggs — as it had adopted cocks and hens — to its own symbolic uses.

The shell became the symbol of the tomb from which Christ had risen and the meat of the egg the representation of resurrection, of the new life of the Christian, and of the hope of eternal life. On Good Friday eggs were brought to the church to be blessed by the priest and eaten by the faithful at the end of the Lenten fast.

Thus, it might be said that most cultures have their own "egg signature" — their own style and form of egg decoration or of fabricating eggs from other materials. While these "styles" were originally religious in character, they have become intricate, elaborate, often costly, and almost uniformly secular. Even within the Western Christian tradition there are, of course, numerous variations in egg decoration. In certain areas of Germany, Easter eggs were hung on trees and bushes, and the Pennsylvania Dutch (really Germans) brought this custom to America, where it still characterizes Easter celebrations.

One of the most common variations of the fabricated (as opposed to the natural) egg is the egg that opens to reveal a "surprise" or treasure. The most spectacular of this genre is probably the famous Nuremberg egg made in 1700. It opens to reveal a gold yolk, which in turn yields an enamel chick, which contains a jeweled egg, and that contains a handsome ring.

The painting of Easter eggs (as opposed to dyeing) dates from the thirteenth century, but the art of fabricating ornate artificial eggs with "treasures" inside was a sixteenth-century invention. Francis I of France (1515–1547) was presented with an eggshell that held a carving of the Passion of Christ. It created a sensation in the court and was widely imitated. Throughout the seventeenth century the kings of France, after high mass on Easter Sunday, gave gilded eggs to their households and to the great lords. Louis XV (1715–1774) secularized the custom by encouraging the decorating of eggs as ordinary gifts.

In his own quarters he had a spectacular pyramid of gaily painted eggs and he gave his favorite, Madame du Barry, a jeweled "treasure egg" with a Cupid inside. The court painters Watteau and Boucher were pressed into service to paint scenes of romantic lovers on eggs. Bawdy verses were painted on others.

On the outside of a white enameled egg made by a Paris goldsmith for a Spanish prince, the Gospel for Easter Sunday was inscribed; the inside contained a mechanical cock that sang two tunes.

This genre — the jeweled egg — was brought to its greatest point of refinement by Carl Fabergé, a Frenchman whose father migrated to St. Petersburg in 1840 and opened a jewelry store. In 1870, at the age of twenty-four, Carl Fabergé took over his father's business and began to specialize in the creation of exotic ornaments; jeweled Easter eggs were his most striking accomplishment. Indeed, the Imperial Easter eggs made for the Czar became an infatuation of the Russian royal family. The Czarina gave her husband, Nicholas II, a fabulously contrived egg in 1897 in commemoration of his coronation and the following year Nicholas presented to his adored Alexandra on the same occasion an egg twelve and a half inches tall, inside of which was a model of the Uspensky Cathedral, where Nicholas had been crowned Czar. The replica of the cathedral contained, in turn, a white enamel egg with a window through which a representation of the interior of the cathedral can be seen. Two clocks on the cathedral tower keep accurate time and toll on the hour. When a button is pressed, the Coronation Hymn plays.

Fabergé rivaled the ingenuity of this creation with an egg ten inches high and fifteen inches long commemorating the completion of the Trans-Siberian Railway. Made of enamel, precious stones, gold, and platinum, it contained a model of the Trans-Siberian

Express. The last car was a mobile chapel. When wound up, the train ran.

Fabergé, who employed a staff of five hundred at the height of his popularity and fame, was ruined by the Russian Revolution and lived out his life in exile in Lausanne, Switzerland.

In recent years the revival of the crafts has brought with it a new interest in fabricated artificial eggs and in the painting and decorating of natural eggs. The fabricated eggs are predominately marble, leather, wood, and porcelain. Painting on natural eggs has displayed a wide variety of styles from abstract to realistic.

At the end of his chapter on eggs, Aldrovandi defended himself against the charge that he had been too prolix on the subject. After all, it might be objected that what he had said of hens' eggs might well be said of other eggs as well. To such a charge Aldrovandi would reply that "nothing included here extends beyond the limits of my subject, that is, whatever pertains to the history of the cock or the hen. For although some things have been said here about eggs which someone too scrupulous or some meddling busybody may declare are valid not only for the hen but also for the eggs of other birds, let him know that the hen's eggs have first place in all parts of the world, are handled daily by all, and are daily in use. . . ."

Hector St. John de Crèvecoeur, whose *Letters from an American Farmer* gave the classic definition of Colonial American society, wrote in those same famous letters, "I never see an egg brought on my table but I feel penetrated with the wonderful change it would have undergone but for my gluttony; it might have been a gentle, useful hen, leading her chickens with a care and vigilance which speaks shame to many women."

The egg indeed might become a chicken, but how splendid that it can remain secure in its own perfection and we therefore can enjoy it as well as its creators.

The Hen and Her Egg

Asked to describe a hen's egg, your first response might be to give an impression of the color, the texture, or more probably the shape — that shape which has about it a sense of the inevitable, for certainly an egg could exist in no other form. What you might not describe is the most obvious characteristic of the egg — it is very big. The ova of most species, including our own, have dimensions which make them barely visible to the unaided eye, and in order to make out detail a microscope is necessary. The ova needed to produce many thousands of elephants would fit comfortably within the shell of even a small hen's egg.

In order to appreciate the physiological commitment the hen makes toward reproduction it is interesting to compare her with mammals. Both modes of reproduction, development of the embryo within or outside the body, occur at the expense of great amounts of energy and materials. The magnitude of this expense has been described as "reproductive effort," a term which is useful in making comparisons between species but which perhaps suggests a degree of conscious dedication that even the hen, with all her virtues, cannot claim. What she can claim is that when compared to other animals of commercial and agricultural importance, none can approach the effort she does make.

In the accompanying table it is seen that the laying hen deposits 1.8 percent of her body weight per day into her eggs. The Jersey cow's commitment is $\frac{1}{100}$ of that, and woman falls in between. By doing the arithmetic in a slightly different way, it may be calculated that a hen in her reproductive prime, laying 275 eggs per year, can deposit seventeen times her own body weight into eggs.

SPECIES	BODY WEIGHT (POUNDS)	AVERAGE DAILY DEPOSITION OF MATERIALS INTO FETUS AND PLACENTA (OUNCES)	AVERAGE DAILY DEPOSITION AS PERCENTAGE OF BODY WEIGHT
Cow (Jersey)	1277	2.9	0.018
Horse	1875	5.7	0.026
Sheep	254	2	0.070
Human	187	0.4	0.019
Dog	16	0.9	0.47
Cat	2.7	0.19	0.25
Rat	1	0.1	0.8
Mouse	0.08	0.03	1.33
Chicken	6.7	(egg) 0.7	1.8

"Reproductive effort" of the hen and selected mammals.

Why is the egg so large — why the tremendous effort? The answer to this must be searched for in the history of the species. It is generally agreed that life on earth began in the oceans. In time, in immense, grinding, geological time, those first amorphous stirrings of life resolved themselves into the kingdoms of plant and animal. Still later both groups gradually invaded the rivers and estuaries, and eventually species evolved which were well adapted to fresh water. Plants invaded the land first. It was much later, and as a result of many hesitant and disappointing steps, that animals followed after and began to exploit the enormous opportunity offered by the soil and its verdant riches.

There were enormous problems in the conquest of the land, most of them having to do with the problems of desiccation. The difficulties were especially acute in respect to reproduction. Primitive fishes, from which all vertebrate life on land has descended, released their gametes into water, where fertilization and later development occurred — a chancy and impersonal matter at best. This pattern is retained by one class of terrestrial animals, the amphibians, which must still retreat to streams and lakes in order to propagate. It was the reptiles, with the development of the cleidoic egg,* who developed the first solution and by so doing established a dynasty which ruled the continents for millions of years. The cleidoic egg was a self-contained unit which, because of the wealth of food materials within, and because of the leathery membrane that slowed drying, allowed reproduction to proceed successfully in even the most arid environment.

An understanding of the real nature and significance of the hen's egg must therefore include a conception, however hazy, of that branch point in the path of evolution when the dominance of the reptiles ended, and birds and mammals roamed or flew over the earth. The mammals deserted the concept of the cleidoic egg and retreated, in a sense, to development within an aqueous environment, the womb. Birds, as if to suggest that learning to fly was enough of an innovation for any single class of vertebrates, retained the basic concept of the self-contained reproductive unit, but in a greatly extended and refined form.

It is worth a few minutes of leisure time to examine an egg with more attention than is usually given it by

---

* The word is from the Greek *kleido,* to lock up, perfectly suggesting the private and insulated nature of the egg interior.

the cook, or even the poultryman. Before the egg is broken into a small bowl in the usual manner, it should remain stationary for some period, perhaps an hour, which will permit the yolk gradually to rotate until the germinal disc is uppermost. It should then be possible to visualize the germinal disc as a small translucent spot located near the middle of the yolk mass. This is the living part of the egg; all the rest, however chemically complex and mechanically ingenious the various components may be, are totally inert. Within the germinal disc is the complement of genes, created by nature but selected by man, which specify the eventual chicken. Inside this insignificant disc also lie the multitude of submicroscopic structures and maze of interlocking metabolic pathways which will allow the information in the genes to convert the amorphous food materials of the yolk and albumin into bone and blood and feathers.

If the egg being examined is fertilized (and if there is a cock about, it is almost certain to be so), it will not appear in any way different to the unaided eyes from its unfertilized counterpart, the commercial egg. In fact, however, it is enormously different, and changes of the most profound sort have occurred. Fertilization takes place shortly after ovulation, and a full day passes before the egg is completed and laid. The fertilized ovum, in the warm, moist interior of the oviduct, has no way to know that this is not the beginning of incubation, and development commences. Cell division within the germinal disc is very rapid in these early stages, and by the time laying occurs, and the sudden cold halts further growth, the embryo has developed to the point where it consists of two layers of cells. A simple structure, to be sure, but many important developmental processes, which must be correctly executed, have already occurred. The germinal disc has been very definitely transformed into an embryo, a fact that comes as something of a shock to those who insist on "fertile" eggs, but who have no wish to dine on a very young chick.

Although a great deal of important biology has been accomplished in the formation of this rudimentary embryo, it is unlikely that the nutritional value of the egg is profoundly affected by fertilization. The germinal disc (now called the blastodisc) has not actually grown, in the sense of increasing in mass, and the embryo has not begun to any significant extent to liquify the underlying yolk for use as food.

Another visible feature of the yolk is the occasional appearance of a blood spot. This may indicate the presence of a more advanced embryo, which usually appears structureless if the egg has been stored for a period. Eggs of this type are objectionable to many people, and in the Jewish tradition they are not considered kosher. There is nothing even remotely harmful in such an egg, however, and in the absence of cultural or personal objections, it remains an excellent food. A second type of blood spot should be mentioned which has nothing to do with the presence of an embryo. This is occasioned by a minute hemorrhage occuring in the ovary at the time of ovulation, resulting in a small amount of blood on the surface of the yolk. Such eggs are perfectly normal.

Because the yolk, together with some contributions from the albumin, represents the only source of materials for the developing chick, it follows that it must be nutritionally complete and well balanced. This is indeed the case, and since nutritional requirements for humans are basically similar to those of the chick (with one interesting exception), the egg is a nearly complete food.

Protein is very much on the minds of nutritionists, and it is significant that almost 50 percent of the yolk mass is protein of very high quality. Egg proteins, including contributions from the albumin, not only contain the essential amino acids but do so in such perfectly balanced proportion that the egg is often used as a standard against which other foods are compared. It is likely that this feature of chicken metabolism — the ability of the hen to lay down in her egg amino acids that man cannot synthesize — has played an important role in the evolution of both species. In areas where the human diet relies heavily, in some cases almost exclusively, upon a particular type of grain, severe amino acid deficiencies can occur. Corn lacks lysine, for example. Because these amino acids are not needed in large quantities, the presence of only an occasional egg in the diet could well change a marginal meal into one that is nutritionally satisfactory.

The yolk is also a marvelous source of vitamins. It contains large quantities of A and D, and provides eight of the B group. Conspicuously absent is vitamin C. The reason for this is either that the chick does not require it in early development, or that it manufactures it from other materials, which it is perfectly able to do. Because of a process of evolutionary dereliction, man has lost a single enzyme which would make him able to manufacture vitamin C from simple sugars, as most other animals are capable of doing. We share our plight only with certain other primates, the guinea pig, and, of all things, the Indian bulbul, *Pycnonotus cafer*.

And the yolk contains minerals, trace elements, some sugar, a moderate amount of fat, and some water. In considering for a moment the needs of the chick, rather than our own, it is easy to overlook its requirements for water. Some water is present in the yolk, amounting to about half of its weight, and considerably more is available from the albumin. It is also the case that the chick makes good use of water that it manufactures itself by the process of oxidizing food materials. In this respect the fatty component of the yolk is of particular importance, because the oxidation of fat produces much more water than can be obtained from equivalent amounts of protein or carbohydrates. (Animals living in very desiccating environments take advantage of this by storing large amounts of fats to be used as a water reserve — the humps on the camel are deposits of fat.)

The hen donates to her chicks, by way of the egg, not only nutrition but protection against disease as well. During the three weeks of development within the shell the chick is, with rare exceptions, never exposed to pathogenic organisms. At the time of hatching, however, the chick emerges into a world that, in addition to being strange, bright, and often terrifying, is also very dirty, with disease-causing bacteria and viruses everywhere. Danger of infection after hatching is lessened by the protection afforded by antibodies, which are manufactured by the hen and deposited in the yolk. During development they are incorporated into the blood of the chick. This type of passive immunization is effective because the hen, having lived in the same environment in which the chick finds itself, has made antibodies against precisely those pathogens to which the chick is likely to be exposed. This protection is temporary, of course, but it provides time for the chick's own immune system to mature and become reactive. Other means of conferring temporary immunity upon the progeny have been devised many times in evolution. In man and other mammals, antibodies are selectively transferred from the mother's blood to the fetal circulation by the placenta. Even after birth this process continues, because in the mother's milk immunologically significant molecules are present, which after ingestion are transferred into the blood.

All of the preceding has been very much in praise of materials found in the egg, particularly in the yolk. It must now be said, alas, that large amounts of cholesterol are also present in the yolk — more than in any other common food. Whether this constitutes a potential health concern is often debated. It is not surprising that the National Council on Egg Nutrition would pronounce, "There is absolutely no scientific evidence whatsoever that eating eggs in any way increases the risk of heart attack." On the other hand, there is evidence that high levels of circulating cholesterol, not necessarily from eggs, are correlated with cardiovascular disorders. Whether there is a causal relationship remains to be confirmed, and many investigators point to other correlations, such as the level of serum triglycerides, as perhaps being equally or more important. There is also opinion that lecithin, also found in the yolk, tends to make the cholesterol soluble and prevent its deposition in blood vessels.

Although prudence might dictate that very large amounts of egg in the diet, or of any other food for that matter, is probably unwise, many of us would not on the basis of present evidence forsake eggs. They are too delicious, too much associated with the good and pleasant aspects of our lives. But now, thanks to yet another miracle of modern technology, there is an alternative, the artificial egg. Available in markets, in either liquid or frozen form depending upon trade name, these products lack shells altogether, and consist of egg whites blended with a complex mixture of materials that are designed to reproduce the color, composition, and taste of yolk, but without cholesterol. To what extent this attempt is successful must be decided individually — a decision based perhaps as much upon aesthetics as upon cholesterol content. Recalling the composition of the true egg yolk as consisting of a perfect balance of natural substances, it is fascinating to learn from the nutritional formulation on the carton of one briskly selling egg substitute that it contains, in addition to many other unfamiliar materials, soybean oil (partially hardened), sodium and calcium caseinate, sodium hexametaphosphate, carboxymethylcellulose, artificial flavor, "Polysorbate 60," and xanthum gum.

The egg white, or albumin, weighs just less than two-thirds of the egg. It is a much simpler material than the yolk, consisting almost exclusively of protein and water. In the chick, as in other species that have been studied, the protein is gradually utilized in the construction of the chick, and the considerable amount of water in the egg white contributes greatly to the body fluids. The white also has protective functions. Mechanically, it cushions and suspends the yolk mass and allows the embryo to rotate to an upright position. Chemically, the albumin layer contains a special protein, lysozyme, which has potent antibacterial properties, and serves as a second line of defense against infection. Because lysozyme causes the physical disruption of bacterial cells, in its purified form it has become an important tool in microbiological research.

The eggshell, separated from the white by two thin, leathery shell membranes, is composed almost exclusively of calcite (calcium carbonate). It performs its protective function so admirably because, first, the shell has no fissures or seams. In *The Hobbit*, Tolkien hinted at this aspect of the physical integrity of the egg in a riddle: "A box without hinges, key, or lid,/ Yet golden treasure inside is hid."

The eggshell is very strong; while it will not withstand the sharp tap against the frying pan, or the onslaughts of playful boys, its strength is perfectly adequate to meet the demands of the nest, or even of the egg factory. Much of this strength comes from the complex curvature of the shell — at no point is it flat. If one imagines an egg with planar surfaces, something rather boxlike, an engineering analysis would not be required to predict that in order for such a structure to have equivalent strength, the shell thickness must be so great that escape by a chick would be impossible.

While on the one hand the eggshell must compartmentalize the embryo and protect it from the ravages of the outside world, it must at the same time provide a means by which gases can be exchanged. From very early in development, but especially as the period of rapid growth arrives, oxygen must diffuse into the egg and carbon dioxide must be voided to the atmosphere. The problem becomes rather complex, because while one can imagine a shell riddled with small holes to allow for gas exchange, these holes would inevitably cause severe dehydration through evaporation. Certainly one of the main challenges facing the developing chick is conservation of its tiny supply of fluids. The danger of desiccation again reflects the central problem of the development of life on land. Without a shell that can successfully provide for the passage of gas without the wholesale exchange of water, everything else would go for naught.

The problem was solved for the chicken by providing the shell with pores, as suggested, but the pores are so minute that they can be visualized only with sophisticated instruments. They are very numerous, averaging two hundred per square centimeter. The size of the pores is critically important, for they provide a potential means of entry for bacteria. As if by design, their measurements are such that it is estimated that only 1 percent are penetrable. Those few bacteria that do enter, and can make their way through the shell membranes, face almost certain elimination in the albumin.

Although the pores are tiny, they are present in such numbers that the total surface area would still allow rapid evaporation. Some slow loss of moisture does occur, but anyone who has purposefully dried eggs to be used for ornamental purposes knows that it requires many weeks. This very gradual rate of water loss is due to the presence of a microscopically thin cuticle, composed of carbohydrates. This cuticle, which gives the fresh egg a waxy feeling, extends across the pores, hindering the movement of water vapors. It may provide still another obstacle to the entry of bacteria.

How ironic that in the processing of industrial eggs, one of the steps that is usually included involves washing the eggs with a detergent. This is apparently designed to remove any trace of fecal material, about which Americans appear to have an exaggerated concern; few people eat the shell. The result of this washing, predictably, would be an egg which dries out more quickly and which is more susceptible to spoilage. Again predictably, the industry rose to the occasion and discovered that if the detergent was not washed away, but was allowed to dry on the egg, its sanitizing activity prevented contamination. If nothing had been done to the egg it would of course be better protected, and if an occasional soiled egg (they appear very infrequently) should escape the inspector's eyes and eventually reach some distant kitchen, a brief rinsing just prior to use would seem a sensible solution to what is not, after all, a very significant problem.

No discussion of the egg would be complete without some mention of shell coloration, which can vary from white to brown to green, and may be solid or dappled. Color, or the lack of it, is a genetic trait and at one time probably had considerable significance. The speckled brown egg would be nearly invisible in a nest made of brown straw and twigs, for example.

Because only white eggs have been marketed in certain parts of this country for many years, a curious customer prejudice has arisen against brown eggs. In other regions and in other countries, colored eggs are considered natural and desirable. Because color is determined by heredity and not at all by nutrition, or other aspects of the environment, the content of the egg has nothing to do with its color. But it seems a pity that foolish prejudices should interfere with what could be one of life's pleasant experiences. Variously colored eggs are a delight. An enterprising breeder could develop a strain in which all eggs were large and of good quality, but in which the genes responsible for coloration were retained, and were distributed throughout the flock in such a way that different hens would lay eggs of different shades and textures. When the cook opened the egg carton, instead of a dozen monotonously white objects there might be a beautiful variety of hues and designs, and the preparation of a routine meal could become a much more interesting experience, one that would be approached with a sense of pleasant anticipation.

It is beyond the scope of this discussion to describe the embryology of the chick, those precisely timed and sequentially integrated series of biochemical events by which amorphous yolk and sticky, slimy albumin are converted into a lively, fluffy chick. A certain amount is known about these processes. Morphological changes accompanying development have been described in vast detail, and gaining an understanding of the developmental anatomy of the chick is one of the major hurdles that generations of biologists and medical students have faced. Something too is known about the chemical events associated with each stage, and how these are regulated by a constantly shifting pattern of gene activity. This knowledge is only a faint glimmer in a vast darkness, however, and the most sophisticated embryologist, observing a wet, scraggly chick laboriously peck an opening in its shell, feels a sense of wonder, and, at many times, surprise.

T. H. Morgan once commented that "to the mind capable of curiosity and wonder, the embryo is the most seductive object in nature." Everyone should have the experience of studying a living embryo, or better, a series of embryos in which successive stages of maturation may be observed. Observation of embryos, so difficult with mammals, can be easily done with chickens in the home, and will provide for everyone, but particularly children, the experience of directly contacting a previously unseen part of the cycle of life.

The observations are most easily made if one owns or has access to a flock of chickens. Lacking that, there is often a commercial hatchery in the vicinity which probably is in the habit of supplying material to schools. Assuming that chickens are available, one may simply set aside six fresh fertile eggs, marked in pencil day 1, day 2, etc., at daily intervals for the remainder. Egg number 6 may then be placed under a brooding hen, or in an incubator if available. On the following day this is done with egg number 5, and on each successive day the next egg in the series is started. At the end of the series egg number 1 will begin incubation, and observations may be made on the following day.

The materials required are several small bowls of clear glass or plastic, a good table lamp and flashlight, a pair of small scissors, a large magnifying glass, a pair of fine tweezers, and an ample quantity of saline solution. The saline solution is made by dissolving 1½ level teaspoons of table salt, using a measuring teaspoon, in each quart of water. Two quarts are probably sufficient, and they should be warmed to body temperature, about 100° F., before using.

When removing the eggs from beneath the hen, or from the incubator, use a pencil marking to indicate which surface is uppermost. This orientation should be maintained in order that the embryo be in a suitable position for observation. The egg is cracked and the contents emptied into a bowl, as in cooking. Warm saline solution should then be added to cover the embryo, which should be visible on the upper surface of the yolk. It may be difficult to make out detail at first, but experimentation with lighting, particularly the use of incident light from a flashlight, should with a little practice produce sufficient contrasts. In order to see internal structures it is necessary to remove the blastodisc and transfer it to another container. Using fine scissors, cut the embryo free of the yolk by making a circular incision outside the region occupied by blood vessels. With some practice, it is possible to float the blastodisc away from the yolk mass, and using a plastic spoon, transfer it to a clean bowl containing a little warm saline solution. By gentle manipulation the entire structure can, with luck, be teased into a flattened position, and by illuminating from beneath, and by experiment with light angle, excellent preparations may be obtained.

If all goes well (and it may not the first time), a series of embryonic stages, from the first heartbeat through the formation of major organs, is available for study. In the day 1 embryo, little may be seen except a slightly thickened line extending across the middle of the blastodisc. This is the most difficult stage at which to observe detail, for there is little to provide color or contrast. At day 2 the embryo should be visible as an elongated, thickened area, distinctly larger at one end, which will form the head. If the heart is not beating at this time, it will certainly be doing so at day 3. It is a memorable sight to see that tiny organ contracting and relaxing, changing color at each stroke, sending blood out of the embryo into a complex network of vessels that picks up food material from the underlying yolk and transports it back to the body. At later stages it is possible to see the development of the limbs, and the gradual appearance of digits. The tail, a transient structure, will make its appearance and later disappear. The brain, huge in relation to the rest of the body, is seen to develop in conjunction with the sense organs — the eyes are particularly easy to observe because of their pigmentation.

There may be some objection to the taking of life for the purpose of mere observation, as perhaps there should be. Whenever an animal is purposely sacrificed for reasons other than food or safety, such questions arise. I personally think that if there does exist a God who counts the fall of every chick, He will not judge us harshly. He might, in fact, be rather pleased that we have taken the trouble to witness some of these wonders.

*The Egg
and the Chick*

THE EIGHTEENTH and early nineteenth centuries in Europe and America were the centuries of amateur science. The spirit of the "scientific revolution" was born and nurtured in the studies of learned gentlemen who collected, in addition to classical authors, curious antiquities, seashells, plants, and flowers (John Locke was a gifted amateur botanist; he observed the stars and the transit of Venus, and took careful note of a thousand other natural curiosities). There was, indeed, a kind of intoxication of inquisitiveness, a delightful dilettantism that periodically ascended to scientific work of the most substantial kind. As Pope put it:

Nature and nature's laws lay veiled in night;
God said, "Let Newton be," and all was light.

The natural world was, for those with leisure, a world infinitely alluring in its perceivable structure, in the apparent harmony of the laws which controlled it. God, if He perhaps seemed more remote than He had in earlier centuries of the Christian era, seemed almost infinitely benign. Genetics and the science of breeding, which was certainly one of man's oldest and most practical sciences, took on a vastly increased significance. In the Age of Reason it was reasonable to suppose that all living creatures, man included, were capable of further refinements, perhaps of almost infinite refinements. Mendel's work lay a century or more ahead, but he had numerous less illustrious predecessors. Any country squire who applied some system to the management of his farm and bred bulls or chickens to improve the strain could claim a place in this burgeoning tradition of amateur science. One of the most conspicuous beneficiaries of the new popularity of scientific breeding was, as it turned out, the chicken. There are few living creatures that offer the same astonishing combination of genetic stability and variability. As soon as this fact was grasped, the chicken was destined to become as powerful a totemic figure in the barnyards of amateur scientists as it had been for centuries in primitive tribes as well as in the high civilizations of the ancient world.

The development and stabilizing of breeds of chicken which began in the eighteenth century was raised to another dimension by the importation into the West of the great Asiatic breeds. The opposition of the Ch'ing dynasty to foreign trade and to foreigners, which had kept China an infinitely mysterious and unknown quantity to the West, was partially overcome with the opening of the port of Canton in 1834. One of the first trading vessels to return with its exotic cargo brought a number of what were called initially "Shanghai" or "Chittagong" (and later "Cochin") fowl as a present for young Queen Victoria. The arrival of these strange-looking birds quite literally caused a sensation in England. That they were presented to the Queen and that she took a queenly interest in them simply heightened the effect. We are familiar with the melanoid skins of these birds, with their dark bones, rose combs, and feathered shanks; but to the Englishman or American, already preoccupied with the breeding of poultry, they were as strange as birds from another planet. What was most disconcerting was that they appeared, at least in the initial astonishment occasioned by their arrival in the West, to be superior in weight and egg-laying qualities to the established European and Mediterranean breeds. Everyone who was a breeder of chickens must have the new Shanghai or Cochin fowl. Since, for a brief time, the Queen had a virtual monopoly on the immigrants, a trio (a cock and two hens) of Shanghai fowl was more treasured than a title. Almost from the moment of its arrival in England, the Shanghai fowl threatened to dominate fowldom. Native breeds — most of them, indeed, relatively new — were rudely shouldered (or winged) aside and the Cochin became the progenitor of a number of new breeds of chicken. A nineteenth-century authority on chickens, S. H. Lewer, declared that "their introduction was the most memorable event that has ever happened in the poultry world; there has been nothing like it before or since."

When the first Cochins were exhibited in Birmingham, they were a seven-day wonder. Tens of thousands of people came to see the astonishing-looking creatures and thousands were instantly converted into poultry fanciers. As Lewer put it: "Previously very few people indeed except farmers kept fowls, and those only scrubs or mongrels. Every visitor went home to tell of the new and wonderful fowls, which were as big as ostriches, and roared like lions, while gentle as lambs; which could be kept anywhere, even in a garret, and took to petting like tame cats. Others crowded to see them, and the excitement grew, and even the street outside was crammed, and *Punch* drew and wrote about the new birds; and before people knew where they were, they were in the midst of the curious 'poultry-mania' of the middle of the nineteenth century. . . . And the Cochin did it all. He is the *father of the poultry fancy*, and none may dispute his place of honour."

The same phenomenon took place in America. Indeed, the Boston Poultry Show held in November, 1849, was a year ahead of the famous Birmingham exhibition and caused quite as much excitement. The exhibit had been arranged by a Boston doctor, John C. Bennett, one of the first American converts to the new fad. Over ten thousand spectators filed through the Public Garden to inspect 1,023 birds of all breeds and varieties. Prizes were given for the handsomest fowl of each breed, and the splendor of the occasion was only slightly tarnished by charges of corruption and favoritism by disgruntled exhibitors. One visitor wrote to a friend: "It would have pleased me amazingly for you to have seen with your own eyes the *vast amount* of Poultry upon the ground. One tent was one hundred and forty-four feet long, by one hundred and fifty wide, filled completely with cages, reserving room enough for the people to walk. It was indeed a magnificent exhibition. . . ."

The highlight of the event was the appearance of the great Daniel Webster who, like any enterprising politician, went where the voters congregated and on this occasion joined in praising the chicken. Not everyone, of course, was captivated by the new fad. One wrote: "The cocks crowed lustily, the hens cackled musically . . . the chickens peeped delightfully, the gentlemen talked gravely, the ladies smiled beneficently, the children laughed joyfully, the uninitiated gaped marvelously, the crowd conversed wisely," and those in the know, who saw through the sham, laughed up their sleeves.

Nonetheless what July 4, 1776, and George Washington are to Americans in their capacity as citizens of the Republic, November 14, 1849, and Dr. John Bennett are to all Americans infatuated with chickens. Every year thereafter for over a hundred years the Boston Poultry Show was faithfully held, displaying each year newe and more marvelous examples of feathered virtuosity. What is more, it was copied in every city that pretended to be up with the times and in innumerable towns and villages throughout the length and breadth of the land. So began the odyssey of the modern chicken propelled out of the obscurity of the barnyard onto the national and the international scene, traded in and speculated on like a growth stock; bred, admired, preened, and exhibited, written about, lied about, even sung about. Vaudeville actors composed chicken skits and sketches, and while professional men — doctors, lawyers, and ministers of the gospel — took the lead in breeding and exhibiting poultry, there were few farmers who did not succumb to the infatuation for rare or improved breeds of birds.

Before a show birds were washed with soap and water, rinsed in three tubs of clear water, and then toweled off. Exhibition fowl had to be taught "the art of showing themselves to the best advantage." A bird to be exhibited was trained daily for a week or two, accustomed to being handled, and "finally made to assume various poses to display her best points."

The newspapers were full of breathless accounts of "rare and curious and inexpressibly beautiful example" of poultry, "every individual specimen of which," a writer and well-known breeder named George Burnham observed sourly, "had, up to that hour, been straggling and starving in the yards of 'the people' about Boston (they and their progeny) for years and years before, unknown, unhonored and unsung."

One of the most successful exploiters of the new poultry mania was our old friend, the Reverend Edmund Saul Dixon, who published his *Treatise of the History and Management of the Ornamental and Domestic Fowl* in the same year as the Birmingham exhibition.

A year later, an edition edited especially for Americans by a Philadelphia doctor named J. J. Kerr appeared and enjoyed instant success.

Dixon had managed to procure some of the first Chittagongs or Cochins imported into England, and he began almost at once exchanging birds with American fanciers — a Mr. Henry Lawrence in Mobile, Alabama, a Mr. Ames of Marshfield, Massachusetts, and others. He began his discussion of breeds with the statement that "the pure, thorough-bred Shanghae Fowl, in its varieties, is, perhaps, the best, all things considered, of any which we know." The page opposite this encomium displayed an etching of a group of Shanghai fowls from the flock of Dr. Kerr. Kerr had gotten his birds from the ship *Huntress*, direct from Shanghai. The cock was "a noble fellow," the hens appropriate spouses for such a bird. Dixon and Kerr were, indeed, rhapsodic in their praise of the Shanghais. They were heavier, more succulent, more fertile, better layers of richer eggs, better feathered than any other breed, and, no less important, of a "quiet and docile temper." "I know not a better Fowl," the author added. "In truth, I might say of it, as the pious Isaac Walton was wont to say of the trout, his favorite fish — 'God might have made a better fish, but he did not;' so of the pure, unadulterated Shanghae."

Along with the Cochins and Brahmas came other Asiatic fowl, the Malay, from that archipelago, and the Sumatra, and, as the passion for breeding, if anything, increased, every combination and permutation of various breeds was explored — Polish, Hamburg, Dorking, Guelderland — varieties beyond calculating. Prize birds brought enormous prices; several hundred dollars for an especially handsome trio was not unusual.

The Malay fowl was especially popular among fanciers of special breeds. The cock was judged "a remarkably courageous and strong bird. . . . His crow is loud, harsh, not prolonged, as in the case of the Cochin China, but broken off abruptly at the termination. . . ." Part of the interest in the Malay fowl was due to the fact that it was "a supposed connecting

link between the wild and the tames races of Fowls."
They were large birds, sometimes weighing seventeen
pounds for the pair — cock around ten, hen seven or
eight — and the "rich buff or brown color" of the
Malay hen's eggs was "much prized by the numerous
epicures who believe that this hue indicates richness
of flavor."

How much "fowl-breeding" was a preoccupation of
gentlemen farmers of means is suggested by Dixon's
comment that a properly appointed henhouse might
cost as much as a comfortably furnished cottage. A
sound structure with a watertight roof was essential,
in Dixon's opinion. "Some people," he wrote, "allow
their Fowls to roost abroad all night, in all weathers,
in hawthorn or elder-trees, that stand near the fowl-
houses. But the plan is a slovenly mode of keeping
even the humblest live stock; it offers a temptation to
thieves, and the health of the Fowls cannot be improved by their being soaked all night long in drench-
ing rain, or having their feet frozen to the branches."
Indeed, a proper henhouse, Dixon wrote, should be
kept so clean "as to afford a lady, without offending
her sense of decent propriety, a respectable shelter
on a showery day."

Dixon described "two classes of Fowl-breeders:
those who rear them for amusement, and for the convenience of having a few chickens at hand to kill, and
a few Hens on the goodness of whose eggs they can
depend; and those whose only object is to increase
their stock as fast as possible, as a matter of business,
and solely for gain and profit." For the latter cate-
gory, Dixon had little but contempt. There would
never, he trusted, be many people with motives so
crass. Even the "poor cottager," who has only a few
hens and depends for her stock on a more prosperous
neighbor, keeps chickens, Dixon argued, "more because she finds pleasure in seeing the good creatures
busying about with their broods," than for any finan-

cial consideration. Even on large farms it was "more as save-alls and collectors of scattered fragments, which would otherwise be wasted," that chickens were useful. They hardly paid their keeping. A good laying hen kept in a pen could be supplied with corn, Dixon estimated, at the rate of two cents a week. Those who were in an extensive run or at large could be raised for half of what they would sell for. Chickens were simply a vital part of the "household routine." In Dixon's opinion, the only people who made any money out of them were the traveling dealers who scoured the country, buying indifferent birds for the lowest possible prices, "the superabundant produce of various housewives," and then fattening them for the market "at advanced prices." Thus it was the middlemen, far more than the breeders, who were "the principal gainers."

Dixon had a conclusive word on the question of whether chicken-raising could be done on a large scale. "When we shall have succeeded in producing peaches and nectarines for the millions for dessert [then expensive luxuries for the rich], we may calculate on rearing Poultry for the millions for dinner." He saw little prospect of "the fulfillment of their great promises." Incubating and hatching chicks "on a great scale" was easy enough. The difficulty came with rearing the newly hatched birds from chicks to mature hens. Here such large numbers of them sickened and died that the purveyors of "Poultry for the Millions" were stumped. Dixon compared the mortality rates among infants in the French Foundling Hospitals with the mortality rates among chicks raised without their mothers. Both were excessively high. What had not been clearly established at this point was the fact that young chicks must be kept warm and dry if they were to grow into healthy birds. The American editor of Dixon's work could not refrain from challenging such an un-American notion. He interjected to in-form his readers that he by no means agreed that chickens could not be raised profitably for the general market. In the past year, he noted, "The gross proceeds of eggs and poultry sold in the U. States amount[ed] to twenty millions of dollars."

Mr. Dixon was a staunch admirer of the Protestant Hen — that embodiment of the Protestant Ethic. Certainly the hen was as notable an example of the Ethic as the animal world could offer. If thrift, industry, and piety constituted the principal ingredients of the Protestant Ethic, the hen plainly incorporated two of those classic virtues — thrift, in the sense that she utilized every morsel of edible and, indeed, inedible matter that could be found in the barnyard or the surrounding woods and fields, and industrious, as we have said, in her indefatigable storing away of nutriments for her precious eggs. As for piety, even here one might imagine that as she sat on her roost at night there was in her demeanor a hint of the reverent and prayerful. As man labored for God, so the hen labored for her master, man and hen each striving in its own way to manifest the bountifulness of the Almighty. Thus it was most appropriate that the American chicken (a New Englander at heart) burst into national prominence at Boston in the middle of the nineteenth century.

In the Reverend C. S. Lovell's *Young Pupils' Second Book*, published in New Haven in 1836, the author included an essay on "The Hen." "Of all feathered animals, there is none more useful than the common hen. Her eggs supply us with food during her life, and her flesh affords us delicate meat after her death. What a motherly care does she take of her young! How closely and tenderly does she watch over them, and cover them with her wings; and how bravely does she defend them from every enemy, from which she herself would fly away in terror, if she had not them to protect!

"While this sight reminds you of the wisdom and goodness of her Creator, let it also remind you of the care which your own mother took of you, during your helpless years, and of the gratitude and duty which you owe to her for all her kindness."

It was a comfort to admirers of the Protestant chicken to discover that the Devil made work for idle chickens as well as idle people. If birds were confined, one poultry manual informed its readers, they needed things to keep them busy. Hanging some vegetables or a split cabbage above the henhouse floor would, they were told, "give *occupation*, and so prevent feather-eating or other vices of idleness. . . . Experiments have shown that a very poor supply of eggs from a pen of birds allowed to become idle and torpid, was soon increased threefold when they were . . . induced to work for their living. . . ."

Not only did the hen symbolize thrift and industry, she also, for Dixon, as for Columella and Aristotle before him and for Aldrovandi in Renaissance Italy, represented motherhood. As Dixon saw it, after serving others her own turn came to be served: "The pleasures of motherhood must be accorded to her. Nature has been sufficiently tasked in one direction; she becomes feverish, loses flesh, her comb is livid, her eye dull. She sees in her heated fancy her young ones crowding around her, bristles her feathers to intimidate an imaginary enemy, and, as if they were already there, she utters the maternal 'cluck' — 'chioccia' — 'glocientes' — 'clock-hens.' . . ." Dixon believed that the "imagination" of the hen gave her an intimation of the joys of motherhood that lay ahead of her.

As the pullets mature, Dixon wrote, "they will grow animated, restless, full of busy importance, as if a new idea had lately broke in upon their minds. By-and-by they will commence prating and cackling, and in a few days the delighted Pullet will lay her first egg. It is hard to say which receives the most pleasure at contemplating the smooth, immaculate production, the Hen or her amateur owner." (Here the practical Kerr noted, "The very first egg . . . which a Pullet lays is seldom quite immaculate, but bears the marks of the effort it has cost. . . .")

For Dixon the egg was the perfect symbol of honest industry and he could not resist pointing a moral: "Those whose inherited wealth comes to them quarterly or annually, without any thought or exertion on their part, have no conception how bright and beautiful the money looks of which they can say, 'I have fairly and honestly earned it; I have done something useful for it.'" So with the hen, a paradigm of industry and thrift, who "rescues from waste many a minute portion of nutritious matter, collects it in her crop, and converts it into wholesome food for Man."

As Dixon put it, "There is nearly as much distinguishable difference between the units in every egg-basket which is carried to market, as there is between the faces in a crowd of men, or the hounds in a pack. To every Hen belongs an individual peculiarity in the form, colour and size of the Egg she lays, which never changes in her whole life time . . . and which is as well known to those who are in the habit of taking her produce, as the handwriting of their nearest acquaintance.

"The tapping which is heard, and which opens the prison doors," Dixon wrote, "is caused by the bill of the included chick." Sometimes, he warned his readers, chicks having succeeded "in making the first breach appear unable to batter down the dungeon walls any further." Here a "rash attempt to help them by breaking the shell . . . is often followed by a loss of blood, which can ill be spared." It is thus better to wait and let nature take its course. Often the chick that cannot struggle out of its shell is damaged genetically and it is kinder to let it die. There are dozens of folk remedies for feeble chicks, from ale and gin to peppercorns and rue, but these are, I fear, more of a consolation to the human doctors than an aid to the chicks themselves. They should be left alone, kept warm and at night smuggled under their mother's feathers; "the next morning," in Dixon's words, "they will either be as brisk as the rest, or as flat as pancakes and dried biffins."

The Reverend Mr. Dixon could never resist the opportunity to make a moral point even in the discussion of lice; from chicken lice he passed on to lice that infest peacocks, a classic case of "apparent magnificence balanced by unseen evil. Like unto them, are the great and powerful of this world, devoured by heart-eating cares and irremediable disappointments . . . the lice in the enameled panoply [of the peacock] remind us that we are in the sight of The Ever-Present."

Dixon had a splendid contempt for nostrums and medical fads whether applied to chicks or human infants. "How wonderful must be the productive energy which is at work in the universe, to replace the myriads of chickens and children that have been laid low by sage nursing! Whole peppercorns, gin, laudanum, tight-swaddling, cramming, dips into cold water . . . make us wonder that either biped, plumed or unplumed, is to be found in any other than a fossil state."

On another point Dixon and Kerr were in emphatic agreement: chickens should not be cooped up but rather be at liberty to range the barnyard and the fields. As one of Dixon's correspondents put it: "It is not possible to compensate a laying Hen for the want of liberty. . . . Liberty and *varied* abundance are the two greatest essentials for poultry, old and young, to promote health, growth, beauty and fertility." In Dixon's words, "Fowls that are kept in close confinement will greatly miss the opportunity of basking in the sun; warmth is almost as necessary for thriftiness as food." Kerr added his own endorsement: "A warm and dry night's lodging is good, but not so confinement during the day, even in the best of poultry-houses. The Hens will always keep themselves out of the wet, and no care can compensate for the exercise and variety of food afforded them by a state of liberty." Another of Kerr's recommendations was for a steady diet of fresh meat, chopped up like sausage or hamburger, "from the time insects disappear in the fall, till they reappear again in the spring."

In his discussion of various breeds — Dixon listed twenty-three — although the author made a conscientious effort to be fair, it was plain that his own preference was for the Cochin Chinas. He quoted with approval one fancier's account of the breed. Judged by "productiveness, easy keeping, laying qualities, size, disposition, beauty of form and plumage . . . they have no equals among the varieties now known in America." The best hens had laid a hundred and sixty eggs in six and half months, or, roughly, two hundred days. A correspondent of Kerr's, E. R. Cope of Philadelphia, was another importer of Eastern fowl, the Shanghai, Malay, and Royal Cochin Chinas. He reported to Dr. Kerr that his Shanghai cock was "very attentive to his Hens, and exercises a most fatherly care over the Chicks in his yard. . . . He frequently would allow them to perch on his back, and in this manner carry them into the house, and then up the chicken ladder."

The Reverend Mr. Bumstead of Roxborough, Pennsylvania, was convinced that if the farmers of Pennsylvania knew of the superior qualities of the imported chickens they would spare no pains to obtain them. One of his white Shanghai hens, he reported proudly, laid a chocolate-colored egg, "and very rich." "She is," he added, "emphatically the hen that lays *the golden egg.*"

As the word spread of the superior laying qualities

of the Shanghais and the Cochin Chinas they were imported in larger and larger numbers. The White Shanghais were even more prized by their owners, who reported that "the eggs are larger, and these Hens . . . more prolific than those of other colors. In their habits they are more quiet and less inclined to ramble." White Shanghais had "quiet dispositions" but they were not "sluggish or stupid"; they were "intelligent and confiding," and thus "invaluable for the purpose of rearing Chickens." The Black Spanish, on the other hand, had little tendency to broodiness and were therefore ideal for laying.

The principal drawback with the five-toed Dorkings, reputably brought to Britain by the Roman legions, was that their shortness of legs and clumsiness made them rather inept mothers, especially when they were given the eggs and chicks of more delicate birds to hatch and rear. Then "the Hen, in her affectionate industry . . . kicks her lesser nurslings right and left, and leaves them sprawling on their backs. Before they are a month old, half of them will be muddled to death with this rough kindness."

Other breeds discussed by Dixon were the Pheasant-Malay, the Guelderland, the Java, the Shakebag, the Jersey Blue, the Polish, the Spangled Hamburg, the Bolton Grey or Creole, the Silky or Negro, the Frizzled or Friesland, the Cuckoo, the Blue Dun, the Lark-crested, and the Dominique.

The attention given to various game birds was evidence of the wide variety of game breeds produced for the recently outlawed sport of cockfighting. Nine of the "breeds" described by Dixon had disappeared by the end of the century, but a hundred and fifty more had been accepted as standard breeds and varieties.

Dixon's book covered all aspects of "the management of poultry" from feeding and butchering to the attentions required by a setting hen. He was frank to confess that there were certain problems connected with the raising of poultry in England that were, for the most, unique to that nation. According to him, "A groom or stable-man almost always despises poultry. A gardener thinks it beneath him to look after them . . . boys are mischievous and untrustworthy as monkeys. . . . Even in public Menageries the man who has charge of a Lion deems it a condescension to tend a few harmless birds." Thus the best poultry-tender was usually "a clever little girl."

Dixon obviously borrowed freely from Aldrovandi and the classical authors — Columella, especially, but also Varro, Pliny, and Aristotle. Like them, he had an unabashed admiration and affection for his subjects. "Next to the Dog," he wrote, "the Fowl has been the constant attendant upon Man in his migrations and occupation of strange lands." Chickens, "independent of all considerations of profitableness . . . are gifted with two qualifications, which, either in man, beast, or bird, are sure to be popular; those are, a courageous temper and an affectionate disposition."

Dixon's book and its numerous imitators gave further stimulus to a movement already running wild. Poultry exhibitions were held in every city, state, and county, and ribbons so bitterly contended for that hardly an exhibition escaped charges of bribery and favoritism. Barnyard mongrels represented as rare breeds were sold at exorbitant prices, and hardly a month passed without someone claiming to have produced a new breed.

In the United States, George Burnham wrote a satiric "history" of the Hen Fever that seemed to hold the nation in thrall. "Never in the history of modern 'bubbles,' " he wrote, ". . . did *any* mania exceed in ridiculousness or ludicrousness, or in the number of its victims surpass this inexplicable humbug. . . ." Burnham's book, published in 1855, purported to follow "this extraordinary *mania* from its incipient stages to its final death or its *cure*. . . ." It was, he declared, written for "the hundreds and thousands . . . . who *may* have been mortally wounded or haply have escaped with only a broken wing" from the speculative frenzy in chickens that swept the country.

According to Burnham, the public were victims of a plot to defraud hatched in his own living room. A friend, inspecting Burnham's flock, had exclaimed over the varieties — "the Chinese, and the Malays, and the Gypsies, and the Chittaprats, and Wang Hongs, and the Yankee Games, and the Gengallers, and Cropple-crowns and Creepers, and Top-knots, and Gold Pheasants, and Buff Dorkings, and English Games and Black Spanish and Bantams," adding, "and I've several *new breeds*, too, I have made myself, by crossing and mixing, *in the last year*, which beat the world for beauty and size and excellence of quality." The notion of producing new *breeds* of chicken in the space of a year seemed to Burnham a bit of harmless chicanery, but before he knew it his friend had arranged for the great poultry exhibition at the Boston Public Garden. This, at least, was Burnham's satiric account of the origins of the Hen Fever. He poked particular fun at the "giant" Cochin Chinas, as the Shanghais had now come to be called. "They resemble giraffes," he wrote. ". . . I let them out upon the floor, and one of the cocks seized lustily upon my Indian-rubber overshoe and would have swallowed it (and myself), for aught I know had not a friend who stood by seized him, and absolutely choked him off."

The author purported to discover a conspiracy among poultry breeders to inflate the price of their birds through press-agentry. After the second great Boston exhibit, according to the writer of *Hen Fever*, "the sales of poultry largely increased . . . and in every town, at every corner, the pedestrian tumbled over either a fowl-raiser or some huge specimen of unnameable monster in chicken shape."

It was, of course, not simply an American "fever." "Kings and Queens and nobility, senators and governors, mayors and councilmen, ministers, doctors, lawyers, merchants and tradesmen, the aristocrat and the humble farmers and mechanics, gentlemen and commoners, old men and young men, women and children, rich and poor, white black and grey, — *everybody* was more or less seriously affected by this curious epidemic." All "joined in the hue-and-cry regarding the suddenly and newly ascertained fact that hens laid eggs — sometimes. . . ." Burnham promised to hold a funeral for "the dead and wounded," those simpletons who had been carried away by the boom. He himself, finding his prize Shanghai cock no longer salable, ate it for dinner; it proved a tough dish.

Certainly the bubble burst; prices for rare and fancy birds dropped precipitously and many breeders lost a bundle, but the fever remained. Or to put it another way, the romance of America and the chicken had just begun. What appeared to Burnham to be the end of the affair was only a lovers' quarrel. The history of the chicken throughout the remaining years of the century was one of what might be called "quiet consolidation of earlier gains." The giddy days were over, but life for the chicken would never be the same. The infatuation with producing new and better breeds of chicken, and handsomer and more particolored varieties of those breeds, remained. Not a year passed without claims for new and improved and more dazzlingly plumaged fowl. Not only was a good deal of fraud involved, but poultry exhibits were often marred by angry contentions over what constituted a breed, and, even more difficult for beleaguered poultry judges to decide: what was the standard of excellence in a particular breed? Old breeds that were new in America were constantly imported, the most notable being the

Leghorn, the classic Italian chicken. For a long time the Leghorn, a small bird — after the Mediterranean style — a reliable egg-layer but without spectacular plumage or an abundance of meat, remained in the background, overshadowed literally and figuratively by the giant Asiatic strains or more alluringly feathered rivals. Classic American breeds, combinations of imported fowl, for the most part, began to gain currency as the years passed. The Wyandottes appeared first in New York State, apparently a combination of Cochins and perhaps a bird of Mediterranean descent. Barred Plymouth Rocks were another breed, a good layer and a good meat bird, which quickly established itself as a favorite. Rhode Island Reds turned out to be efficient and durable birds, resistant to disease and energetic layers. But the problem of identifying and certifying breeds remained a source of bitter contention in poultry circles.

The amateur, the dabbler, the gentleman breeder was gradually replaced by the working farmer who, to the dismay of the fancier, had every intention of making a profit from the sale of eggs and chickens. Such profits were, to be sure, always supplementary to a general farm income, but it gradually became clear that birds properly raised and cared for could produce that vulgar commodity, money. As a consequence a more professional — one might even say, scientific — temper made itself felt. The next important development in the history of the chicken in America had no such single hero as Dr. John Bennett of Boston.

The phenomenon, of course, was, as we have already noted, by no means exclusively American. England was a serious rival in the chicken mania, and other nations followed suit. In Britain the principal authority on the chicken came to be Lewis Wright, who began raising Minorcas at the age of nine. "These chicks," a contemporary wrote, "were the delight of their young owner's heart . . . and Lewis Wright used to watch them by the hour, until, as he told me, 'I could almost have acted a chicken myself.' This close observation of their ways and individual peculiarities, doubtless cultivated a quickness of perception which stood Mr. Wright in good stead in later days," according to his biographer.

Wright went to a grammar school where a "kind-hearted schoolmaster" permitted the pupils to keep chickens in the coal cellar. As a young man he kept the enormously fashionable Brahma fowl and then began a "shilling monthly" entitled *The Book of Poultry*, which "scored a tremendous success," and brought him fame and a modest fortune as "the foremost . . . amongst poultry *litterateurs*." The issues, handsomely illustrated and soon collected into a book, became the authoritative work on Fancy Poultry and a model for quite literally innumerable imitators on both sides of the Atlantic. A new edition appeared every three or four years, and it was translated into a number of foreign languages. Finally, in 1901, after almost fifty years of devotion to the chicken, Lewis Wright was given a testimonial dinner at the International Show of Fancy Poultry and there hailed as the man who had "introduced a new spirit into the poultry world and lifted the entire pursuit to a higher plane than it had occupied before. . . ." "Yours," the master of ceremonies declared, "were the hand and brain which opened a new era in poultry journalism. . . . Your fearless exposure of fraud, wherever found [has] done much to strengthen and purify the exhibition world and make the path of the wrong-doer more difficult."

Lewis Wright was also a student of optics, the inventor of the projection microscope, and "a contributor to theological literature." He died crossing the train tracks at Saltford Station in 1905, doubtless preoccupied by reflections on chickens or, perhaps, on God, and it is perhaps not too much to say that his passing marked, coincidentally, the beginning of the decline of his beloved fowls.

As we have already noted, in Dixon's *Treatise on the History and Management of Ornamental and Domestic Poultry*, cocks and hens in the nineteenth century were endowed with all the virtues and attributes of Victorian ladies and gentlemen or, more particularly, Victorian husbands and wives. The attentive and courtly cock was described as the kindly arbiter of the barnyard, the keeper of order, the defender of the female. And she, of course, was, in her plump, comforting shape, the epitome of the uxorious, the dutiful wife who laid her eggs and faithfully attended to her children, never presuming to intrude into her husband's world. The splendor of the cock and the simple comeliness of the hen comported almost ideally with the Victorian male's image of himself in relation to the opposite sex, and there is no doubt that the popularity of "domestic fowl" with upper-class Victorians was in part a consequence of the relative ease with which they could be transformed into symbols of domestic felicity in human society.

There was still another dimension to the human-chicken analogy. One wonders how many Victorian males, contemplating the cock in his relentless and inexhaustible pursuit of the hen (who more often fled with terrified squawks than tamely submitted to his brutal advances), were moved to speculate on their own sexuality. The truth, never very successfully repressed, was that the Victorian male usually treated his wife with that tender, asexual solicitude which he credited to the cock (although the terror of the wedding night rape was a persistent element in the imaginations of carefully nurtured Victorian girls), but he, in many instances, pursued serving girls, prostitutes, and lower-class women generally with an avidity not wholly dissimilar to that of the cock for the hen.

Indeed it is interesting to ruminate for a moment on the violence of the cock's assault on the hen. Hens certainly vary, like females of every species, in their sexual responsiveness. The nearest a hen comes to being in "heat" is a certain patient submissiveness to the rude attentions of the cock when the hen has her mind on setting and hatching eggs. After the hen has laid an egg she is often particularly approachable. I would not, in fact, be surprised to learn that her triumphant cackle after having laid an egg (the cackle, of course, is not necessarily related to her having laid an egg; there are lots of different kinds of cackle, and cocks cackle as well as hens) is a signal to the cock that she is available. The cock seizes the hen by the nape of her neck and mounts her in an act of copulation as hasty and precarious as it is violent. Much of the time, as we have seen, the hen has nothing on her mind so much as flight. The cock pursues with a notable singlemindedness, wings half-opened and trailing backward, the very picture of sexual aggression, or, more plainly, of the intent to rape, to take by force the sexual favors of the hen. It must be said for the reader with anthropomorphic inclinations that the hen, once captured, seems to find the experience not wholly unpleasant, though it is certainly true that she often uses every stratagem to avoid intercourse. After the fowl deed has been done, literally in seconds, the hen crouches at the spot where she has been crushed to earth, with a posture both resigned and reflective, and then rises, ruffles up her feathers and rearranges them (much as a woman might arrange her hair after making love), and then proceeds to look for a worm or bug.

And here one is tempted once more to speculate on the thoughts of a Victorian female as she observed the activities of cock and hen in the barnyard. Certainly, it is clear that many Victorian wives took refuge in childbearing from the persistent and unwelcomed sexual attentions of their husbands. It would perhaps be going too far to suggest that they learned such a strategy from female chickens, but I find it difficult to believe that they were entirely unconscious of the analogy.

The less sentimental or more scientific observer of chickens questioned the desirability of having cocks loose in a flock of hens if it was the intention of the farmer to produce the maximum number of eggs and the plumpest table birds. It took no great powers of deduction to conclude that a hen that spent a substantial part of her time running for dear life was apt to be as lean and tough as an Olympic sprinter. Nor was she apt to be quite as productive in the egg department. The notion of exiling the cock appalled the Reverend Mr. Dixon, who, doubtless thinking of the horrors of divorce and broken homes, dismissed it indignantly. Without a kindly, superintending cock the hens would lack all order and organization and spend their time gossiping and quarreling. The cock was the principle of order in the barnyard. "Any one whose Hens have from accident been deprived of a male companion," he wrote, "will agree with me in saying that they have not done so well till the loss has been supplied. During the interregnum, matters get all wrong. There is nobody to stop their mutual bickering, and inspire an emulation to please and to be pleased. The poor deserted creatures wander about dispirited, like soldiers without a general. It belongs to their very nature to be . . . marshalled by one of the stronger sex, who is a kind, though a strict master, and a considerate, though stern disciplinarian." The thought of his hens in "melancholy widowhood" was almost more than the parson could bear.

There is some truth in Dixon's notion. While cocks, with their insatiable sexual appetites, create a good deal of disorder, they also *preserve* a kind of order. And if they sometimes drive hens to distraction, hens

without cocks do look, it seems to me, rather forlorn.
But then, of course, I have no doubt that I am Victorian at heart.

One need not belabor the point. It is plain as the
comb on a cock's head that a great many nineteenth-
century Victorians, whether in the United States or
across the Atlantic, found the chicken a creature of
infinite allure, indeed, one might say, a bird of magic
properties and potentialities. In this respect they were
not very different from those primitive tribes which
kept (and keep) chickens for purely ritual purposes.
Chicken fanciers of the Western world had no explicit
taboos against eating eggs or chickens, but it is clear
they often preferred to use them for ritual purposes
— to breed them and groom them and exhibit them —
rather than to eat them. And the magic that the
chicken revealed was the magic of genetics, scientific
magic whereby a man (much less frequently a woman)
could shape and mold and modify another living creature to his own desire and intent.

The nineteenth century was intoxicated with the
more mundane magic of science, the alchemist's gold,
a power of apparently limitless potential. At the end
of the scientific spectrum it produced the fine gold
pocket watch and the crossbred chicken, objects that
an ordinary man could touch and possess; if he could
not make a marvelous Swiss watch he could make a
chicken, and what was more he could make it (and
did) in his own image. (Had not Socrates described
man as a featherless biped?) Chickens and humans
had lived in the closest proximity for as long as civilization had existed, and the chickens' migrations were
almost as strange as the human migrations which they
had accompanied, as moving and inscrutable and irresistible. In the nineteenth century man and chicken
entered into quite a new relationship. They both lived
in a competitive society, a society involved in an extraordinary industrial and technological flowering, a so-

ciety that experimented with submarines and dreamed of trips to the moon, a society that increasingly worshipped technology as the protean producer of *things* in inconceivable abundance. Therefore they must produce and compete. Some chickens must be judged better than others and the lesser must, eventually, lose out.

The chicken must be not only a magic bird, a ritual bird, a bird whose domestic life replicated that of the human family; it must be a productive bird. It must earn its keep and that of its master. In that fact would lie its downfall, but before that fall it rose to dizzy heights.

In England the Reverend Mr. Dixon and in America Dr. Kerr and his correspondents characterized an era in the history of the chicken in which the perfection of various "breeds" came to be a major preoccupation of those gentlemen farmers who represented the best spirit of experimentation balanced by affection for their charges. They spoke of chickens, as we have seen, much as they spoke of people. They viewed cocks as the same kind of stern but benevolent father that they thought themselves to be; hens they compared, with amiable condescension, to their wives. The fecundity of the hens suggested the fecundity of their own docile and productive spouses. The new scientific spirit of the age had entered into their relationships with their fowl but had not yet corrupted it. As featherless bipeds they observed their fine-feathered friends carefully, systematically, and lovingly and found nothing odd in this combination. Their observations and speculations were, to be sure, often casual and superficial by modern standards, but they marked a considerable advance over anything of the kind that had been done before. Dr. Kerr was thus a more scrupulous researcher than Aldrovandi, though not so catholic. At the same time the Dixons and the Kerrs were, as we have seen, learned men who were familiar with the speculations of the ancients and with Aldrovandi's work.

From the point of view of the chicken, the situation could hardly have been better. The chicken, in addition to being closely and respectfully observed, was pampered and cherished, weighed, measured, fattened, and improved until cock and hen, chick, pullet, and matron dominated the barnyard.

The development of fine breeds of poultry was also congenial to the growing spirit of democracy. A farm wife or farmer of the most modest circumstances could compete on almost equal terms with the wealthiest breeder. And while it was true that prize birds brought large prices, eggs from blue-ribbon hens could be bought relatively inexpensively and hatched and raised to win ribbons in their own right. The same concern with science was evident, of course, in every area of animal husbandry but nowhere more conspicuously and agreeably than in the keeping of chickens. Various breeds had, as we have seen, their enthusiastic advocates. The ideal hen was the hen who was a steady and industrious layer and delicious roasted or fried. And although there might be disputes about the breed that best conformed to these criteria, there was no argument about the criteria themselves.

In 1873, twenty-four years after the Boston poultry show, a group of breeders from various parts of the United States and Canada met at Buffalo, New York, and formed the American Poultry Association. Their primary purpose was "to standardize the varieties of domestic fowl so that a fair decision could be made as to which qualities marked prize winners." The amateur spirit was still very much in evidence. Breeding fine birds and showing them in poultry shows had only a tenuous monetary implication. Better birds, of course, produced more and larger eggs and more meat, but certainly the endless experimentation with coloring and feathering rested on purely aesthetic grounds. And it was this persistent, indefatigable breeding by tens of thousands of devoted breeders that became the most conspicuous part of the story of the American chicken in the latter half of the century.

The year after the formation of the American Poultry Association, a manual — *The Standard of Excellence* — was published with detailed drawings and descriptions of the strong and weak points of forty-one varieties or breeds of bird. *The Standard of Excellence* was replaced in 1905 by *The Standard of Perfection*, which is still the handbook of poultry breeders. Its purpose, like that of its predecessor, was "establishing and illustrating of the Standard fowl. . . . The aim of the [American Poultry] Association has been to stabilize our economic and commercial breeds to uniform size, shape and color, with good production and practicability; with provision that ornamental breeds, including the Bantam, be attractive, productive and meet requirements of the Standard breeder."

The Standard of Perfection is a mine of information about the conformation of various breeds, their coloring, size, weight, combs, wattles, feathers, and so on, a sober, factual compendium designed for practical use. It is at the same time a symbol and measuring rod that can be used to calibrate the astonishing rise and subsequent decline of the chicken. For the uninitiated the concentration of chicken fanciers on producing exotic feathers on standard breeds is perhaps most striking. The gold and silver feathers of the Sebright are the exemplars of this fad. Basically white and golden brown with a rim of black, these feathers have been produced on a number of breeds. The purpose is, of course, purely ornamental.

As we have said, the late nineteenth century was the heyday of the chicken. No respectable farm was without its panoply of handsome birds, a fine flock of vigorous fowls for eggs and meat and prize creatures for showing at poultry exhibitions and at county and state fairs. The best birds went to regional and national exhibitions and came home loaded with honors, with cups and ribbons and enthusiastic encomiums. Perhaps Robert Frost has best described such a bird, the pride of her owner and the envy of the neighboring farmers:

Such a fine pullet ought to go
All coiffured to a winter show,
And be exhibited, and win.
The answer is this one has been —

And come with all her honors home.
Her golden leg, her coral comb,
Her fluff of plumage, white as chalk,
Her style, were all the fancy's talk.

It seems as if you must have heard.
She scored an almost perfect bird.
In her we make ourselves acquainted
With one a Sewell might have painted.

Here common with the flock again,
At home in her abiding pen,
She lingers feeding at the trough
The last to let night drive her off.

The one who gave her ankle-band,
Her keeper, empty pail in hand,
He lingers too, averse to slight
His chores for all the wintry night.

He leans against the dusty wall,
Immured almost beyond recall,
A depth past many swinging doors
And many litter-muffled floors.

He meditates the breeder's art
He has half a mind to start,
With her for Mother Eve, a race
That shall all living things displace.

'Tis ritual with her to lay
The full six days, then rest a day;

At which rate barring broodiness
She may well score an egg-success.

The gatherer can always tell
Her well-turned egg's brown sturdy shell,
As safe a vehicle of seed
As is vouchsafed to feathered breed.

No human spectre at the feast
Can scant or hurry her the least,
She takes her time to take her fill.
She whets a sleepy sated bill.

She gropes across the pen alone
To peck herself a precious stone.
She waters at the patent fount.
And so to roost, the last to mount.

The roost is her extent of flight.
Yet once she rises to the height,
She shoulders with a wing so strong
She makes the whole flock move along.

The night is setting in to blow.
It scours the windowpane with snow,
But barely gets from them or her
For comment a complacent chirr.

The lowly pen is yet a hold
Against the dark and wind and cold
To give a prospect to a plan
And warrant prudence in a man.

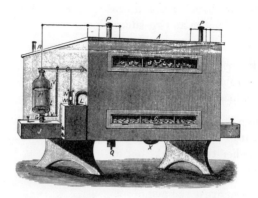

THE INCREASED DEMAND for eggs was less a by-product of aesthetic and scientific fascination with chickens than a consequence of the rapid industrialization of the Western world in the course of the nineteenth century. The processes of production determine, Marx taught, the character of a society. The chicken was not to escape this iron law. The accelerating growth of industry required, as a corollary, the mass production of cheap processed foods, in many of which eggs in some form — dried, powdered, or later, frozen — were an essential ingredient.

By the end of the nineteenth century the national preoccupation with chickens had induced many farmers substantially to increase the size of their flocks and the proportion of their incomes derived from the sale of eggs and chickens. (As late as 1910 a farm census showed over two hundred eighty million chickens on five and a half million farms. Eighty-eight percent of all farms kept chickens — an average of 80.4 chickens per farm.) The numerous poultry journals carried an unending supply of "scientific" information about the most advanced methods of raising chickens — designs for improved poultry houses, better feed, ways of combating common diseases, etc. Chickens that had ranged the barnyard and the farm found themselves confined in large outdoor areas, their activities and their output, once natural and uninhibited, now increasingly controlled.

This was especially true of farms and farmers adjacent to large cities, where there was a constant demand from city dwellers for fresh eggs. At the same time it should be noted that chickens were very widely raised in large towns and cities, so that a "census" of chickens in urban areas in 1906 disclosed that such an area had one chicken for every two people, a very substantial number considering that an urban chicken is a rarity today.

To put the matter simply, by the end of the nineteenth century industrial technology had advanced to a point where the chicken could, increasingly, be utilized as a commodity rather than as a uniquely interesting element in the economy of the farm. However, there was first the question of the transportability of eggs and chickens to be solved. Railroad transportation had been available for decades, and eggs and chickens in modest numbers had long been shipped by rail. But by and large there was little interest in shipping large numbers of eggs or birds. As we have noted, near every large city were farms where eggs in sufficient numbers were produced, carried to the city, and sold with other farm products. The refinement of breeds of chicken had, moreover, resulted in certain breeds that were superior as meat producers and others in which the size, uniformity, and number of eggs laid by an average bird clearly dictated their use primarily for the production of eggs.

The unlikely setting for the next act in the universal drama of the chicken was the little town of Petaluma, the center of a farming area in the Petaluma Valley of California, seventy miles north of San Francisco. The mild climate of the Petaluma Valley was ideally suited for year-round farming, and farms (or ranches, as their owners preferred to call them) filled the valley in the last decades of the nineteenth century. They were at first classic small farms with a variety of crops. Since the Petaluma River ran to the Pacific and freighters could make the run to San Francisco in a day or so, that city was the natural market for the produce of the Petaluma Valley. Soon eggs proved to be one of the most profitable items picked up by the market-bound ships, and Petaluma farmers in consequence placed increasing emphasis on the poultry side of their produce.

By the 1880's a chicken-boat put into Petaluma daily to deliver grain for chicken feed and carry fresh eggs to San Francisco. In the same period Christopher Nisson, a Danish farmer who had come to Petaluma by way of Panama to work as a nurseryman, began to take an interest in poultry "ranching." In the words of a reporter for the *Petaluma Argus-Courier*, writing in the eighty-fifth "Anniversary and Progress Edition," Nisson "disapproved of chickens that hung around the barn and laid eggs in the mangers and under the porch. He also considered it unethical to leave eggs lying around, completely undated, until the farmer's wife, ready to go to town, sent the children to scare up all available eggs to sell for what they used to call 'pin-money.' " To the thrifty Nisson the time that his hens spent setting on, hatching, and tending baby chicks in order to replenish the flock was time far better spent laying those eggs to be marketed in San Francisco.

A small, primitive incubator which hatched ten eggs at a time had recently been produced and had caused a sensation when it was exhibited at county fairs. Many visitors refused to believe that it was capable of actually hatching eggs and were convinced that properly hen-hatched baby chicks were simply concealed in a part of the incubator, from which they emerged as though hatched by the odd-looking box itself. It was at best a curiosity, at worst an intrusion on the realm of Mother Nature.

Nisson was not a sentimentalist. One of the first to see the commercial potentialities in the device, he bought a ten-egg incubator and began to reproduce his flock himself, leaving his hens to lay for the market, uninterrupted by maternal cares. Neighbors, so the story goes, brought eggs of their own to be incubated and soon came round to urge Nisson to sell them baby chicks hatched from his eggs. Almost inadvertently Nisson shifted from producing eggs to producing baby chicks. He added incubators and then built one capable of hatching a substantial number of eggs, thus establishing his claim to be the proprietor of "America's first commercial hatchery." Coincident with Nisson's venture came the great incubator boom.

Perhaps stimulated by Nisson's experiments, some enterprising citizens of Petaluma established a factory to manufacture incubators. They were simple gas-burning apparatuses in which the eggs had to be turned three times a day by hand to simulate the hen's turning of her eggs with her beak, but they were soon in great demand. They won prize after prize when pitted against rival incubators and were soon being shipped to the East Indies, to Alaska, "by fast freight," and to Germany to the great circus tycoon Carl Hagenbeck, who intended to use one to hatch ostrich eggs.

Following Christopher Nisson's lead, six hatcheries were established in Petaluma within the next ten years. At first the sales of hatchery chicks were limited to chicken ranchers in the immediate vicinity, but it was soon clear that baby chicks could be safely shipped within a two-day railroad radius of a hatchery. This was because chicks do not need food or water for roughly forty-eight hours after they are born; and this, in turn, is nature's way of coping with the fact that eggs, although laid over a period of as much as three weeks, all have to hatch within forty-eight hours of each other. The fact that the newborn chick does not need food and water initially enables the mother to remain on the nest and act, to a degree at least, as midwife for her hatching babies without leaving to rustle up food for those just out of the egg. In addition, the baby chick is one of nature's hardiest infant creatures, crammed with various antibodies and immune mechanisms that enable it to survive the first few traumatic weeks outside the shell. Capitalizing on the hardihood of the newborn chick, hatcheries began shipping their output as far as three or four hundred miles by rail express.

Decades of competition between various breeds of birds in the matter of egg laying had by the 1890's produced a clear winner, the Leghorn, most typically white, though not necessarily so. The conjunction of the egg-laying champion Leghorn with the development of the hatchery might be said to mark the modest beginning of the poultry industry or at least the egg-producing division of it. In place of the medley of birds of uncertain ancestry, many of them remnants of the earlier obsession with rare and unusual breeds, it was possible now to breed pure strains with the aid of a simple arrangement called a trapnest. In trapnesting, hens pushed aside a light wire barrier to enter the nest. Once inside, the hen, her egg laid, was trapped until her master released her. It was thus possible to identify a particular egg with a particular hen (hens were also numbered and banded to help in identification). Now it was possible to produce eggs on a rather large scale — from a flock of several hundred hens — and keep careful check on which hens laid which (and, more important, how many) eggs. This, in turn, meant that the top layers could be chosen selectively as parents of the next generation and the strain progressively improved, provided always of course that one paid proper attention to the right "line" in mating so as to prevent excessive inbreeding.

The result of these developments was a shift from

the production of eggs and meat as part of the general production of a farm to making a living by the specialized raising of nothing but chickens. It was soon clear that this was a far more efficient method of production. Feed was cheap. Little land was needed (an acre or two would take care of a thousand chickens) and hardly any capital was required to set up business; a man handy with tools could readily build a simple chicken house. In California, the chickens stayed out of doors in all but the most inclement weather. Moreover, once the henhouse had been built and the flock established, there was much less work to do than on the average farm. The chickens had to be fed and provided with a constant supply of fresh water — this was accomplished by gravity-flow pipes and devices of various kinds that relieved the rancher of the labor of hauling water — and the eggs collected, cleaned, candled, and packed. Children could do many of these chores before leaving for school and after they returned home. (I have met dozens of middle-aged Americans whose irrational loathing for chickens stems from their childhood performance of such chores.)

Harry Lewis, professor of poultry husbandry at Rutgers University, writing in 1913, described the advantages of "greater concentration and specialization." First of all "exclusive egg farms" had placed the business on a "scientific basis" and guaranteed the customer "a strictly fresh and clean product." In place of the haphazard methods or nonmethods which brought eggs to the market often in poor condition, improperly handled or graded, the new science of poultry management had produced an egg of uniform size and color, reasonably fresh from the hen.

What the opportunity to raise chickens in comparatively large numbers of the production of eggs or meat meant, almost immediately, was that it was impractical and uneconomical to allow the hen to lay a clutch of eggs, set on them, and hatch and raise the

chicks. If she was permitted to follow this old-fashioned procedure she would be out of production for an
intolerably long time; the number of days it took her
to lay her clutch (if we take fifteen eggs as a suitable
number, this would be twenty to twenty-five days depending on her laying rate); plus twenty-one days to
hatch the eggs once she set; plus five to ten weeks to
raise her brood to the point where they could fend for
themselves. Thus the total time that a broody hen, allowed to set, would be out of production ranged from
a minimum of two and half to three months to more
than four. Since the productive period of egg laying
for a hen is not much more than two years, to allow a
hen to set and hatch her own chicks would be to use
up a substantial portion of her productive life. Of
course, only a relatively small number of hens in a
flock would need to function as mothers to keep a
flock at a steady size. In a flock of five hundred chickens, for example, no more than two hundred would
need to be replaced each year. With normal luck (that
is, allowing for a mortality rate of ten percent among
chicks and pullets) twenty-five hens out of the five
hundred could replenish the flock and keep it up to
full strength. But viewed another way, since the output (of eggs) of a good laying hen was worth perhaps
four dollars a year, to lose the output of twenty-five
hens for a substantial period of time was uneconomical
when eggs could be collected, hatched in a home-made
hatchery, and raised in a brooder at very little cost.
Or, more conveniently, baby chicks could be bought
from a hatchery which specialized in developing the
finest breeding birds for twenty or twenty-five cents
apiece. So the first casualty of the commercial poultry
operation was the classic motherhood of the hen. Economics required that she be reduced to the role of
egg-producer and her mothering function taken over
by machines — incubators and brooders.

Not only that. The hen's broodiness, her determination to set, hatch, and raise chicks, became a negative quality. Some stubborn hens, confined to henhouses with their eggs collected daily, so that they never had a chance to accumulate a clutch of eggs to set on, nonetheless insisted on setting on something, on one egg or, not infrequently, no eggs, and this, of course, interfered with their productiveness. Farmers thus preferred those breeds such as the Leghorn which inherently had the least tendency to broodiness, and considerable pains were taken to breed broodiness out by selecting the eggs of hens who in the face of active discouragement showed no inclination to set.

In the words of Harry Lewis: "It was not so many years ago that the American hen ruled supreme in the capacity of incubator and brooder, faithfully sitting out the twenty-one days on the nest, cautiously leading her tender brood of fluffy youngsters through the early stages of their development. . . ." But times had changed. "The hen," Lewis wrote, "is too valuable as an egg machine to allow her to waste weeks and months in hatching eggs and brooding chickens. Then, again, the hen is too fickle, too unstable, too variable in her whims and desires, to entrust to her the hatching of chicks on a large scale. . . . Credit for making possible our great commercial poultry industry should go in large measure to the modern mammoth incubator, equipped with automatic ventilation and temperature control. . . ." To Lewis, "the real romance of modern poultry husbandry" had been "the unprecedented growth in the production and shipment" of eggs and chickens.

As for Petaluma, it found itself on a giddy financial ascent that must have surprised its most enthusiastic boosters. By the turn of the century it was turning out the *Petaluma Poultry Journal*, a weekly publication with a wide circulation to poultrymen in every part of the country. The lesson it preached was a simple and enticing one: "Poultry Farms of the Family

Type, The Only Successful Kind, Provide Daily Cash Income. . . ." The specialization which was the key to the success of Petaluma could only bring greater prosperity — that was the constant pitch of the Chamber of Commerce and of the poultry growers' association of the city. The White Leghorn, with her "large egg . . . smoothly textured pure white shell and desirable light yellow yolk," was the agent of Petaluma's wealth and fame.

Those interested in trying their fortunes in Petaluma were assured that "our poultry farmers will remain of the family type." "Extensive production on a large scale with hired help, has been tried," prospective ranchers were told, "but it has always failed. This industry seems to require a special technique to be found only in the personal supervision of the hardworking but happy poultryman who tends his flocks with far better results than he could expect to get with the aid of a host of hired men." It was that — the alliance of the hardworking, happy farmer with the hardworking, happy hen — that made the poultry business such a potentially attractive one: the cheerful cooperation between man and bird.

It was an intoxicating prospect certainly, a kind of answer to the American dream of the independent entrepreneur, self-employed, self-reliant, able by thrift and hard work to make a decent living; not a wage-slave or a time-clock puncher as so many Americans had become, but a businessman who had set himself up in a profitable venture with an absolute minimum of capital. The life was a healthy one — the Petaluma Valley was a lovely spot if one were fortunate enough to be able to realize his dream there, outdoors much of the time. While raising chickens was no job for the shiftless or lazy, it was certainly not physically arduous and the hours were good; one went to bed and got up with the chickens, and early to bed and early to rise, as Doctor Franklin said, "makes a man healthy, wealthy and wise."

It seemed too good to be true and of course it was. But for a time the truth was concealed by the boom psychology of the new converts, those who believed that poultry raising was as close to the American dream as an imperfect world was likely to allow. Certainly one of the most attractive features of poultry keeping for married couples was that in contrast to the vast majority of jobs where the husband rushed off to a remote office or factory and returned in the evening exhausted and preoccupied to a wife who felt somehow left in the lurch, poultry keeping was a task ideally shared by husband and wife. It was as though a way had been found to retrieve that period, now largely in the American past, where husband and wife shared the responsibilities and the pleasures of a rural economy and held each other, perhaps as a consequence of common tasks, in mutual affection and regard.

Between 1899 and 1909 the value of poultry produced in the United States had increased by forty-eight percent. Vineland, New Jersey, and Hunterdon County in the same state were the eastern rivals of Petaluma. These communities produced eggs and chickens for the New York market. Indeed, despite the spectacular success of Petaluma, the production of poultry was concentrated in the East, especially in the Middle Atlantic states and in Ohio, Iowa, Illinois, and Missouri. In 1905 the value of poultry products in the United States had been estimated by the Secretary of Agriculture at $500,000,000. Five years later it was second only to corn as a revenue-producing agricultural crop.

A process had been started which could not be stopped short of its ultimate rationalization. Modern techniques for the manufacture and distribution of eggs and chickens had been set in motion. By the time they had run their course the small, independent poultry farmer and the chicken would both be flattened by the juggernaut of modern technology.

Much of the story can be traced in the *Petaluma Weekly Poultry Journal* or in any of the dozens upon dozens of similar publications. First, the feed companies entered the scene. Poultry farmers must be prevailed upon to use high-quality feeds; only by doing so could they get proper production of eggs. To skimp on feed was to practice the most short-sighted economy.

But there was already a note of anxiety; the message that the *Petaluma Poultry Journal* brought its readers in much of the literature was that "the time has passed for making money with poultry by old fashioned methods. The farmer and poultry keepers who are making any money today are wide awake, progressive men and women, who study their business, who take advantage of the best facilities, latest improvements, modern methods, etc. In short, they keep up with the times." That was surely reasonable enough. Americans were great at keeping up with the times; they were known around the world to be whole-hearted advocates of progress. The trouble was that "the latest improvements" and "modern methods" seemed to change every day, so that even "wide awake progressive men and women" began to find it increasingly difficult to keep up.

In 1903 land in Petaluma was advertised for a hundred dollars an acre; "ninety dollars cash, balance 3 and 5 years at 6 per cent" or one could rent a ten-acre farm for one hundred dollars a year. The price of eggs varied from twenty cents a dozen in the prime laying months to as much as sixty cents a dozen in the winter months. And prospective poultry keepers poured into the valley.

In 1904 the Petaluma Incubator Company built a new plant sixty-two feet wide by one hundred eight feet long, two stories in height, "the acme of convenience in factory construction," the *Argus* proudly announced. The opening was celebrated by a lavish banquet for the employees and their wives "and many of its warmest friends." By the end of the first decade of the new century, Petaluma was able to proclaim itself "the largest poultry center in the world" and then, "the egg basket of the world." The town's official insigne was designated as a wire basket of eggs. Each year the production figures mounted, often astronomically. By 1913 the poultrymen of Petaluma were shipping a hundred million eggs a year and one million chickens.

But not everyone prospered. Rumors circulated of failures and bankruptcies so that a somewhat defensive tone crept into the promotional literature of the town. The author of a prospectus written in 1913 and entitled "Petaluma, the Poultry Center" was careful to say that he could not assure anyone who came to Petaluma and entered the poultry business that he was sure to get rich. "But listen," he added; "you must say for yourself whether or not you can succeed. Many men have succeeded [the implication was that a number had not] and many are now making good money with chickens in the neighborhood of Petaluma. If the chicken business were not a paying proposition here it would gradually decrease in volume, as there are not enough 'suckers' beginning to keep it up. On the contrary, the output of eggs from Petaluma is constantly increasing and everything in connection with the industry here is growing." The victim of "hen fever" who hopes to make his fortune in the poultry business must realize that it is "a difficult undertaking . . . and many a man, thinking it to be an easy snap has 'bitten off more than he could chew.'" The beginner was warned that he must have "infinite patience. He must be willing to give constant and vigilant attention to seemingly unimportant little details. He must be willing to 'labor and to wait.' . . . He must be a 'Johnny-on-the-spot' three hundred and sixty-five days a year. He must know that one hundred cents make a dollar. . . . He should have (though perhaps he might struggle along for a while without this item) a wife who is also endowed as above stipulated — and some more."

All these exhortations were written by Frank Snow, editor of the *Petaluma Journal,* for a prospectus for the Chamber of Commerce, which was clearly uneasy about the growing number of failures among poultry keepers. There had been angry accusations from embittered poultrymen who had lost their shirts that "the poultry business is a big sell, every man who says anything good for the business is a liar, and no one, except the feed dealers, is making a cent out of it." There was an increasing number of such individuals who pronounced an anathema on Petaluma and chickens wherever they subsequently went.

Superficial and romantic notions, the editor of the *Petaluma Poultry Journal* warned, had drawn many into "the business" who had little idea of its real nature. Such a novice poultryman was described by the editor in these words (they are worth quoting at some length because they give a vivid picture of an earlier era in the history of the chicken): he (the novice poultryman) "hears about what a big thing the chicken business is at Petaluma, and is interested. He is tired of his present daily grind and thinks how much easier it would be to raise chickens. He remembers that when he was a small boy on the old farm the labor of raising chickens was small and the cost almost nothing. He does not remember or take into account the fact that the old home was a general farm, with horses, cattle and hogs, while crops of corn, wheat, barley and oats were raised. . . . The mother of the family set the hens in the spring and managed the hens and chicks when they came off. There was plenty of room and the chicks thrived under ideal conditions. There was the manure pile for the chicks and hens to scratch in — and of course they often got into the garden, while there was always a nice place to wallow and a few tender green sprouts or some bugs under the berry bushes and grape vines.

"There was the ash heap, containing also bits of charcoal and burned bone. The old, half-rotten straw sack afforded some bugs and some green sprouts, while the new straw stack of the grain yielded grain and exercise. There was variety and more exercise in the barn, around the corn crib and the granaries and in the stubble fields. There were more bugs and worms and green sprouts among the bushes and willows along the brook and around the spring. Besides these there were good things to eat which the hens knew where to find but about which no one else knew or cared. There were also cosy, sheltered places in the winter and shady places in summer. Thus the greater part of the hens' good was found by themselves and consisted of things not noticed by the boy. He scattered grain once or twice a day, and that was all he knew about the hens' food or requirement."

Walter Hogan, editor of *The Call of the Hen*, a treatise on poultry raising published in 1913, sounded an even more somber note than Newton. It was his estimate that only one out of a hundred succeeded in making a living in the poultry business. It was his view that there was "no other business which calls for so many qualifications as that of the poultry-farmer . . . ," among them "detailed knowledge . . . an unlimited reserve of perseverence, determination and resource, a genuine love for fowls, the capacity for hard, continuous work for seven days a week . . . and thrifty management." It was Hogan's advice to "poultry-keeping aspirants" to keep birds in their spare time and to concentrate initially on breeding birds for exhibition purposes. Only then, when they had determined that they have a "genuine love for the work," should they consider keeping chickens for a living. The life of a poultry keeper was, "contrary to popular belief, far from being a bed of roses. Practically all men who are today making a living from poultry," Hogan wrote, "commenced keeping fowls as a hobby, and the knowledge and experience which they gained in this way enabled them to found the establishments which are to-day of world-wide reputation." It was, he wrote sternly, no occupation for "the idle, the thriftless or the pleasure-seekers of this holiday-making age. . . ."

Under the pressure of rising feed prices and falling prices for eggs, some of the shrewder poultrymen in Petaluma, as we have seen, moved from the production of eggs to the production of baby chicks. The proximity of the incubator factory provided an irresistible opportunity to turn out baby chicks for sale to ranchers who were starting in business or who, increasingly, found it more convenient to buy chicks rather than produce their own. Chicks were much less subject to the fluctuations of the market than eggs. This pattern, like most of those set in Petaluma, was soon followed by poultrymen in other parts of the country. The largest hatchery in Petaluma produced a hatch of over one hundred fifty thousand birds every three weeks. As soon as the newborn chicks were dry they were placed in boxes holding a hundred chicks. As the Petaluma Chamber of Commerce's brochure put it, "It is certainly a lot easier for the beginner with a bad case of 'chicken fever' to buy his chicks already hatched than to do the trick himself. . . . Many old poultry raisers . . . take very kindly to the idea, being able in this way to increase their flocks much more rapidly than their own hatching alone. . . ."

In 1910 there were sixty-five colleges and experimental stations doing research in poultry husbandry, from Alaska to North Carolina. The research activities of the state universities were most helpful even if sometimes confusing in their contradictory advice, and if they were written up in language that was often impenetrable to the layman (such as "The Relative Efficiency of Beta Carotene and Vitamin A for Growing Chicks," or, even more unnerving, "Physiological Factors Associated with Genetic Resistance to Fowl Typhoid" or "A Study of the Coliform Group of Bacteria in the Intestine of Diseased Chickens"), there was usually an agricultural agent available to explain what new feed or vaccine was called for.

So indefatigable were the researchers on poultry matters in the land-grant colleges and universities of the United States that between 1896, when such research could be said to have properly begun, and 1950, over twelve hundred "poultry theses" alone were presented in fulfillment of the requirement for advanced degrees in poultry husbandry. And these were, of course, just a drop in the thirsty chicken's water bucket. Thousands more were produced in other colleges and universities and additional thousands by the professors in such institutions and by researchers employed directly by the federal or state governments and by large feed companies. So for even the most "progressive men and women," dedicated to "the latest improvements" and "modern methods," keeping poultry — the preferred designation of the occupation of the raiser of chickens — became more time-consuming and, for the great majority of poultry keepers, more and more expensive.

In addition to formal "research" on the raising of chickens and the production of eggs there were, by 1915, sixty-one journals devoted exclusively to poultry. They included such general publications as the *Golden Egg*, the *Intermountain Poultry Advocate*, *Profitable Poultry*, the *City Farmer*, *Poultry Success*, *Happy Hen*, *Industrious Hen*, *Poultry Life of Amer-*

ica, Feathered World, and the *Advance Poultry Journal*, in addition to magazines devoted entirely to one breed, such as the *Ancona World* and the *National Partridge Wyandotte Journal*.

In addition to the flood of scholarly pamphlets detailing the results of scientific research on the chicken there was an increasing number of manuals, books designed to guide the novice poultry keeper through the increasingly complex procedures and techniques required for the successful raising of chickens. The degree of specialization was still, to be sure, minimal. Most poultrymen produced their own birds from incubators through brooder to mature bird. The emphasis in the manuals was heavily on egg production, and the "culled" birds, those that were indifferent and unprofitable layers, were removed from the flock, killed, and sent to market, or, more commonly, sent alive on special poultry trains — freight cars which had been converted to carry four or five thousand chickens, to city markets and butcher shops, where they were slaughtered and sold to customers as demand dictated.

The most typical method of keeping laying hens was in small individual houses with separate "runs" or yards. Birds could thereby "range," get ample light and sun and yet have a place to lay, to roost at night, safe from predators and protected from inclement weather.

There were indeed dozens of plans for improved henhouses. All agreed of course that the open sides of the houses should face south in order to get the maximum amount of sun and that drafts should be avoided at all costs.

Through all these publications one heard always the insistent voice of the feed producer declaring that with his improved feeds chickens could be made to lay as many eggs in two years as an ordinary hen would lay in four. That of course meant twice as much profit for the farmer. Feed was the touchstone of successful poultry management. There was a seemingly endless stream of articles on the properties of particular feeds, and one of the great changes in "management" came with the shift from wet mash to dry mash. Success or failure, the poultryman was assured, rested on the use of the proper feed. So if poultrymen prospered or failed, grew wealthy or were forced, by depressed prices for eggs and chickens, to tighten their belts, the feed companies continued to show a rising curve of profits on a vastly increased volume of business.

Agricultural experiment station bulletins, scholarly monographs, poultry journals, and newspapers were supplemented by classes and courses. Poultry husbandry was introduced first into the high schools as part of general programs in animal husbandry and then, in the progressive farming states, in elementary schools, where children learned "the functional activities of birds of all kinds and poultry in particular." The missionary word was carried from state fair to state fair and from town to town by an "agricultural Gospel train," and educational exhibits prepared in one instance by the New York State College of Agriculture and Cornell University, famous for its work in agriculture and animal husbandry.

Harry Lewis, reviewing the accomplishments of the past decade in 1913, could "but marvel at what has been attained in the development of our domestic species of poultry through scientific mating and rearing."

S CIENTIFIC MATING AND REARING" was only half the matter; the rest was marketing. Petaluma, which had led the way in incubating eggs, took the lead in establishing a marketing cooperative, the Poultry Producers of Central California. This organization represented some 5,500 poultrymen, roughly forty-five percent of those involved in the industry in that area. The producers' association ran eleven packing houses, where its members' eggs were candled, graded, and packed, and forty-three depots where eggs could be delivered from farms and brought to the packing houses. After several earlier attempts had failed, the association was organized in 1916 in response to a general decline in the price of eggs due to overproduction and the manipulation of the egg market by wholesalers. In the spring, when the supply of eggs was abundant and indeed, increasingly, overabundant, dealers bought eggs for ten cents a dozen, put them in cold storage, and then, when the price of eggs rose in the fall as birds began to molt and laying dropped off sharply, the dealers brought their eggs out of storage and sold them at premium prices, often fifty and sixty cents a dozen. The Poultry Producers assessed each member one cent per dozen eggs delivered to the association's depots until ten dollars had accumulated. Then a share of stock was issued bearing six percent interest. All profits for the association were returned to its members after a certain working capital had accumulated — $750,000 by 1940.

Within a year the Poultry Producers of Central California were handling over two hundred thousand cases of eggs a year. The price of eggs was largely stabilized and the poultrymen were protected from exploitation by the wholesalers. The Petaluma cooperative was copied in many other regions and it undoubtedly was a landmark in the development of the industry.

Having dealt successfully with the exploitation of the wholesale egg dealers, the cooperatives next took on the feed companies. To most poultrymen struggling to stay in business, the feed companies had become the principal villains. Increasingly, newly formed marketing cooperatives established mills to produce feed. Now the poultryman could be assured of a regular market for his eggs (indeed, he had to sign a contract to sell his eggs to the cooperative) and a supply of grain at bargain prices. In return, of course, he lost a substantial measure of that "independence" that he so treasured, the promise of which had been a substantial inducement to enter the "Poultry World." Once he was free of the machinations of the egg dealer, the chicken farmer was often painfully aware of the constraints imposed by the cooperative. Many doggedly independent poultrymen refused to join cooperatives and sometimes did better outside than those who were members.

Of course, the cooperatives themselves were subject to a certain amount of manipulation. And disgruntled members often seceded to form rival cooperatives. Even the cooperatives could not in the long run do anything about the increase in the price of feed. They were undoubtedly responsible for lowering the profit margin of the large feed companies, but when new and more expensive feeds were developed that were certified to produce better chickens and more eggs, the cooperatives had to fall into line or lose members. Moreover, as the cooperatives grew in size they became increasingly bureaucratic and unresponsive to the needs of their clients.

The success of the poultry cooperative and the entry of the United States into World War I brought a boom in the poultry business and prosperity of Petaluma. In 1918 the Chamber of Commerce, in a buoyantly optimistic mood, put out a new brochure that showed none of the wariness that had characterized the brochure of 1913. Now, the Chamber proudly announced, "The very atmosphere of Petaluma throbs with the activity of the poultry industry, although to the casual observer in this beautiful little city with attractive homes, splendid schools and wonderful gardens, there are no obtrusive signs of chickens and eggs. . . . The banks are busy receiving the deposits. The business houses who are almost dependent upon the poultrymen who must purchase the necessities — yes, and the luxuries of life — are busy receiving their patronage. On Wednesdays and Saturdays the streets are lined with parked automobiles and other rigs of the poultrymen and families doing their shopping." And outside the town, everywhere one looked, "for miles around, are the homes and yards of the celebrated White Leghorn dotting the landscape. Their snow white plumage crowned with the blood red of their breed reflecting their health and the prosperity of the community. Surely some land, a comfortable home, independence and contentment is worth striving for in this land of success."

Petaluma was intoxicated by the success of National Egg Day, instituted by the Chamber of Commerce and held on the thirty-first of August, 1918. The theme of National Egg Day had been Why People Should Eat More Eggs, and this theme, emphasizing "the nutritive and necessary body-building qualities in the egg," had plainly helped to stimulate consumption throughout the country. Petaluma had "proved that the lowly hen is without peer in food value. . . . For invalids and children and for the man who works, it has been and will be almost indispensable. And eggs contain more nutriment per ounce for less compared to other food in ounces and cents than any other food product known." Stimulated by wartime demand, production of eggs had risen to four hundred and fifty million in 1918, and some ingenious soul had calculated that the eggs shipped from Petaluma would, if laid end to end, circle the earth. It was a slightly delirious image — a line of hens, stretching as far as the eye could see, over mountain and valley, laying their precious eggs all the way around the world.

To the question of when was the right time to start keeping chickens there was (in the opinion of the Petaluma Chamber of Commerce) only one answer: "NOW!" The season of the year didn't matter "if you have a shelter and a small place for them to run. The quicker you get some chickens the more pleasure and profit you will have. . . . What does one want better in this life," the author of the brochure asked, "than his own little farm, good home, with his family, plenty of eggs and other produce of the farm, to make money, and be independent of the larger cities, the strife and everlasting struggle to get along."

The brochure of 1918 had hardly issued from the press before the cheerful optimism of that document had changed to something close to despair. By the spring of 1918 poultry farmers everywhere were in desperate straits. The increased demand for eggs created by the war, which had brought a sharp rise in the price of eggs, had stimulated overproduction. Now the price of eggs fell to twenty and twenty-five cents a dozen. Pleas were fired off to the head of the National Food Administration, the various officials in the federal government, and the California congressional delegation. The request was for a minimum price for eggs or a maximum price for corn and barley, as the principal elements of chicken feed. In a letter to the National Food Board Administrator, the Petaluma poultrymen stated that for the previous ten years the "fair average profit made by successful poultrymen" had been between sixty-five and seventy cents per bird per year. In the past year that profit had been replaced by an average loss of thirty-five cents a bird, a loss which had forced some farmers into bankruptcy and others into desperate financial straits. The cost to maintain a hen for a year had jumped from $1.75 per year in 1917 to $4.35, a rise of almost 150 percent. Meanwhile the price of eggs had gone up only 7.7 cents — from a ten-year average of 27 cents per dozen to 34.7 cents, an increase of only 28.5 percent.

The seriousness of the situation was proclaimed by the headlines in the *Petaluma Argus:* "Destiny of Poultry Industry in Hands of Food Administration." The Food Administration took no effective action; its only response to the importunings of the poultrymen was to issue periodic bulletins announcing that the situation was improving. The improvements were imperceptible to the poultrymen themselves. They grew increasingly bitter and contentious. The rest of the country was enjoying a boom while they withered on the vine. Conditions remained so serious that when the convention of California mayors met in Sacramento on the twenty-sixth of October, 1919, they were faced by an angry contingent of poultrymen, who "so vigorously presented the case of the poultry industry" that the convention broke up in disorder "after some six hours wrangling" when the mayor of Los Angeles declared that "the farmers had 'egged' the convention to death."

According to the reporter for the *Argus,* "Nothing was accomplished by the convention but the spirit of

antagonism toward the agricultural producer. . . ."
The message was unmistakable: it was "a timely warning to every poultryman" that "if he would expect to live upon his ranch and enjoy a reasonably prosperous existence . . . he must join with his progressive neighbors in our local cooperative association."

The majority of poultrymen weathered the storm. By 1920 feed prices had dropped and eggs held steady. Improved methods of production with a lower cost per egg enabled farmers once more to make a profit. Euphoria replaced despair.

The year 1920 was a banner one for the poultry industry generally and for Petaluma in particular. The town shipped 22,250,000 dozen eggs, an increase of 28 percent over the previous year, and three million chickens, an increase of 52 percent. In five years the valley's production of eggs had doubled. The average price a dozen had risen to 50.5 cents per dozen, an increase of 1.5 cents over the previous year. The highest egg yield in the town's history was accompanied by the highest price. The president of the Poultry Keepers' Association attributed the rise in profits to improved methods of "culling, feeding, and housing," but it was plainly due far more to the vagaries of the market. The average gross income per bird was $6.12 (this included the profit from selling hens that had stopped laying, from culled birds sent to market, and from selling chicken manure). The cost of keeping a hen was estimated at five dollars per year; the profit per bird was thus calculated at $1.12, up from the sixty to seventy cents' average of the decade prior to 1918. In all of the United States the value of poultry products exceeded a billion and a quarter dollars.

With the price of eggs at 94 cents a dozen in San Francisco and $1.15 in New York for "Petaluma Extras," the poultrymen looked forward to a time of unparalleled prosperity.

The optimism produced by the record prices for

eggs in 1920 soon evaporated with a bear market and a postwar recession that saw five million unemployed. Eggs dropped to thirty cents a dozen in the spring of 1921, lower than they had been for five years. And over the Western horizon lay a new kind of yellow peril — the untold millions of Chinese eggs. The eggs sold as fresh eggs to customers in groceries and markets were, of course, only a portion of the eggs sold each year. Several hundred million dozen eggs were bought by "egg breakers," the yolks and the whites separated by hand, the "meat" frozen and sold to bakers and a wide variety of processors. Vast numbers of eggs were also bought by brokers and placed in cold storage, a largely speculative venture. Chinese eggs were "meat" eggs, used exclusively for large-scale baking and cooking. A survey revealed that there were more chickens within easy access of Chinese port cities than in all of the United States; Chinese eggs sold for the equivalent of six cents a dozen.

By 1922 the spokesmen for the poultry industry were in full cry after greater governmental protection. The *Argus* in January of the new year carried banner headlines: "Adequate Tariff Rates on Agricultural Products Essential for the Prosperity of American People," and in smaller type: "Poultry Industry Must Have Help to Prosper." A box on the front page described "The Condition" and "The Remedy." The Condition was that "American Agriculture [faced] the most menacing condition in history; Increased production with narrowing market; Either no market at all for many products or ruinously low prices; The Poultry and Dairy Industries being drawn into a whirlpool of disaster." The remedy, of course, was "the immediate enactment of a genuine Republican Protective Tariff law levying on all competitive imports."

Each year, S. S. Knight ended his report to the Petaluma Poultry Keepers' Association with a reminder of the importance of high tariffs. He repeated his warning in 1923: "The future of the poultry industry of our nation, as well as of California," he wrote, "is indissolubly bound up with the maintenance of an adequate tariff — a customs duty schedule carrying rates which effectively protect our farmers against the poultry products of China and all other countries having standards of living greatly below our own." S. S. Knight expressed alarm over the fact that although volume once more was up — 35 percent more eggs exported from Petaluma and 100 percent more chickens than the year before — prices and profits were disastrously down, the latter to 38 cents per bird as against $1.26 the prior year. While it was admitted that unemployment, strikes, and "disturbed industrial conditions" had sharply reduced the consumption of eggs in the face of a rise in egg production nationwide of almost 15 percent, the spokesmen for the poultry industry seemed unwilling to draw the conclusion that overproduction lay at the heart of the poultryman's problem. Instead the cry was for higher and higher tariffs, as though such a measure would guarantee the prosperity of poultry farmers.

Among other rising costs that squeezed the chicken rancher was the cost of labor. In 1912 a man could get all the help he needed at fifteen cents an hour. By the mid-twenties wages had risen astronomically to forty and fifty cents an hour, and "indifferent" labor at that. Where a dollar or a dollar twenty-five a day in wages once commanded an honest day's labor, three times that sum was no guarantee of decent performance. Knight still calculated that while a farmer got only four cents more per dozen for his eggs than he had ten years ago, the wholesale price of a hundred commodities had risen seventy-five percent. Therein lay the story of the plight of two million poultrymen scattered around the country.

Congress had responded to the importuning of millions of farmers through their lobbying organizations by passing the highest set of tariffs on agricultural products in the country's history — the Fordney-McCumber Bill (which by its dampening effect on world trade would help bring on the Depression of the thirties). Poultrymen did not get their desired twelve cents per dozen tariff on shell eggs, but they got a whopping eight cents. It did them little good and it produced within two years a strong reaction that led to the lowering of tariff barriers on many imported foodstuffs, eggs included.

With the great increase in the size of flocks and their increasingly close confinement, disease became a critical problem. In 1924 a disease, known for want of a better name as the "fowl plague," had broken out. Two-thirds of a shipment of meat birds for the New York market arrived at that city dead. Loss by death in the average flock rose from an average of 5 or 6 percent in the earlier years to 20 percent, "a percentage hitherto undreamed of." Some poultrymen felt sure that the high death rate in flocks was due to the increased emphasis on production, and S. S. Knight wrote, "Strange as it may seem this percent [of dead birds] has increased tremendously within the past four years or since definite and determined efforts were made to increase the productive capacity of our hens." The poultry departments of state universities were hastily enlisted to combat the epidemic. Although the immediate threat was met by new vaccines, poultry mortality became a perennial problem for farmers.

The Chinese civil war of Sun Yat-sen brought a sharp drop in the importation of eggs from China to the United States, but 1927 was nonetheless a bad year for poultrymen. The price of eggs dropped to twenty-nine cents a dozen, its lowest since 1916, leaving the farmer with a profit of twenty-four cents a dozen as compared with seventy-four cents for the preceding year, a decline of 67 percent in income.

S. S. Knight believed that the real problem was under-consumption of eggs by the American public, a consequence, in large part, of the publicity given in the national press to the "fowl plague" and other poultry diseases. The average consumption by Americans was estimated at one hundred sixty eggs per year "due to the pernicious news stories and false propaganda which is attempting to discredit the highly nutritive value of eggs as an article of human diet."

The year 1928 was an "up" year for poultrymen, due, in large part, to "a larger mortality than probably was ever known before in poultry husbandry." Thus while the price of eggs advanced only a cent a dozen, a decline in the price of feed and labor and a modest increase in productivity brought the profit per hen up to fifty-four cents, an increase of thirty cents per hen in a year. It was just these fluctuations, of course, that encouraged poultrymen to persevere. What the figures do not reveal is the large number of poultry keepers who were "shaken out" by a succession of several bad years, not to mention those who lost their flocks through disease. But there were always new venturers to take their places. Moreover, production of eggs increased year by year, good years and bad. (Between 1925 and 1928, for example, it rose from thirty million dozen to forty-five million dozen in Petaluma.) In addition, a greater measure of financial stability was given to the district by the constant growth in the number and size of hatcheries, which were much less affected by fluctuations in the market.

If 1928 was a good year for poultrymen, 1929 was a bonanza. The price of eggs rose but, more important, the cost of feed fell once more; so while the grain producers cried havoc, the poultrymen grew fat. Profit per hen more than doubled from 54 cents in 1928 to $1.19 in 1929. The stock market crash and the onset of the Great Depression brought the price of eggs down to 26 cents a dozen in 1930, but grain prices continued to decline and poultry profits remained good, though well below the sensational showing in 1929. Once more the cry for higher tariffs was renewed. It was an incantation, a panacea for everything that ailed the industry.

From 1930 on, the effects of the Depression made themselves felt in the poultry industry as elsewhere. In only one year between 1930 and 1940 did the price of eggs rise above twenty-two cents a dozen; the low was fifteen cents in 1933, and the profits that year were calculated at an average of seven cents per hen. Still, depressed as general prices were, the same extraordinary fluctuations persisted through the Depression years. Feed declined, if anything, more rapidly than egg prices, and labor costs dropped to half of their pre-Depression level. In 1935, in the depths of the Depression, with eggs selling at twenty-three and a half cents a dozen, the profit per hen to the average poultryman rose to sixty cents a bird (in part a reflection of the Japanese invasion of China), the highest (with the exception of 1929) since 1926. The next year eggs were down to thirty-seven cents and then to thirteen cents and then back up again to sixty-one cents and down to twelve cents in 1939. During the Depression years food that many humans could not afford was fed to chickens. Carrots became a staple of a hen's diet by the early forties, along with wheat, oats, barley, cottonseed meal, soybean meal, peanut meal and dehydrated alfalfa, fish meal, and fish liver oil.

The year 1936 was the first one in which baby chicks at the Petaluma hatcheries were sexed. Two million day-old baby cockerels were drowned at the hatcheries.

If the Great Depression checked the pace of chicken technology, it also attracted an increasing number of the jobless, or those with modest savings, into the ranks of small-scale chicken farmers. People who could not afford more expensive foods found relatively inexpensive nourishment in eggs and chickens. A couple with a thousand well-managed hens could expect to gross as much as three or four dollars a hen and net perhaps half as much. In a survey of a hundred and twenty poultry farms in New York in 1940, the cost of the farmhouses themselves averaged $3,598, the poultry buildings $2,858, and land $3,032. The equipment requirement for poultry raising averaged $624 and the value of the flocks $2,059. Egg sales averaged $4,596 in a thousand birds and meat sales $972. A study made by Cornell Agricultural Extension in the 1930's stated that of all who tried the poultry business only 5 percent fully utilized the available technology, and these did well financially. For the rest it was a marginal enterprise at best, but in the Depression years salvation often lay in the "marginal."

A chicken farmer had, after all, his own eggs and chickens. Typically, he had a vegetable garden and some fruit trees. The eggs and those chickens he sold for meat gave him a modest cash income. Nevertheless, he found increasingly that he needed not only the prudence and energy of a farmer but the management skills of a successful businessman. County farm agents pressed into his reluctant hands the results of the latest researches, which made clear that his cost-accounting and cost-control procedures were seriously obsolete. He needed to keep better records of productivity, to follow breeding charts and tables more closely, to catch up with the latest (and most expensive) processed feeds, to calculate his hours of labor per bird, the weight of each hen as compared with its production of eggs, the mortality rate, and the ratio of feed per dozen eggs produced. In addition he had the fluctuations of the market to contend with and an increasing mortgage debt as he was tempted (or forced) to increase the size as well as the efficiency of his operation in order to earn the same return. If he had Rhode Island Reds or Barred Plymouth Rocks he must contemplate switching to White Leghorns because of their greater efficiency or because, increasingly, the public was demanding white eggs instead of brown ones (unless of course his farm was in New England, where people preferred brown eggs to white ones. Elsewhere white eggs brought a cent or two more per dozen).

One of the most famous references to chickens dates from the Depression: the Republican Party promise of 1928 to put "a chicken in every pot." This classic example of a politician's pre-election promise is interesting from two perspectives. First, it reminds us that chickens were once a comparative luxury. Much more than steak, chicken on Sunday was a symbol of a certain widely desired level of economic well-being and was so generally recognized as such that it could be incorporated in a campaign speech with confidence that the audience would understand and respond. The promise was made in the 1920's. Since that time what we have called chicken technology, while, in our view, destroying the chicken, has, nonetheless, made it a common item of food on the table of the poorest families. From having been a luxury food chicken has in the space of less than fifty years become the poor man's high protein–yield food and beef has replaced it as the luxury food item. To promise a chicken in every pot today would seem to the American electorate a very paltry promise indeed.

Beyond this it is worth noting that the promise was not a new one. In the sixteenth century, Henry IV of France noted: "If God grants me the usual length of life, I hope to make France so prosperous that every peasant will have a chicken in his pot on Sunday." That simple measure of prosperity thus remained in effect from the sixteenth to the twentieth century.

By the end of the decade of the 1930's the stage was

set for the last act in the tragic drama of the hen. Refinements in genetics and new developments in immunology had prepared the way for her to become no longer a free and lively creature but merely an element in an industrial process whose product was the egg.

The
Industrialization
of the Chicken

263

The Fall
of the Chicken
(*and Almost*
Everything
Else)

264

THE YEARS of the Great Depression saw a development in the area of egg production, the consequences of which were only gradually felt. This was the discovery, probably the most important single discovery in the history of the domesticated chicken, that the production of eggs was directly related to light. Researches soon made it clear that this was an important reason for the low rate of laying in the winter months when the days were short (the other was that hens molted in the fall and ceased to lay for several months). It followed, as the day the night, that if hens were exposed to light during normal hours of darkness their production of eggs would increase. Light stimulated the hen's pituitary gland, at the base of the brain, resulting in a greater amount of hormone, which in turn stimulated the ovaries of the hen. If there was ever a bit of research fatal to the hen it was this.

For a time the discovery was not fully exploited. An extended argument raged over how much light a hen should be subjected to and, above all, when. There were moral overtones to the argument, even, one might say, theological overtones. Most of the people who raised chickens were pious, God-fearing people, pious and God-fearing in a substantially higher proportion than in the general population, one suspects. They were the kind of person disposed to worry about "unnatural acts." The image of the happy hen basking in the sunlight, luxuriating in a dust bath, her feathers glistening and shining, was one dear to the heart of any poultryman who loved, or even tolerated, chickens.

Tests of various periods of light were made by the Cornell University researchers and other experimental agencies — a few hours after dusk; between eight and nine at night (to encourage the hens to have a little "lunch"); all night, and so on. In a book, *Modern Poultry Management*, first published in 1928, Professor Louis Hurd, professor of poultry husbandry at Cornell University, a man still sentimental about chickens, approached the subject warily: "The operator," he declared, "may use lights at any time of day that is most convenient, and, according to his judgment, adds most to the comfort of the birds." Light will cheer up a dreary henhouse on a winter evening, making it "pleasanter both for the hens and the feeder." It was plainly a problem. To keep a faithful Protestant hen up half the night for the sake of a few extra eggs — if it was not immoral it was at best ungrateful. It helped considerably if one could think that it added "to the comfort of the birds."

The fact was that Hurd's manual breathed much the same spirit as its predecessors had thirty years earlier. It was dedicated to his mother, "whose courageous and progressive spirit was an inspiration to me to undertake this work" — an expression of filial piety in keeping with the tone of the book. "Poultrykeeping," Professor Hurd wrote in his opening lines, "is interesting because it gives pleasure as well as profit to persons of both sexes, all ages, all walks of life in all sections of the country. It is useful alike on the farm and in the city back-yard, in the cold North and in the sunny South, in the hill and mountain country, or on the plain. It may be conducted as an exclusive business or as a side line. It affords pleasure and profit for rich and poor alike. In fact, it is the universal agricultural industry. . . . It is a health-giving recreation to thousands as well as a means of support."

It was thus the ultimate, democratic, a-hundred-percent American calling, toward which, it might be thought, the whole of American history had tended. Thomas Jefferson, infatuated with the yeoman farmer and fearful of his decline, overshadowed by urban industrialism, would surely have applauded the "independent yeoman farmer" who had been metamorphosed into an "independent chicken farmer." Thoreau also would have been pleased. He wished to see man immersed in nature; a poultryman immersed in chickens was perhaps the next best thing. So it promised everything — growth and progress, nature, science, independence, and, finally, money in modest amounts.

Professor Hurd belonged in spirit to the old dispensation. His devotion to the Protestant hen was apparent in his description of the temperaments (or character) of various types of layers. First, there was "the highly excitable hen that squawks, flies and thrashes about when caught. This type is usually a very poor producer. Second come a class of birds less active than the first but still lacking the aggressiveness of the best layers. They cannot endure heavy and continuous production over long periods. Next comes a group of birds that are quiet but ambitious; they are always working, yet they lack the snap and pep of the best producers and are inclined to be mechanical in their movements. Such birds just fall short of attaining what is expected of really good layers. Lastly come the type that combines all the good points of the other groups. This type is intelligent, friendly, and aggressive. There is no noise or violent struggling when caught, for, although their nervous systems are active and sensitive, they are under control. These hens are hearty eaters and tireless workers, and, as a result, are usually found on the outside perches at night for they are the last to go to roost and the first to come down for food in the morning." They are the exemplars of the Protestant Ethic in the chicken. The composer of this hymn of praise to the "tireless workers" of the chicken world — it might serve just as well as a guide for personnel director of a large corporation — was more akin in spirit to Samuel Sewall and the Reverend Edmund Dixon than to the new generation of chicken technologists pressing onto the stage.

Another rationale was that artificial lighting provided "a perfectly uniform day and night, thus overcoming the constantly changing sunrise and sunset which is going on throughout the entire season" (and, presumably, worrying conscientious hens into a decline). "In any case," Hurd wrote, "it is unwise to give hens more than a fourteen-hour day unless all night light is used. . . ." The dilemma was that even a difference of fifteen minutes in the length of a hen's working day had an effect on a hen's production.

The use of light brought more problems than simply moral ones. It forced production and thus weakened hens and sometimes brought on a premature molt. Or made them particularly susceptible to disease. Finally, and most unfortunately, at least from the hen's point of view, artificial illumination led, inevitably, to keeping hens in confined, windowless buildings where the light could be completely controlled. It was becoming increasingly evident that sun, breezes, dust, the random foraging of birds at large — that all these were unscientific, that is, uncontrollable, elements in egg production. Pleasant as they might be for the hen and picturesque as they might be to the eye of her master and mistress, they had nothing to do with the scientific production of eggs. They were, to put the matter plainly, a distraction.

The cock had long since been relegated to the breeding pens. He was a definite minus in terms of scientific egg production. He chased hens and wore them out; moreover, impregnated eggs were considered by many consumers to be decidedly inferior to nonfertile eggs. The almost imperceptible spot of male sperm seemed to make the egg somehow less "pure." Now the hen was to have a very much bleaker life. Improved technology indicated that she should do as little as possible — simply eat and lay eggs. This required a controlled environment in which sun, wind, rain, bugs, worms, sprouts, and growing things had no place. For the rays of the sun a few extra vitamins in the hen's food and an electric bulb, burning ceaselessly, would be substituted; for the breeze, air conditioning; for the bugs and worms and sprouts, additives (minerals and chemicals of various kinds). "Sunlight," Hurd wrote, revealing the depth of his own ambiguity, "warms the house in winter and makes it more cheerful and pleasant at all times. Sunshine is a better egg producer and tonic than any of the condimental foods on the market."

There was one final problem. Birds so confined were inclined to cannibalism; out of boredom and frustration they pecked each other to death. The remedy for that was mutilation. Part of the bird's beak was clipped neatly off. She could eat the enriched mash that soon passed before her endlessly on conveyor belts, but she could not peck her sisters.

Despite Professor Hurd's obvious uneasiness about the use of artificial lighting, he concluded his chapter on the subject with an argument that proved ultimately irresistible: "Frequently poultrymen with large flocks have been able to pay for the installation of a private lighting plant in one season, from the increased returns from their hens." (One almost anticipates the word "grateful" before "hens.")

One would think that the scrupulous poultryman

might have resisted the confining of his birds and the use of artificial light on the moral grounds that we have mentioned. It was important to him to think of himself as friend and, indeed, benefactor of the chicken — he was committed, in most instances, to what we might call the "chicken mystique." Yet harsh economic realities forced him to fall in line or quit. All hope of profit or even bare survival revolved around the feed–egg ratio. The successful poultryman was the one who could get the most favorable ratio of eggs to feed. Since his costs rose constantly (with a whole series of "shots" or vaccinations for chicks, the introduction of more elaborate and costly new procedures, the rising costs of feed, and so on) while the price of eggs remained low (with continual and unpredictable drops), the poultryman had no choice but to adopt every new development in chicken technology which would (or even might) have the effect of reducing his costs per bird. The standard procedure thus came to be that of starting laying hens on a twelve-hour "day," and increasing the time the lights were on by fifteen minutes a day until the lights were on and the hens, it was hoped, eating and laying for twenty-one and a half hours in every twenty-four.

Every great movement deserves a literary memorial. What we might call the Great Democratic Poultry Movement of the 1920's through the 1950's had its chronicler in Betty MacDonald's best-selling book *The Egg and I,* the story of a young wife carried off to a chicken farm in the Northwest. On a remote Washington headland she reflected, as a good many other wives must have reflected: "Why in God's name does everyone want to go into the chicken business? Why has it become the common man's Holy Grail? Is it because most men's lives are shadowed by the fear of being fired — of not having enough money to buy food and shelter for their loved ones and the chicken business seems haloed with permanency? Or is it that chicken farming with each man his own boss offers relief from the employer-employee problems which harry so many people? . . . Again I repeat, why chickens? Why not narcissus bulbs, cabbage seed, greenhouses, rabbits, pigs, goats? All can be raised in the country by one man and present but half the risk of chickens."

Betty MacDonald found only one saving element in the chicken business: "If a hen is lazy or uncooperative or disagreeable you can chop off her head and relieve the situation once and for all. 'If that's the way you feel, then take that!' you say, severing her head with one neat blow. In a way I suppose that one factor alone should be justification for most men's longing for chickens. . . ."

The illusions that created and sustained the Great Democratic Poultry Movement persisted through the years of the Great Depression. While prices in general fell precipitously, the price of eggs and chickens, already low because of improved methods of production and a tendency to overproduction, fell, as we have seen, less than most other commodities. There was, of course, a limit to the number of one's own eggs and chickens one could consume but there was always barter, and since the units of poultry production — the individual farms or ranches — were, in the vast majority, of modest size and modestly capitalized, the husband and wife who, typically, ran them tightened their belts and persevered.

Perhaps the exemplar of the spirit of scientific egg production was a young man named John Kimber, an amateur musician and a trained biologist. In 1934 John Kimber started a hatchery at Fremont, California. It was his inspiration to apply the most modern discoveries in the rapidly expanding field of genetics to the breeding of chickens for specific purposes

*The Fall
of the Chicken
(and Almost
Everything
Else)*

270

— meat or eggs. The first task that he and his associates undertook was to "*identify* the genes or 'hereditary elements' possessed by all living creatures." The next and incomparably more difficult problem was "how to combine the various genes to the best advantage, to determine 'how the chemicals should be mixed together.' " Would a chicken that was the result of "extreme inbreeding followed by hybridizing give better results" than birds bred in the conventional way? And, most important, "How do different breeding techniques compare with regard to various traits of economic importance?" The modern research laboratory was brought to the farm with the founding of Kimber Farms.

The term "Farms" was obviously a concession to sentiment. The gleaming laboratories and offices and, eventually, computers that filled the administration buildings of the Kimber operation had little to do with traditional farms. Nor did the bright young Ph.D.s in genetics recruited from the outstanding graduate schools in the country have much relation to farmers. Kimber Farms, nonetheless, revolutionized the breeding of chickens. It had been possible for years to produce large numbers of chicks in a single hatching, but breeding had remained comparatively hit-or-miss. Now it was made relentlessly scientific. Kimber proved that quality and size of egg, thickness of shell, and production of eggs could all be controlled by scientific breeding. Kimber Farms began to number its strains K-22, K-43, and so on, and the poultryman could order hybridized White Leghorns whose eggs would have a guaranteed thickness of shell.

Hybridizing had, as in every area of genetics from wheat to hogs, certain disadvantages. Perhaps the most notable in the area of poultry was a lessened resistance to disease on the part of hybridized birds. This, plus the increasingly crowded conditions under which birds were kept and the proximity of flocks to

*The Fall
of the Chicken
(and Almost
Everything
Else)*

271

each other in chicken-growing areas, made poultry disease more and more of a nightmare for the rancher or farmer with large numbers of birds. Kimber Farms replied to this challenge by developing a whole line of vaccines to deal with the most common diseases of chickens. It inoculated its baby chicks before it sent them out to its customers and it adopted the novel practice of guaranteeing healthy chicks, replacing any that died of disease, and performing autopsies on birds brought to its pathologists.

The efficient, white-gowned workers in the antiseptic laboratories of Kimber Farms had little time for sentiment. To them the baby chickens (half of whom were killed at birth and incinerated or fed to the hogs) hatched by the million in their enormous incubators had to be seen primarily as items on an assembly line. The fact that they were alive was, it seems fair to suggest, incidental.

So it was that the chicken, from being an object of veneration, of pleasure, of curiosity or delight, was in the process of becoming a product not much different from a galosh or a bar of soap. My contemporaries who have such dismal memories of chickens from the unpleasant chores of their youth had experienced already the consequences of putting living creatures in circumstances that are inherently uncongenial to them. Chickens confined, and especially chickens confined in large numbers, like people confined in large numbers, are at their least appealing. In such circumstances, chickens, like people, give off offensive odors; disposing of their cumulative wastes becomes a major problem; they behave badly to each other, bedeviling and pecking each other in boredom and frustration; they become neurotic and susceptible to various diseases of the body and the spirit.

This is what happened to chickens, or, more precisely, it is what happened to White Leghorn chickens, because these Mediterranean birds, small, active, energetic, economical feeders and big producers, turned out to be the exemplars of the Protestant Ethic in the henhouse. All their rivals — the giant Brahmas, the good-natured Dorkings, the sturdy Barred Rocks and Rhode Island Reds, the delicately marked Wyandottes, the exotic Polish, the Hamburgs, the Sussex, Sultans, Sumatras, Cochins, Dominiques, Minorcas, Andalusians, Spanish, Hollands — all had to give way before the hybridized Leghorn.

The average poultryman, preoccupied by his chickens, by the fluctuations in the price of eggs, by certain droopy-looking hens in his henhouse, was only dimly aware of the import of these developments. The war years from Pearl Harbor to Hiroshima were good years for the poultry industry, as it was increasingly referred to. World War II was, like the first, a stimulus to the poultry industry (among many other things). Eggs could be processed — dried and powdered — and millions of GIs consumed such eggs in thoroughly unappetizing form, watery and tasteless, the dimmest imitation of a real egg. Demand for eggs soared and the price of eggs stayed high. Production rose to over three *billion* dozen eggs — thirty-six billion eggs — and there seemed to be no end in sight. In the year 1942 New York City alone managed to put away 174,456,000 dozens of eggs and 253,091,193 pounds of dressed poultry.

The end of the war found a new generation of war workers anxious to get out of the "rat race" and returning veterans tired of a regimented life. A substantial proportion of these young men and women looked, as their parents had done a generation earlier, to poultry farming (or, in the West, ranching) as the answer to their desire for a modest competence and for independence. The small unit was still viable. The enormous volume of information and advice on how to raise chickens which threatened at any moment to bury the established poultryman appeared to give an advantage to the newcomer who, not wedded to archaic ways of doing things (such as letting chickens range) could start in with the newest and most up-to-date methods. The county agricultural agent was ready to give him all the help he needed; the bank and the feed company were most attentive. Together they would provide know-how, money, and a guaranteed market for his eggs.

So tens and then hundreds of thousands and, finally, millions of men and women built their chicken houses, bought their chicks, and set themselves up in business. It was almost too good to be true — so much help, so much interest, and such fair promise of success. Poultry keeping was that thing so close to the hearts of Americans, a growth industry. Every year there were more poultry-producing units — one hestitated to call them farms — more eggs and more chickens. Every year production was increasingly rationalized. In the years immediately following the war, a flock of a thousand chickens could be expected to produce in a good year an income of, roughly, four thousand dollars clear. Four thousand dollars with perhaps some vegetables and a few fruit trees to augment the family larder was a "comfortable" income in the late forties and early fifties.

Poultry keepers formed a close-knit fraternity (and sorority). They belonged to the same poultry organizations (usually a feed and marketing cooperative was the most important of them); they socialized together and they even intermarried, though it was notable, as I have observed elsewhere, that the children of poultry keepers to whom fell many of the less rewarding chores on the ranch had little of their parents' enthusiasm for chickens. And, indeed, it may be suspected that the parents in many instances had little enthusiasm.

We have already taken note of the growing concern among poultrymen at the devastating effects of various epidemics. The problem grew more acute as use of hybridized birds became more common. Moreover, chickens were now so closely confined that disease spread quickly through an entire flock. As we have already seen, the large hatcheries met the threat of disease by constantly producing new vaccines to cope with new viruses. In addition, hatcheries with valuable breeding stock began to bar all outsiders and to institute elaborate precautions against germs being brought onto their grounds. The pathology laboratories to which diseased birds could be brought for diagnosis and the prescription of a proper vaccine to protect the rest of the flock were established at some distance from the hatcheries themselves. Employees were disinfected when they came to work, wore sterile clothes, and in the performance of their duties observed procedures often similar to those of a surgeon before operating. Even feed at many hatcheries was brought to delivery stations at the end of the hatchery and disinfected before it was allowed on the premises. Thus the poultry ranch became, like the hospital, or indeed even more than the hospital, a sterile environment and the keepers, in a sense, the victims of their charges.

A classic example of the consequences of crowding and confining chickens was the spread of coccidiosis, a disease caused by intestinal parasites. Coccidiosis, in one form or another, is common to most avian species and has doubtless been in the intestinal tracts of hens since there have been hens. Among closely confined birds, coccidiosis became a serious menace to the survival of baby chicks and pullets. Since it was transmitted by chicken droppings, the obvious remedy seemed to be a strong emphasis on cleanliness. At this point chickens began to be raised on wire, which allowed the droppings to fall through and be collected. The method kept the baby chicks and later the mature birds from infecting themselves with their own manure.

The problem was that baby chicks in their normal state develop an immunity to coccidiosis by gradual exposure to it. When they are placed in hygienic growing pens or cages they fail to develop immunity and thus as mature birds are much more vulnerable to the disease. The answer of the poultry researchers was antibiotics in the feed of the chickens to kill the coccidiosis parasites. The effect was to lessen the resistance of hens to diseases other than coccidiosis, and once more the cycle of searching for vaccines for the new bacteria was set in motion.

So we enter, in the years from the mid-forties to the end of the decade of the sixties, into what might be called the last, or at least the penultimate, act of the fateful drama of the American chicken. It was increasingly clear in this era that virtually every new development was unfavorable to the chicken and, indeed, to his master, the small poultryman. A cutthroat spirit began to predominate among poultrymen themselves, expressed chiefly in the warfare between rival cooperatives (often the cooperatives were not genuine cooperatives but in fact dummy organizations, set up and controlled by the feed companies). Warring cooperatives cut prices on feed and on the market price of eggs to drive the opposition out of business. New technological improvements were usually expensive. Automated conveyor belts which carried feed past hens cramped in small cages (one of the fiercest debates was over how many hens to keep in a single cage; the theories range from one to ten; each number had its champions) were obviously borrowed from the industrial assembly line. The dry mash feed, full of egg-producing additives, filled the air with a choking dust; expensive air-conditioning units were needed to keep the houses properly ventilated (chickens need three or four times the amount of air in volume that human beings do). The constant "retooling," such as the installation of cages, was costly.

*The Fall
of the Chicken
(and Almost
Everything
Else)*

276

After the conveyor-belt feeder, the next innovation was the conveyor-belt egg collector. Before the advent of the automatic collector, eggs were collected in the morning and at night from the nests built along the central aisles of the typical chicken house. On small farms and ranches this was a chore usually assigned to the children of the family. A friend who had such an assignment as a child before he left for school and after he returned in the afternoon (as well as cleaning and candling the eggs) recalls to this day the dreadful apprehension with which he put his hand into each nest to collect its egg, unable to see whether the nest was occupied and anticipating with each a bruising peck from an indignant hen. With the conveyor-belt egg collector, the cages of the hens are at a tilt sufficient to cause any egg laid by one of the four occupants of the nest to roll gently through an aperture onto a moving belt. The belt carries the eggs to a machine that grades, cleans, and packs them.

In this automated process the thickness of the eggshell is, of course, crucial. It does not much matter what the egg tastes like, but in order to survive all this tumbling about, it must have a shell of requisite thickness. The trouble is that the poor hens' already overstrained systems have trouble, despite all the high-powered feeds, converting enough material into calcium to give their eggs sufficiently tough shells. Thus, we are told in an article in the *Petaluma Argus-Courier*, much research still needs to be done "to keep California housewives from cracking up over cracked eggs" (it is of course the egg ranchers, not the housewife, who are in danger of cracking up. The housewife does not receive cracked eggs; they are cracked in the collection and packing operation). Thin-shelled eggs, the article tells us, cost the poultry industry seventy-five million dollars a year.

For a time egg ranchers in the middle range were able to keep pace with the mass producers by emphasizing efficiency. A Petaluma poultryman, Oscar Miller, attracted wide attention in 1940 by his almost completely automated "egg factory." Although he had over two hundred and fifty thousand chickens, he confined his automation initially to 35,680 birds housed in a structure seventy-two feet long which cost ninety-six thousand dollars. The building was insulated by Styrofoam with feeder and egg-collecting conveyors and the facilities now typical of such a structure. Miller's principal innovation seems, according to the newspaper report, to have been that his chicken house is on stilts six feet off the ground, enabling chicken droppings — "the bane of existence for chicken ranchers" — to be removed by heavy equipment.

The Fall
of the Chicken
(*and Almost*
Everything
Else)

278

This is probably as good a point as any to comment on the use and disposal of chicken manure. The reader will recall that chickens are almost as remarkable for the quantity and potency of the manure they produce as for their eggs. With one chicken producing as much as sixteen or seventeen pounds of droppings a year, the problem of disposing of the manure can become acute.

When small-scale farmers lived in proximity to suburban residents, the matter of chicken droppings was often a bitter bone of contention between the ranchers and their neighbors. The principal complaints were over the odor of the excrement and the flies attracted by it. Since the chicken ranchers typically had established themselves on the periphery of large cities, they soon found themselves in the path of the suburban developers. In many instances, as soon as enough nonfarmers had moved into the area (Van Nuys, California, would be a typical example) to outvote the chicken ranchers, they voted out the chickens as a nuisance. The chicken farmer was thus the victim of the hostility or resentment of the new immigrants into the area and the concomitant rise in land values and, correspondingly, in taxes. Gradually, he was forced to sell and go out of business or retreat farther into the country and wage what turned out, invariably, to be a losing battle against rising costs and steady prices.

The decade of the fifties and the early years of the sixties were the Golden Age of the industrial chicken and its manufacturer, Kimber Farms. A splendid new plant was filled with shiny machines — tabulators, computers, sensitive scales, microscopes, machines for testing shell strength, laboratories for analyzing blood and tissue, laboratories for making new or improved vaccines, laboratories for the research staff to pursue obscure problems of genetics. Highly trained technicians and their assistants discovered each year new facts about the hen and new ways to extract more eggs from her. When the Kimber laboratory (or Farm) turned its attention to increasing the output of eggs per hen, that output averaged one hundred fifty to one hundred sixty eggs in a twelve-month period. Some hens did better (there were fabled layers who were reported to have produced three hundred and thirty or three hundred and forty eggs in three hundred sixty-five days) ; some did worse, but taking an average flock, one hundred sixty eggs a year was considered good production. (This was in the first year of laying, since a pullet begins to lay at five or six months, lays for a year, and then molts.) In a period of less than ten years the Kimber geneticists produced a hybridized bird that was guaranteed to lay two hundred fifty eggs a year. It is not hard to imagine the effect of this extraordinary increase in the productivity of the average pullet. Traditionally, a normal hen molted in the fall, ceased to lay for several months, and then began again at a reduced rate, so that a mature hen in her second year of laying would, before the new dispensation, lay perhaps a hundred

and twenty or a hundred and thirty eggs and, thereafter, far fewer, finally in the fourth year laying none
at all. It was then that she, traditionally, was con-
signed to the soup pot or the stew pot. The Kimber
hen could be expected to lay in her second year fewer
eggs, of course, than in the first, but still in the neighborhood of two hundred to two hundred twenty eggs.
After the second year of laying, she was sold for
pet food.

Meanwhile some ingenious experimenter discovered
that a forced molt could be produced by giving a hen
no feed or water for a period of four or five days.
The hen would then begin to molt, its molt would be
briefer, and it could be brought more rapidly back
into production. The control of the molt, the development of a much greater egg-laying potential by hybridizing, and the use of close caging and artificial
light all contributed to a spectacular rise in the rate
of egg production; these combined with the continual
refinement of feed to the same end. Since the hen sat
or stood all day, with her mutilated beak, usually in a
small cage with five other birds, her appetite was not
apt to be as good as if she had been free to range in
an enclosed yard or more widely in plowed fields and
barnyards; chemicals must therefore be added to the
feed to stimulate her appetite.

A by-product of these developments was the split-
ting off of meat-bird production from egg production.
Two entirely different birds were required: for egg-
laying the small-bodied White Leghorn with its remarkable production record of large, white eggs;
for meat production a much larger bird hybridized to
give the maximum growth in the minimum time. Since
nature could not anticipate the domestication of the
chicken and the development of the modern poultry
industry, it provided for a roughly equal number of
male and female chickens to be born. Cocks, with their
insistent sexuality and combativeness, have always

*The Fall
of the Chicken
(and Almost
Everything
Else)*

280

been, aside from their capacity to impregnate the female, a drug on the market (it will be recalled that one cock can take care of the impregnation of ten or fifteen hens). It has thus been the custom in every culture that has kept chickens for meat to kill the young cockerels when they are fifteen weeks old and eat them as what today are called, commercially, "broilers"; or to castrate or caponize them, in which case they grow fat and tender and make excellent roasting chickens. Since White Leghorn males (cockerels) are virtually useless as meat birds, the so-called chicken-sexer became a key figure in the production of chicks for laying purposes. As soon as the baby chicks are hatched, the chicken-sexer divides the males from the females. (This is a most arcane science, as any one who has observed baby chicks will know; secondary sexual characteristics in chickens seldom appear even to the practiced eye until the birds are at least five or six weeks old.) The sexing of chickens has been a virtual monopoly of Japanese-Americans, as has been the impregnating of turkeys. An experienced chicken-sexer can sex as many as a thousand chickens an hour, and he is usually paid at the rate of a cent a chick. The male chicks, as we have noted, are thrown into a garbage can and fed to the hogs or burned up in special incinerators.

The development of chickens for eating lagged far behind egg production. Initially meat birds, as we have seen, were a by-product of the laying hen — the culls and the young cockerels (spring chickens) and castrated males fattened to four or five pounds as roasting chickens. This remained the practice until the White Leghorn, a poor meat bird, began to dominate egg production. At this point the same process of hybridizing was applied to birds bred for meat. Here, again, the feed–conversion ratio was crucial. As late as the early fifties it took fourteen to sixteen weeks and twelve pounds of feed to bring a bird to the three or three and a half pounds required for marketing it as a broiler. Year by year the length of time required to achieve marketable weight in a meat bird declined and the ratio of feed consumed to the weight of the bird at marketing improved. By the mid-sixties the time was down to ten weeks and two and two-tenths pounds of feed for each pound of weight of the bird. Now it takes seven or eight weeks, and the food conversion ratio is even lower, two pounds or less to produce a four-pound bird. The geneticists have thus created a bird which seems to confound common sense; it eats less and fattens faster — three and a half to four and a half pounds in eight weeks by "enriched" feed. For one thing, such birds are, like laying hens, very closely confined. They get virtually no exercise; moreover, they have appetite-stimulating chemicals added to their feed. The question not unnaturally arises as to whether such birds are indeed chickens. They certainly bear very little resemblance to the archaic, almost extinct, chickens that we still see occasionally scratching around in remote farmyards, in zoos, or on old movies on TV. Many of them cannot stand up for long; their bones and muscles have not kept pace with their flesh. These monsters are doubtless more tender than the old-fashioned fryer or broiler that was usually a cockerel or a cull, but it is also plainly the case that they taste much less like a chicken than their predecessors did. Almost all that they retain of a genuine chicken is the surface appearance and the yellow color of a normal chicken, which is produced, as one might expect, by a chemical — xanthophyll.

Many of the same automated techniques that had been developed for laying hens have been applied to meat birds. Feeding is done by conveyor belts, and by 1965 one man could operate a plant producing forty thousand birds a day.

The large producers of meat birds keep between sev-

The Fall
of the Chicken
(*and Almost*
Everything
Else)

282

eral hundred thousand and a million laying hens and one-tenth as many cocks. Some 85 percent of the eggs laid under such circumstances are fertile. When the baby chicks are two weeks old they are given their shots and debeaked (the cocks, incidentally, are allowed to keep their beaks since they need them to mount the hen; the cock, the reader will recall, grips the hen by the nape of her neck when copulating). The birds are then, typically, distributed for fattening to small farmers on a contract basis — Mom and Pop operations reminiscent of the earlier days of poultry raising — where their care and feeding is carefully supervised by the parent corporation. After seven or eight weeks, when they have reached the desired weight, they are retrieved by large trucks holding up to five thousand birds, which come at night when the birds are drowsy and spirit them away. Frank Perdue, the largest chicken manufacturer on the East Coast, often kills as many as three hundred thousand birds a day.

All parts of the chicken abattoirs are, of course, automated. In the Perdue plant the chickens are taken from the trucks at six-thirty in the morning at Accomac, Virginia, and hung upside down by their feet on a conveyor belt. The belt then moves through an electrically charged solution, which, in Christian Adams's words ("Frank Perdue Is Chicken," *Esquire*, April, 1973), "shocks almost all of them senseless. From there they move to the Kill Room where a knife-like instrument cuts their throats; then down the 'bleed tunnel' where their blood drains away into a vat of hot water which loosens the feather sockets and then past rubber finger-like pluckers which remove most of the feathers [and] through a flame that singes off the fine fuzz." Next in the processing, the head and feet are removed. In the Eviscerating Room, the birds are gutted by machines and inspected and graded by government inspectors. Finally, they are chilled, weighed, and packaged. Nothing is wasted. In that respect, at least, the Puritan Ethic is still observed. Those parts considered inedible by humans are made into pet food, or, as in the case of legs, considered a delicacy in the Orient, exported. Even the feathers are processed and made into a component of chicken feed.

Technology has also overtaken a by-product of the chicken — manure. Chicken manure has always been one of the most prized products of the chicken. Properly seasoned, it is invaluable as fertilizer and every prudent gardener covets it. When, after World War I, the small barnyard flock was replaced by a larger, commercially significant flock as a valuable auxiliary to the farm income, chicken manure was carefully collected and used in home farms and truck gardens. When chicken raising and egg production became specialized enterprises, the chicken rancher had to contract with vegetable farmers to buy his manure and haul away his manure crop. For a time there was a precarious balance between the poultryman's need to dispose of his chicken manure in some systematic way and the truck farmer's desire to utilize it. But as chemical fertilizers came into wider and wider use, their relative cheapness and above all the ease and efficiency of their application to the soil brought, first, a drop in the price of chicken manure, and, finally, a complete lack of marketability in many areas, so that poultrymen had to pay to have it hauled away or dispose of it themselves.

We have mentioned waste disposal through heavy wire henhouse floors and periodic gathering of the droppings. Another method was to make the floors of the houses of concrete and scatter, most commonly, dry rice hulls on the floors to absorb the moisture in the droppings and thereby render them relatively inoffensive. They would accumulate over the course of a year to a depth of several feet. When a new flock was to be brought in to occupy a house the manure would be shoveled out and offered for sale, and the premises cleaned, fumigated, and thoroughly aired.

The present uselessness of chicken manure, once so prized as an "organic" fertilizer, goes along with the systematic killing of male chicks.

We have digressed from the topic of the increased egg production that resulted from improved technology. As the principal architect of this marvel, Kimber Farms was known, admired, envied, and copied. In 1955 it capped its achievement by establishing, through the National Academy of Sciences, the most prestigious scientific association in the United States, the Kimber Genetics Award, a "magnificent gold medal and two thousand dollars in cash." The medal was designed by Malvina Hoffman, the well-known sculptor and pupil of Rodin, and it showed in bas-relief Charles Darwin, Gregor Mendel, the father of modern genetics, William Bateson, the English geneticist whose work with chickens confirmed Mendel's experiments, and Thomas Hunt Morgan, winner of a Nobel Prize for his studies of inherited characteristics. The prize was awarded in 1955 to William Ernest Castle for his work, among other things, on the "continuity of the germ plasm," and to Hermann Joseph Muller, already winner of a Nobel Prize, for his work in the genetic patterns of fruit flies. Sewall Wright, Alfred Sturtevant, Theodosius Dobzhansky, George Beadle, and John Haldane were among the winners in subsequent years.

On a more practical level Kimber Farms published the *Kimberchik News* and a series of bulletins and catalogues describing the research work that went on at the Fremont laboratories and advertising its various strains of chicken. The *News* for December, 1958, was emblazoned with a colorful seasonal border of rein-

*The Fall
of the Chicken
(and Almost
Everything
Else)*

285

deer in green and red and a message from John Kimber, president. "As the year 1958 draws to an end," Mr. Kimber wrote, "it brings a season when business cares, political conflicts, even world tensions, give way, to some extent at least, to a concern for others, greetings to friends old and new, gifts large or small to those we hold dear. A revaluation of conditions which affect our lives helps to put into more nearly accurate perspective many things which may at times have appeared distorted or unbalanced." The message ended with best wishes for the coming year. But there was, oddly enough, no mention of chickens, and readers may have been excused if they puzzled over this rather Delphic utterance.

*The Fall
of the Chicken
(and Almost
Everything
Else)*

286

In addition to the newspaper and the medal, Kimber Farms, in their Niles plant near Pomona, California, instituted a series of "open houses," where poultrymen and their wives were invited to attend day-long conferences on improved methods of poultry management. The open house on June 3, 1959, drew over six hundred people to the "new ultra modern hatchery building . . . which covers more ground than a football field and houses an auditorium seating about five hundred people." Guests were taken on a bus tour of the plant, the autopsy lab where dead birds were examined to discover the cause of death, the bacteriological laboratory where vaccines and viruses were worked with, a pedigree house, the egg quality laboratory, and the new hatchery capable of hatching several million eggs at a time. Lunch was, most appropriately, a chicken barbecue, for some eight hundred people, including the one hundred seventy-five employees of the hatchery. The afternoon was devoted to lectures "pertaining to today's breeding, management and disease problems . . ." and "a lively question and answer session participated in by the audience which brought out many interesting points."

Many of the poultrymen may have reflected upon

the contrast between their own economic state (precarious) and the obvious opulence of the Kimber operation. Perhaps they thought it more than mildly ironic that the principal benefits of the poultry boom in the United States seemed to have fallen on the technical specialists rather than on the producers of eggs and chickens for the American consumer. Certainly there was a moral there for anyone to read it. While the immaculate laboratories, the white-coated researchers, and the serious and prosperous-looking managers were impressive testimony to the success of the poultry industry, there was a disturbing ambiguity at the heart of it all. Here, more than anywhere, the industrialization of the chicken was displayed in a manner that no one could miss. The rows upon rows of neat, clean birds, with their mutilated beaks, in the small cages, were like a glimpse into an Inferno as terrible in its own way as any of the circles of Dante's hell.

Yet the managers and technicians who showed the visitors around so proudly were seemingly oblivious to such analogies. They had done what they had done in the name of science, progress, technology, indeed, of Americanism. They boasted discreetly about the Kimber Award, the medal designed by the famous sculptor, and showed their visitors an enlarged photograph of it hanging on the wall of the main offices. One would like to think that some of those more than six hundred poultrymen and their wives, seeing the handwriting on the henhouse wall, went home resolved to get out of a business which had reduced the hen to no more than an egg-laying element in what was in fact an industrial process; the process of making eggs — a process in which the hen was turned from a creature of its own quite particular charm into a living machine. There is unfortunately no record of the discussion. Perhaps some of the "lively" questions put by the visitors in the discussion period had to do with such notions. More probably it seemed inappropriate and ungrateful in this shrine of chicken-science to raise issues that were essentially moral ones.

Certainly the visitors had an opportunity to learn about the qualities of K-137, K-141, K-155, and K-222. (The old Model-T chickens of K-43 and K-82 had long since been superseded.) "Today's K-137," a brochure informed them, "incorporates even better performance and balance than earlier models." Disc brakes and power steering? A chart gave the weight of the birds at various ages, their "livability" (98 percent growing; 92 percent laying); their egg production, "245 to 285 eggs to 18 months of age, henday basis," whatever a "henday" may be, and, most important of all, of course, "Feed Conversion (½ lb. less feed per 24 oz. of eggs than average of all stocks)." K-141 was a tough bird, well adapted to "adverse conditions," which produced a kind of knockabout egg. Moreover, its feed conversion ratio was 1:7.

In addition to their main hatcheries at Fremont and Niles, Kimber had another hatchery at Sanger in northern California, and a network of "authorized associate Hatchers . . . in other States and Counties," including two permanent European agents dedicated to helping bring that continent out of the Dark Ages of poultry raising into modern times.

There was one somber note to the festivities and good cheer of the 1959 open house. Many smaller poultry raisers felt themselves being pressed to the wall by rising costs, part of which were due to an inflationary spiral in the country at large, part to the increasing expenditures required for the technology that held down cost per egg to a competitive level, and part due to the constantly rising cost of land and the almost yearly rise in taxes that accompanied it.

This process was well under way by 1959 and John Kimber, president of Kimber Farms, showed a certain fortitude in tackling the question, "Can California

*The Fall
of the Chicken
(and Almost
Everything
Else)*

288

Poultrymen Survive?" The question was not, it might be noted, whether they could "prosper" but rather whether they could "survive." "When a hard year comes along, and I have seen many of them," Kimber declared, "some poultrymen find they are not making a satisfactory profit. Some find they are losing money. They naturally wonder whether they can pull through, whether they can survive indefinitely in the face of ever-increasing competition from such areas as the Middle West and South." Unfortunately, a number would not. "It is, of course," Kimber added, "very sad to see anyone lose one's life savings or even take a big loss on a business operation. However, in the long run, business principles and economic laws apply to agriculture as to any other business. If they are heeded and obeyed, success usually follows. . . . I believe California poultrymen can survive, provided they use good business judgment and demonstrate the other abilities necessary for success." After listing three favorable factors — growing population, good climate, and moderate cost of feed — Kimber listed three unfavorable ones: higher land costs, higher taxes, and higher labor costs than other states. "California poultrymen," he concluded, "should . . . hold their own indefinitely, provided they have what it takes." There was an ominous ring to the words. To merely "hold their own" was not a cheering prospect. And it was by no means clear to many hardworking, struggling poultrymen "what it took" to survive in an industry moving toward larger and larger units of production as the only means of making a decent profit.

Dr. Kermit Schaaf, a doctor of veterinary medicine, sounded another ominous note in his talk about disease. Disease was becoming more and more of a problem to many farmers, especially those who could not afford an expensive program of inoculation.

Behind John Kimber's hardly reassuring words was an assumption common to most of the members of the audience. In America if a man was reasonably intelligent, worked hard, saved his money, didn't drink to excess, and went to church on Sunday, he could expect to make a decent living. If he did these things and still failed, it must be because of some flaw in his character. Perhaps he didn't really work hard enough, or wasn't shrewd enough, or tough enough, or, perhaps, even pious enough. When times were good it seemed that everyone talked in inflated, optimistic terms about all the money to be made in this or that; just a little of that good old American know-how, and enterprise and success and prosperity, if not wealth, must follow. When times were bad, when failures were numerous, then the spokesmen, the successful businessmen and the politicians, talked about character and hard work and "having what it takes" to succeed in the world.

So John Kimber was talking the kind of language that his audience understood and by and large agreed with, though many of them must have wondered subsequently what they were doing wrong and why they suddenly no longer "had what it takes," when they had had what it took in earlier years.

What followed that memorable Kimber Farms picnic in 1959 was an accelerating race with disaster. What resulted was the farmer or "keeper" (and increasingly the couple with chickens became "keepers" as in jail-keeper) was spurred on by two complementary motives, desire to make more money — known as "maximizing his profits" — and the even more pressing desire to avoid bankruptcy.

It went something like this: Poultryman A kept a thousand birds which returned him, in a good year (that is, a year when the price of eggs was high, no serious diseases were around, and the price of feed reasonable, let us say four dollars a bird), four thousand dollars, a very decent income through 1946, perhaps even to 1950. With chicken technology constantly expanding, it was possible to keep two thousand, or even three thousand, birds at very little extra labor. Indeed, with the greatly increased profits a reliable boy or an old man could be employed to help out. The feed company and the bank were both encouraging if they did not, as they did in innumerable instances, whisper the suggestion in the rancher's ear. The trouble was that Poultryman A's neighbors were listening to the same siren song, responding to the same agents of the feed companies (who guaranteed them feed at bargain prices and promised to market their eggs for them). When Poultryman A was joined by B and C on down through the alphabet and back again, the inexorable law of supply and demand entered the scene like the rent-racking landlord in the classic melodrama. The price of eggs fell as the supply rose. Now Y, who, content with his four thousand dollars, had resisted all temptations to increase the size of his flock, found that the ambitions of his neighbors had brought a drop in the price of eggs, with the result that his thousand hens now brought him only three thousand dollars a year, while the price of feed crept up inexorably. At this point he had several choices: he could follow the leaders, "the wide-awake progressive men and women"; he could borrow some money from easy lenders and double the size of his flock; he could stand fast and accept (at least for a while) his diminished profits; or he could get out of the chicken race (which he had gotten into to get out of the rat race), cut his losses, and go back to the nine-to-five job. If he took the first option, he simply dug himself in deeper and only delayed the day of final reckoning when he would lose much more of his investment.

Uncontrolled production was, of course, only one factor in the general cataclysm that overtook the small poultry rancher. The other, perhaps in the long run more fatal, element was a runaway technology, a technology that year by year grew more expensive. Encouraged by the feed co-ops and banks, which preached interminably that there was no choice but to grow or die, to double production or go under (and which stood ready to lend money without stint to those hardy souls determined to grow), thousands of poultry keepers plunged on in a course that led, almost invariably, to disaster.

There were a few notable exceptions. In Santa Cruz County, California, where hen fever was once rampant and almost fifteen hundred chicken ranches existed in the mid-fifties, one poultryman — Vernon Miller — is left. His story is an interesting one and he is clearly pleased to tell it. One day in 1968 a bank representative came to him to offer the support of the bank if he would double his flock of six thousand birds to twelve thousand (even then a very small flock). His present flock was uneconomical he was told. Only by expanding could he hope to survive. Vernon Miller ordered the representative of the bank off his land and delivered a few homilies on good financial practice to the discomfited official. Not only had he no intention of increasing his flock, he told the bank representative, he was, in fact, determined to cut its size in half — from six thousand hens to three thousand. He would collect and pack the eggs himself, load them in his station wagon, and deliver them to neighbors within a five-mile radius who wanted fresh eggs, direct from the farm.

When I first talked to Vernon Miller eggs were selling for thirty-five to forty-five cents a dozen and he was barely scraping by. But the big boys were in real trouble, he noted with some satisfaction. Rumor had it that Nulaid, the biggest egg marketing enterprise in central California, was nineteen million dollars in debt to the banks.

Vernon Miller's experience at least suggested an

*The Fall
of the Chicken
(and Almost
Everything
Else)*

292

alternative to giantism: rather than get larger and larger, get smaller and restore the classic relationship of the producer to the customer. Three thousand hens is still a large number. They require the full-time attention of Miller and a boy who helps him. But Miller is not afraid of work. He is full of the Protestant Ethic and his face grows grim when he talks about the bankers, the plungers, the get-rich-quick operators, the pseudo-marketing cooperatives, and the industrialists of Egg City in Moorpark, California, where two and a half million chickens produce well over a million eggs a day. He has been raising chickens all his life and he has seen all the vagaries of the industry: the change from the still rural atmosphere of the twenties and thirties to the boom times of the forties and fifties and the deadly efficiency of the great egg factories.

*The Fall
of the Chicken
(and Almost
Everything
Else)*

293

He believes we may walk into our favorite supermarket someday in the not-too-distant future and be told that they no longer carry eggs. The giant producers have been losing too much money; the banks have foreclosed. No more eggs. But, of course, before that happens, the federal government will step in and impose limitations on production designed to keep the prices of eggs at a level where big poultrymen can stay solvent. That means eggs, the greatest and most consistent food bargain in the housewife's shopping basket for some seventy-five years, will rise sharply in price.

Of all those tens of thousands of poultry keepers (or egg ranchers) in California and hundreds of thousands in the United States, only a handful of very large producers remain. The rest have failed, lost all that they invested, or gotten out before disaster overwhelmed them.

Perhaps if we revert, for the moment, to Petaluma we may be able to measure the magnitude of the catastrophe. Today, the "egg basket of the world" is virtually empty. There are a few ranches left in the thirty-thousand-to-one-hundred-thousand class (once they would have seemed enormous; now they are strictly small potatoes). One man with a few thousand birds has a gift and curio shop adjacent to his henhouses. He, like Vernon Miller of Santa Cruz, sells retail and specializes in large brown eggs, somewhat of a novelty in California, which is white-egg country. Petaluma is near enough to San Francisco (seventy miles) so that it has become a bedroom community for the city. The developers are pressing the former egg capital hard. Recently the city council passed an ordinance limiting its growth to five hundred new dwelling units a year and forbidding high-rise apartments. The ordinance is being challenged in the courts by developers who claim that it impairs a man's God-given right to dispose of his property as he wishes.

The lovely Petaluma Valley is still filled with the weathering gray husks of buildings once used to house happy and industrious hens. There, indeed, one can trace the changing styles in poultry keeping like a kind of archeological museum: the small detached huts, the larger houses, first open and then, with the advent of artificial lighting, closed; the long single-story buildings, and then the two-story structures. In a few years they will have given way, ordinance or no ordinance, to tracts of split-level houses, and the days of the hen fever that made Petaluma famous around the world will be only a memory. Indeed, they are not much more than that now.

Even the library reveals little of the history of chicken and egg in Petaluma. A local newspaperman and history buff, Ed Mannion, is unofficial custodian of Petaluma minute books, old records, and journals having to do with the poultry industry in its prime. The town insigne, with its wire egg basket and the inscription "the egg basket of the world," was quietly dropped several years ago on the ground that it was no longer a legitimate claim. Antiquarians argued that it should be kept for sentimental reasons, but the memory was too painful to perpetuate consciously.

There is, of course, no reliable way to calculate the money lost in the failures of the small and medium-sized poultrymen in Petaluma and a thousand similar communities. Many went broke and many got out while they could. A number switched to other jobs — went back to the nine-to-five routine — before the final pinch. I suspect between five and ten million Americans tried their hands at poultry keeping in the eighty-year period from 1890 to 1970, and of that number the vast majority failed, often at the cost of all their investment and savings as well. In a sense, their failures could be said to have subsidized the low price of eggs and chickens. If we calculate their failings at many millions of dollars a year, especially in the period from the early 1950's to the end of the sixties, it is evident that if they did nothing else they kept down the price of eggs, both by overproducing and by failing.

What is also apparent beyond question is that very few succeeded in the long run. If the poultry business was, for a time, the American dream, a striking form of the "promise of American life," the dream became a nightmare and the promise turned to ashes. And the reasons seem plain enough in retrospect. The classic American faith that science and technology, combined with intelligence and diligence, must result in success, prosperity, and happiness — America's particular version of the Protestant Ethic — this simply turned out not to be the case. Technology is neither wicked nor benign. It is neutral. It was the assumption that it must be benign that was fatal to the chicken entrepreneur. It was the touching, blind faith that the ultimate order in the universe was a scientific and technological order rather than a moral order that brought all down into dust and humiliation.

And there, of course, is the moral of the story. What

has been said of technology and the chicken can be said of many other aspects of modern life, from the motor car to a head of lettuce. The case is simply more poignant with the chicken because the relationship between man and chicken — now so besmirched and, in truth, virtually destroyed — is older than human history and one of the most agreeable relationships that has existed between man and any element of the natural or nonhuman world.

One way to view the advance of chicken technology is to see it as a process which, at each stage, made life bleaker for the exploited hen by reducing it more completely to an element in egg production. The chicken, in turn, fought back passively by various forms of neurotic behavior (such as excessive pecking) and susceptibility to disease. The farmer, for his part, backed by a formidable array of poultry specialists, pathologists, researchers, and, increasingly, geneticists, struggled to cope with the most common diseases of the hen. Various vaccines were developed and baby chicks were inoculated shortly after birth to insure immunity from the most common diseases. But it was all to no avail. The "poultry ranch" was replaced by the "poultry factory."

The human side of the "fall of the chicken" will (for understandable reasons) never have its historian; it is a uniformly depressing and lackluster tale of frustration and defeat experienced, for the most part, by obscure and "unimportant" people who, proud of their "rugged individualism," had no effective power, no ubiquitous lobby, no friends in court; people who were victims of a process of which they had little understanding, people who believed in "progress" and "free enterprise," and in the inevitable triumph of American technology and American industry: in short, American "know-how."

In any event, by the end of the sixties the situation was such that the small poultryman about whose survival John Kimber had been so guardedly optimistic a decade before was almost as extinct as the mourning dove. The production of eggs was concentrated in huge factories housing hundreds of thousands or even millions of hens. It was just at this point that a new and more virulent strain of the once feared Newcastle disease appeared in flocks in southern California. The constant refining of strains for egg production had resulted in birds that, as we have seen, were peculiarly prone to disease and especially to the most deadly viruses. This, in turn, had produced a race in the laboratories to come up with vaccines and medications to stave off disastrous epidemics. In 1972 the Newcastle virus appeared in an especially devastating form that appeared immune to the available vaccines, at least when used in mature birds. Over nine million hens reportedly had to be destroyed in southern California alone, two million eight hundred thousand of them in Egg City, to prevent the spread of the disease.

Some research scientists, whose task it was to make vaccines to combat the Newcastle disease, among others, were convinced that the slaughter was unnecessary, that the threatened flocks would have been protected and the disease checked by vaccination. They believed that an important element in the action of agriculture officials was the desire to boost the price of eggs by destroying large flocks. Since the egg manufacturers were handsomely compensated by the government and since, indeed, the exterminations were bound to have the effect of raising prices, thereby saving them from incipient bankruptcy, they, not unnaturally, kept their mouths shut and cooperated with the government agents in the mass killings. Prices of eggs and of chickens did indeed rise steeply in the aftermath of the killings, aided by a general rise in the price of food and of beef in particular. The trading in egg futures was brisk and the industry took a new lease on life.

*The Fall
of the Chicken
(and Almost
Everything
Else)*

298

The killing and disposal of nine million hens is *gallocide* on a scale too vast for the average imagination, a true horror story for the owners of the birds (however little sentiment they may have for their chickens), and perhaps, above all, for those human beings charged with actually destroying the birds. Chickens are not people, but perhaps the destruction in our age of millions of human beings who were thought to carry a kind of racial virus in their genes has inured us to the horror of killing so many living creatures and left us equally indifferent to the strange developments which make such a solution seem inevitable if not commonplace.

As for the hen, undoubtedly the virulent new strain of Newcastle disease will be (if it has not already been) contained by a new antidote concocted in the computerized laboratories of the chicken-makers. But what has been done to the life and the essence of chickens cannot be so easily undone. Some of the classic breeds, developed lovingly and ingeniously over generations, indeed over centuries, are nearly extinct, to be found only in the pens of a few breeders or in zoos along with other endangered species. They have been driven from our lives and even from our consciousness by the terrible and apparently irresistible logic of technology. We have already raised a generation of human beings many of whom have never seen a hen or a cock in its natural state, who have never heard a cock's crow or a hen's triumphant cackle, who have never eaten a "natural" egg, or munched on a genuine chicken. The chicken can thus, with its immemorial association with man, be taken as a symbol of our heedless manipulation and exploitation of the universe we live in and, particularly, of the planet we live on. The authors of this work have come to feel that somehow the fate of all of us is entwined in the fate of that once familiar and commonplace bird, the chicken, an endangered species. Surely creatures, raised like those we have described, feathered bipeds bearing a superficial resemblance to the chicken, will continue to exist under the auspices of our technological society, but, and one must insist on this, *they will not be chickens and their eggs will not be eggs*. It is certainly not inconceivable that people will come to recognize this fact.

It is not simply that manufactured eggs laid by birds filled with chemicals are far less appetizing than natural eggs, it is also that the consciences of people will be increasingly touched by the treatment of chickens in modern egg factories; their mutilation and their cruel confinement runs against the grain of our newly discovered respect for the natural world and our determination to make a decent use of its bounty. I suspect that people will not accept indefinitely a process which so abuses a creature that symbolizes, in its natural state, the bounty of nature.*

The purely practical man will, of course, be quick to point out that one of the consequences of the chicken boom is that the price of eggs and the price of chickens have remained constant over the last fifty years. The chicken and the egg are perhaps the only food items on the American housewife's shopping list that cost little more than they did in the depths of the Great Depression; in any event they are clearly, in dollars and cents, if not in quality, the best food bargain available today (or they were yesterday).

Thus the history of the chicken and her egg might

* An ancient fable repeated by Aldrovandi tells of the woman who had a hen that laid an egg every day. Hoping to get twice as many eggs from her, the woman fed her twice as much grain. "But the hen grew fat and was not able to lay even one egg a day. This fable hints at those who, because of avarice, are desirous of more and lose that which is at hand."

A more apt fable to describe the history of poultry raising in the last fifty or sixty years could hardly be found. Not satisfied with the bounty that a normal hen produces for her master, men, with their greedy ways, set about to squeeze more and more eggs and more and more meat from her. They abused her in dreadful ways and made her life a burden to her and to all those who attended her. In doing so they showed a callous disregard for a living creature and a reckless confidence that their insidious new technologies would make them all rich.

be taken as a classic vindication of the virtues of the open market. "Look," someone (not we, certainly) might say, "the history of the production of hens' eggs is a perfect model of the relation between supply and demand on the one hand and technological advance on the other. It would be hard to find in the whole vast and varied realm of industrial capitalism a more striking instance in which our society has mustered all its resources to produce more of a particular item at lower cost to the consumer." This much must be acknowledged. But we would insist that economics aside the story has a much deeper moral: unrestrained technology, fueled by the desire for larger and larger profits, exacts a price in terms of human values that we can no longer afford to pay. There are invisible costs as well as visible ones in the destruction of nature by technology.

*The Fall
of the Chicken
(and Almost
Everything
Else)*

PART THREE

Raising one's own chickens is a thoroughly rewarding enterprise. Chickens are certainly the most
easily managed of domestic animals — they are smaller
than goats or cows, and more practical than white
mice. Anyone who has a suburban lot (and reasonably tolerant neighbors) can keep enough chickens to
provide eggs for the family. Ten or a dozen good laying hens will produce an average of six to eight eggs
a day, seven days a week, seven or eight months of the
year. They can be kept in a henhouse, six by six feet
or so and two to three feet off the ground, with a
larger area on the ground fenced in by chicken wire.
The fence should be about seven feet tall and, if the
area to be fenced is comparatively small — say, ten
by twenty — it might very well be covered on the top
to prevent the more enterprising birds from flying
out or predators (especially cats and owls) from getting in. If it is impractical to cover the chickens' pen
with wire, their wings can be clipped. This can be
done by cutting the long flight feathers at the edge
of each wing. The feathers on one side can be cut
about half their normal length. This will keep a hen
from flying, but it will also make it difficult for her
to mount to her roost unless it is very low. Clipping
a hen's wings, as the phrase suggests, is a mutilation,
however mild, of the bird and it is much better to let

her fly. Once a plump laying hen has reached maturity she has trouble getting very far off the ground. Young pullets and cockerels are the best flyers as well as fryers.

The Reverend Edmund Dixon recommended perches made of rough poles two or three inches in diameter with the bark left on them to give the roosting birds a better toehold. He also endorsed "hen-ladders": boards with crossway slats to enable the chickens to mount to their roosts. This seems to me somewhat of a refinement. I prefer lower roosts. Even the heaviest and most cumbersome bird should be able to get two or three feet off the ground.

For cold climates, the pen or roosting place of the chickens should be entirely enclosed or with sides that can be raised when the weather is fine. Since drafts are bad for roosting chickens, only one side of the coop, of wire, should be open, and where there is danger of predators the wire should be heavy-gauge as, of course, should the wire constituting the floor of the cage if it is up off the ground. If it is on the ground, a cement floor that can be hosed off periodically is most desirable, but this should be kept covered with straw or some other kind of litter, since a bare cement floor is hard on the feet of chickens and almost impossible to keep clean.

The Reverend Mr. Dixon proposed a series of nests built of brick up against the side of the henhouse with wooden bottoms that could be removed like drawers to be "scoured and scalded and the brickwork washed and whitewashed." Dixon also had the practical suggestion of "small separate fowl-houses about a cubic yard. . . . Into these each breeding fowl, with her young, can be separately driven from the coops at night, and remain there without disturbance or quarrels till the proper time to go abroad next day." (I may say, parenthetically, that driving a hen and her brood into a particular henhouse or enclosure requires a good deal of tact and patience.) Dixon recommended that the floor of the henhouse be swept every day and sprinkled with fresh sand, gravel, or ashes.

If you must confine your birds, perhaps the best arrangement is a chicken house or coop with an entrance at each end and a dividing wall in the middle. Each door opens onto a separate pen or run or fenced-in area, areas as large as the situation permits. The chickens are allowed in one area while the other restores itself, green things grow, dust holes fill in, and manure diffuses in the soil. Then the areas are reversed. In this way you assure your chickens of the best conditions for health and happiness, short of being completely at large.

If you want to start a small flock in your backyard (or on the terrace of your apartment), you can order a dozen chicks or so from a number of places that sell chicks by mail. Sears, Roebuck has a good stock of Rhode Island Reds that are excellent laying birds. You can also buy baby chicks a few days old in most rural feed stores. (If you live in a rural area it is simple enough to buy from a neighbor.) Feed stores often have a bulletin board that advertises livestock for sale. Or the proprietor of the feed store can direct you to a reliable seller and usually give you advice as to what breed does best in the area.

The word *reliable* I use advisedly. There is nothing that gives some farmers more pleasure than sticking a city slicker. When I first set out to buy chickens I didn't know a pullet from a hen or even how long a hen could be counted on to lay. As a consequence I got thoroughly taken by a shrewd old lady. To do her justice, I was really begging to be swindled. When I picked out a matronly hen who appeared to my innocent eye to be the kind of bird that should lay good eggs, her owner offered to give her to me. This should have aroused my suspicions, but I attributed

it to an excess of neighborly good will and insisted on
paying for it. "Oh no," I said, overcome by her generosity, "I couldn't do that. I want to pay you for it.
What should I pay?" The lady, doubtless hardly
believing her ears, said, "Oh, I guess about three dollars." Needless to say the hen's egg-laying days were
over. It never laid an egg for me and died (of old
age, I suspect) several months later.

When you buy your chicks you will buy either
"straight run" or "sexed" chicks. Straight run are
chicks just as they come out of the egg, so to speak,
and since out of every clutch of eggs or incubator
load of eggs approximately half will be males (cockerels) and half females (pullets), you will have to be
prepared to dispose of the surplus cockerels, most
typically by eating them when they are still fryer or
broiler size or by caponizing (or castrating) them. A
beginner will thus do better to buy sexed chicks although they cost more — thirty-five to fifty cents as
opposed to twenty-five to forty for straight run (depending always, of course, on the breed and the state
of the market).

One "home method" of sexing chicks consists of
holding baby chicks upside down by their legs. It is
said (but I cannot vouch for it) that the male chicks
will try to bend upward while the females will hang
down passively. (I suspect this may simply be a male
canard.) A better-established method is to breed dark-
colored cocks with light-colored hens (or vice versa).
The dark-colored chicks will then be male and the
light-colored ones female (or vice versa).

There is also the question of what breed of chicken
to keep. The most readily obtainable breeds, of course,
are the hybridized commercial birds (they are not
really breeds), although few big hatcheries (if there
are any in your vicinity) will bother to sell you a few
dozen hens. Besides white and brown Leghorns, Rhode
Island and New Hampshire Reds, and Barred Rocks,

there are, the reader will recall, dozens of classic breeds, only a few of which we can mention here. The Wyandotte is a classic American bird, slender, tasty, and a good layer — named after the Wyandotte Indian tribe of the St. Lawrence Valley.

The Dorking is a large, awkward, untidy bird of English origin, interesting primarily because of its fifth toe and the fact that its progenitors were probably carried to Britain by the Roman legions that invaded that island in the first century. In its present form it was developed as a popular meat bird in the town of Dorking in the late nineteenth century. The residents of Dorking tried to preserve their monopoly by making it illegal to sell live birds to "outsiders."

The Buff Orpington, also English, is good eating and a good layer — a smooth-feathered giant, which, like the Dorking, is tame and amiable.

The Australoup is an excellent layer, developed in this century in Australia. The Houdan and the Polish have exotic feathered headpieces. The Brahma and Cochin have feathered shanks and are, like the Dorking and the Orpington, heavy-bodied birds.

The point is that if you are to have the pleasure of keeping chickens without any special concern about "production" you might as well play a modest part in restoring the classic breeds. You can proceed by experimentation — by trial and error — or you can solicit the expert advice of the Society for the Preservation of Poultry Antiquities at Owatonna, Minnesota.

When a dozen sexed chicks arrive at your house, the most important thing is to keep them warm. Poultry farms have electric brooders where the temperature can be maintained at an even 95 degrees and then gradually lowered until the young chickens are ready to be turned outside (usually at four or five weeks, again depending on the outside temperature). An amateur can accomplish substantially the same effect by suspending an electric light bulb in the box. Needless to say care has to be taken to see that the bulb is protected and does not start a fire. If you suspend an electric light in the chicks' box or cage, the chicks will regulate the temperature for themselves by the distance they stay from the light bulb. In addition to warmth, all you need is some mash, chick scratch, and water. Since baby chicks are indefatigable scratchers, they will scatter any meal or food put in a plate or bowl, and it is much simpler and cheaper in the long run to buy a metal chick-feeder which has small holes that inhibit, if they do not stop, the chicks from scratching and thereby scattering their food all over the place. The bottom of the box should be covered with soft paper toweling and this should be changed every day. The best waterer is a mason jar with a plastic trough. If you use a bowl it will soon be filled with the feces of the chicks. Indeed, even the narrow trough of the waterer collects fecal material very rapidly and must be cleared and refilled every day.

Ancient and modern writers are in agreement that cleanliness is essential in the raising of chickens. This is especially true of henhouses, of course, and of drinking water. As Aldrovandi writes, "The water must be very clean, for water that is filthy with excrement causes the pip. . . . The caretaker should be very careful lest the dung gather and torment the hens, and, since the water should be very clean, vessels made for drinking purposes only should be [used]." (These were, typically, lead, wood, or earthenware and had to be scrubbed at least once a week.) The principal enemies of the baby chick are dirt and cold. If the chicks are kept warm and clean they will, almost invariably, grow into healthy birds.

If the weather is mild, the young pullets can be transferred to their outdoor quarters when they are about five weeks old. If they get chilled when they are very small, they will simply die of the cold (75 degrees is too cold for a small chick) ; if they are put out when they are larger but not yet ready for the outdoors (especially for cool nights) they will get pneumonia and usually die of it. Prior to being left to face the fluctuations of temperature on their own, they should have the temperature gradually reduced until it approximates the temperature out of doors.

When the pullets are established in their outdoor quarters, they can graduate to processed pellets or various forms of commercial chicken feed. If they are fortunate enough to be what the Italians call *polli ruspanti*, that is, free-ranging chickens, they of course find their own food, primarily by scratching up the ground, but also, and very importantly, by eating green things, grass and tender leaves for the most part. They are indeed omnivorous. However, left to their own devices they are very efficient feeders. They eat corn and grains as well as buds, seeds, blades of grass, vegetables, flowers, garbage, eggshells, oyster shells (where available), sand and pebbles (for their gizzards), bugs, worms, grubs, termites, and so on. The green things they eat give the yolks of their eggs a characteristically dark yellow or orange color that is absent from the yolks of industrialized hens.

Chickens will eat almost anything in the nature of a table scrap. They will eat bits of leftover meat (they love cat and dog food), rotten (or ripe) fruit, wilted lettuce, stale bread, eggshells and, I fear, even chickens. They have one of the toughest digestive systems in the animal kingdom; they fill their gizzards with small stones and pebbles, which help them digest their food and strengthen the shells of their eggs. If they are free to scratch for themselves they will take care of their own need for bits of stone, pebble, and shell. If they are confined, they need to have these elements made available to them. Chickens especially like, and profit from, stale or sour milk and cream. In short, almost anything that goes down the disposal can go down a chicken's gullet; the chicken is the world's greatest recycler. Chickens will eat human as well as animal waste, and many thrifty farmers used to take advantage of this fact by having their outhouses in the chicken yard. Even when your chickens are ranging and the feed they find is supplemented with garbage and stale vegetables scrounged from the waste bins of local supermarkets, they should receive some grain each evening before they go to bed. They sleep more comfortably with something in their crops and have more amiable sentiments toward their master or mistress.

We have already described the potency and utility of chicken manure. Mixed with straw or rice husks and allowed to season, it makes an excellent organic fertilizer for flower and vegetable gardens. On the other hand, chicken manure is so rich in nitrates that if it is applied directly to growing things it will burn them. Lately some ingenious inventors have found ways to convert chicken (and other) manures into methane gas and use it to run trucks and automobiles. Properly treated, it makes an almost wholly non-polluting fuel, but you should not count on running your car with the manure produced by a dozen chickens. It would take the year's output of manure from your twelve chickens to make enough methane to run your car for a day or two.

When your pullets are six months old (or more) they will begin to lay eggs. Their initial eggs will generally be rather small and they will lay, when they are in a good mood, between a hundred and twenty and a hundred and sixty eggs a year. They will lay quite comfortably on straw placed in a box with low sides, and more than one will lay in a single nest. They form an unusually cooperative little community, taking turns at the nest, with two hens often crowding or trying to crowd into a single nest at the same time.

Ideally one would have a cock presiding over a flock of hens. This means fertile eggs, which epicures and health-food advocates from the days of the Greeks to the present have insisted are better than infertile (wind) eggs. Fertile eggs, for one thing, keep better. On the other hand, a hen has only to set on a fertile egg for twenty-four hours to start the incubation process, which makes the egg less appetizing although no less nutritious. A hen, conversely, can set for three or four days (or more) on an infertile egg without spoiling it.

The problem with a cock is that he of course crows and your neighbors may not share your pleasure in his nocturnal music. Most people will soon accustom themselves to the crowing of a cock, which by almost any standard is, after all, far less offensive than the slamming garbage cans, ambulances, police and fire-engine sirens, screeching tires, grinding trucks, buses, and automobile horns that characterize most urban and suburban environments. A sleeper will readily adapt himself to noises that occur at the same time each night (like the tolling of church bells), and thus most people will soon sleep undisturbed through the crowing of a cock, or cocks. At the same time it may very well be that a neurotic or impatient neighbor will be unwilling to put the issue to the test. In that case it is not difficult to build a lightproof coop for your cock and hens to roost in. My experience (by no means scientifically tested) has been that cocks usually crow in response to changes in the light. Although they commonly crow three times during the night, as we have already noted, it seems to me their most strident crowing and the crowing that most typically awakens the slumberer is at dawn. Thus, shutting them up, after they have gone to roost, in a lightproof coop discourages or checks their crowing.

And if it does not check it, it muffles it so that even the lightest sleeper can slumber on undisturbed.

But to take things in order. Let us assume that through preference or necessity you have a flock of hens unattended by a cock. Once your flock is established and laying you should have no problems. Your space should, of course, be adequate to your flock. By the same token you probably should not have more chickens than you can consume the produce of. Twice as many eggs as you can eat are too few to sell to a neighbor or to dispose of in any systematic way. You can, of course, always give them to grateful friends.

The relation of space to the number of birds is very important. If birds are crowded into too small a space (as they are on huge poultry farms) they become restless, bored, and somewhat psychotic. The famous pecking order, which under normal conditions is no more than a method of establishing the kind of order that characterizes any group of creatures living together, becomes unpleasant bullying of the less aggressive hens by the more aggressive and can degenerate, as we have seen, into cannibalism, where the weaker hens are literally pecked to death. In a well-regulated pen with plenty of air and light and things to do and with hens who have grown up together, pecking is a minor problem. If it threatens to become serious it can usually be solved by dividing the pen and separating the hens.

The surest way to prevent boredom is to give your chickens the largest possible area to roam in. At the very least they should have access to the ground. Above all things a chicken treasures a dust bath; a cock or hen loves to squinch down in a dusty depression and, with its wings and legs, stir up a small cloud, fluffing up its feathers until the dust penetrates to every part of its anatomy. A chicken taking a dust bath is an image of sensual enjoyment. Luxuriating in a manner no seraglio with a perfumed bath could surpass, it also protects itself against the mites and lice that would otherwise make it miserable. The latter is a point worth stressing. With no dust bath, chickens are subject to verminous infestations and should be checked periodically; when infected they should be treated with a powder to kill mites, lice, and other such creatures. Their roosts should, in addition, be sprayed periodically with nicotine sulfate.

To put the matter succinctly, chickens, like people, need sunlight, air, clean water, exercise, and, if constrained, diversion. An attentive master or mistress will devise simple games for chickens to play when they are confined to a relatively small area and are not free to seek their own diversions. These games may simply be a ball or bright-colored object suspended from the top of the cage. Or a game with a reward. Chickens are not the stupid creatures they are sometimes painted. As distinguished, apparently, from man, they know all they need to know to live happy, productive lives if they are left largely to themselves with a minimum of interference by human beings. In addition they are quick learners and have that cunning natural to all living creatures.

It should be said at this point that there are at least two other ways in which you may start your own flock of chickens. First you can skip, if you wish, the "chick" stage and buy young pullets that are within a week or two of laying or that have already started to lay. In the Reverend Mr. Dixon's words: "It will add to the amusement derived, if, in the first instance, strong three-quarter grown chickens are procured, instead of adult birds, so that an opportunity is given of watching their progress to maturity." You should assure yourself that they are indeed pullets no more than a year and preferably nearer six months old. The disadvantage of purchasing pullets just as they are starting to lay is that the birds, taken from a large flock, may not know each other and will have to go through the process of establishing their pecking order. This may result in several of the less aggressive birds being seriously abused by the rest. The problems of a pecking order are minimized by raising chicks together.

Another alternative, and in our view by far the best, is to buy a trio, a cock and two hens between a year and two years old. If the crowing of the cock is not a problem because of your location or because you can keep him in a light- and relatively soundproof coop at night, you will be guaranteed fertile eggs and, what is more important, you can raise your own chickens. After a period of adjustment to their new quarters your two hens will doubtless lay in the same nest and one of them will eventually decide to set. If your hens average an egg every day or two, it will probably be two weeks or ten days before one of them settles down on the eggs and if you are reluctant to wait for your eggs you can steal a few from time to time without upsetting the hens. Indeed, your only control over the number of eggs a hen sets on is by taking eggs out of the nest when she has started to set. One thing should be noted: the egg laid the first day and the egg laid the last day before the hen begins to set (the interval may be three weeks) hatch, of course, at the same time. The first egg laid remains "fresh" enough to hatch a chicken, and of course fresh enough to eat, for two to three weeks.

In the interval when she is laying the eggs, the hen gives no particular indication of what she has in mind but at the moment when she decides to set, she becomes "broody," and this is a public declaration of her impending motherhood. She fluffs up her feathers until she appears to be almost twice her normal size. She will elevate and expand her tail feathers until they form an inverted V.

The number of eggs a hen should set on has been a subject of discussion for several thousand years, as the reader may recall. The Reverend Mr. Dixon recommended eleven to thirteen eggs, adding, "If a Hen is really determined to set, it is useless as well as cruel to attempt to divert her from her object." What can be done with a hen that cannot be dissuaded from setting is to let her set on infertile eggs (or on false ones) for a week or so, meanwhile saving eggs that you would like to try hatching, and when you have collected five or a dozen, place them under the hen.

The setting hen is very protective of her eggs, and while a hen that is merely laying will abandon her nest with an indignant squawk when disturbed, setting hens will sit tight, peck at an intruder, and make angry noises. Still, the less interference with a setting hen the better. If you follow the prescriptions of Aldrovandi and fuss every day with a nest, the hen may very well abandon it entirely and leave you with a clutch of useless eggs. It is, however, sensible to dust your setting hen with some lice powder.

A hen setting on a clutch of eggs is a very comfortable sight. It is indeed one of the commonest expressions of the animal in art of all kinds. Dozens of useful and useless objects from casseroles to tea caddies are rendered in the form of a setting hen. (I have among many such curiosities a child's TV pillow in the form of a hen; the child is supposed to set on the hen in this turnabout.)

The setting hen is a kind of living incubator; her temperature goes up and her metabolism goes down when she sets. Moreover, she is by no means idle. She must turn every egg three times a day — this she does with her beak — and keep her nest in order. Mother hens are as different in skill and temperament as human mothers. Some keep a clean and tidy nest with everything in good order; others foul their nests, break eggs in getting in and out (especially where the nests are in awkward places or the sides are too high), and are generally slovenly and improvident. It is very ancient wisdom that pullets should not be allowed to set and raise chicks, though they will certainly try to in most instances. Apparently this injunction is based on the notion that they are not yet ready for the responsibilities of motherhood; their eggs are not as large as they will be when they are mature hens and it is thought that the chicks hatched from them are not as large and healthy. Presumably pullets are too giddy to make the best mothers.

The reader will recall that the hen's period of incubation is twenty-one days, give or take a day. When she is setting she should have handy (or beaky) water and food. She will get off her nest for ten or twenty minutes a day to forage for food and stretch her wings. When she does come forth, she comes forth bristling with ardent motherhood. Her attention is fixed on getting nourishment as quickly as possible and getting back to her nest. (So ingeniously has nature arranged the development of the egg, that eggs incubated artifically have to be cooled for fifteen or twenty minutes a day to correspond to the period of time the mother hen is off her nest feeding and getting water.)

The twenty-one days finally pass — very slowly for the anxious chicken owner, perhaps even more slowly for the hen, who has only henlike thoughts to occupy her time but never seems restless or impatient. About twenty-four hours before a chick is due to hatch it will begin to peep in its shell. Researches have suggested that these peeps, which have already established a barely audible "communications network" between chick and chick and between the chicks and their now thoroughly expectant mother, are the way in which the chicks, locked in their respective eggs, notify each other that it is time to emerge.

The nature of the egg, as well as the details of how

the chick emerges from it, are discussed in another chapter. In effect it saws its way out with its egg tooth, a rough kind of edge that disappears after it has served its purpose. The mother hen now reaches the most delicate part of her duties. She does not break the eggs herself, and in fact she can give only a minimum of help to the emerging chick. More difficult, she must maintain her poise and balance while this process goes on underneath her and out of her sight. As each chick emerges from its shell in the dark cave of feathers underneath its mother, it lies for a time like any newborn creature, exhausted, naked, and extremely vulnerable. And as the mother may be taken as the epitome of motherhood, so the newborn chick may be taken as an archetypal representative of babies of all species, human and animal alike, just brought into the world. At this point a clumsy or nervous mother may quite literally stamp out the chick's life by shifting her weight in the nest and placing a heavy foot on the still-helpless chick. Some do. Moreover, if the mother has kept a dirty nest the new chick has a smelly and unpleasant environment for its first home. But within minutes, as soon as its down has dried, the new chick is on its feet, peeping away. If its mother should step on it it gives an immediate message by a series of frantic peeps. Assuming this particular chick of whom we have been talking is the firstborn, it has to stand by for as much as two more days while its brothers and sisters struggle out of their shells.

During all this time the chorus of peeps goes on virtually uninterrupted, the unborn chicks peeping away, the newborn ones singing their less muffled song. Since some of the eggs may be infertile or may have aborted in the shell at some stage of their incubation, the peeps keep the mother informed of how long she needs to continue on the nest. The last two or three days she has been unable to leave the nest even for a few minutes to get food or water. It seems safe to assume she is tired and hungry. And what about the chicks themselves? By the time all the eggs have hatched, those that were born first may have been without food or water for almost two days.*

As soon as all the eggs are hatched, or all those in which there is a living chick (and here human intervention can be useful; if a hen does not want to leave eggs that will not hatch, her master or mistress, after listening to make sure there is no live chick in the egg, should remove it from the nest), the mother hen is ready to sally forth with her brood and make her and its way in the world. If she can be turned out, it is certainly best to do so. Her nest will almost inevitably need cleaning. It will be filled with bits of broken eggshell, which she, to be sure, will eat, and sometimes with manure. Fresh straw should be put in the nest. Water should be available in special chick watering jars. If it is in a pan or bowl some chicks may fall in and drown.

There is, of course, no mothering like the mothering of a competent and experienced hen. The hen delights in its function and the chicks prosper. They plainly like having a mother.

A cautionary word. Mother hens who have a brood of their own chicks to manage can be very harsh with the chicks of other hens. If two hens and their broods are at large they should be watched closely for several

---

* Columella knew what close observers of mother hens and their chicks have always known — that for the first two days baby chicks do not eat or drink. After that he recommended putting them in a sieve and fumigating them with pennyroyal, "since this seems to prevent the pip which kills the young birds very swiftly." Then they are to be returned to their anxious mother and fed with boiled barley flour or "spelt flour sprinkled with wine." And each day their throats should be inspected. Varro recommended that for the first fifteen days they be fed polenta with nasturtium seed and kept from water, a very dubious prescription. Another ancient writer (Didymus) recommended the tenderest of leeks ground up with fresh cheese. Democritus proposed that worms from cow or donkey manure be collected and kept for ten days until they were large enough to feed to the chicks.

days to make sure that they do not fight and kill each other's chicks. This is a particular problem with game hens, who are much more belligerent, generally speaking, than their country cousins. The Reverend Mr. Dixon also counseled against keeping a hen and her chicks confined. "A Hen of active and energetic disposition confined in a coop will soon reduce her brood by the blows given in scratching. The Chicks are knocked right and left, and those few which may survive the confinement are destroyed by dew and rain, lost in the grass, or, becoming tired, are left by their dam, who, in exuberance of her delight at her escape from confinement, forgetting that her Chicks are not as strong as she is, goes on her way rejoicing, till, finding a fat worm or grub, she seizes it and while seeking for her little ones, her attention is attracted by some fat grasshopper, and away she darts in pursuit." This poor hen then, finding she has outdistanced her chicks, rushes about trying to find them, "by her loud cries drowning out the feeble chirpings of her little ones," and finally returns to her coop alone.

Indeed, from the moment they begin to eat, scratching and peeping are clearly innate forms of behavior in baby chicks. Their eyesight is excellent; they can see minute objects and their aim is unerring. The interesting thing is that the basic need supplied by the mother is less food than warmth. Periodically the mother squats down, perhaps alerted by some change in the decibel range of her chicks' peeps — a peep, say, that indicates they are chilled and in need of warmth — and they all dash under her outspread feathers and stay there until they are thoroughly warmed; then out again to continue the search for food and the adventure of exploring the world. The chicks are quite enterprising — some, of course, more than others. They venture a considerable distance from their mother, keeping contact always through peep and cluck. The hen seems to have some kind of computer that enables her to keep track of the chicks by counting the peeps of each chick. A missing peep or a frightened peep will bring her on the run to find the wanderer, to extricate it from some tangle of weeds or a hole in the groud, or to defend it if it is threatened by an animal or by a human.

The mother hen needs the protection of a pen or coop or cage at night. Both she and her chicks are extremely vulnerable to every kind of predator. A hen will almost invariably fight to protect her chicks; thus she is tempting to a stray dog or cat; not, of course, to mention her delectable chicks. She must nest on the ground rather than on a roost and, beyond that, the peeping of the chicks attracts the attention of any passing predator. At night she and her chicks should be shut up in a sturdy coop. A raccoon or 'possum can reach through the wire of a cage and pull out the baby chicks. I have lost more than one that way.

As the days pass and the chicks grow larger and larger, it is more and more difficult for the mother hen to accommodate them under her feathers at night. Finally, when she feels they are ready to be on their own, she flies up to her roost and abandons them as casually as if they were complete strangers. Her feathers, which have, from the time she first began to set, proclaimed her militant motherhood, now subside. Even stranger, her chicks show no continuing state of dependency. They do not even seem to recognize their mother. This may very well be because heretofore they have identified her by her shape. Now she has altered her shape and appears indistinguishable from the other hens in the flock.

If we assume that half of, let's say, sixteen chicks born are males (cockerels) and half are females (pullets), the problem that now confronts the amateur chicken raiser is what to do about the cockerels. Since he already has a cock, he does not need another one, let alone seven more. Indeed if his birds are confined he can hardly accommodate two cocks without the dominant older cock making life miserable for the younger one. The two classic methods of dealing with the problem are, as we have noted, first to segregate the cockerels as soon as they are identifiable — that is as soon as their secondary sexual characteristics begin to appear — and fatten them with an especially rich diet of broiler mash and milk. At about thirteen or fourteen weeks they should be killed as broilers or fryers. Killing a chicken puts to the supreme test the amateur chicken raiser who believes that the dirty work of the world should be done by somebody else. But it is either kill the cockerels or accept a state of almost constant warfare between the growing cockerels.

The second alternative is even more harrowing. It calls for castrating the cockerel and thus making him into a neuter bird, which will develop more like a plump hen than a cock, which will leave the hens alone (and, equally important, not fight with or threaten cocks) and concentrate on growing fat and tender.

As we have seen, cockerels have been caponized since classical times and have always been considered a great delicacy. With the proper feeding a capon will grow to four or five pounds by the time it is twenty weeks old and will make a fine roasting chicken.

In Europe in the sixteenth century the Dutch had developed a technique for fattening hens and capons by substituting beer for milk. At the time Aldrovandi wrote, he noted that "our age fattens capons rather than hens," and prescribed the same methods for fattening them.

I would add only a few words to the owner of confined chickens. They may be acquired in the three ways I have described: bought as sexed chicks, bought as laying pullets, or acquired in a trio and raised from scratch, so to speak. Each course has its problems. The first and last alternatives are plainly the most rewarding. In each instance the chicken keeper is faced with the problem of broodiness. A broody hen is an obstinate, uncooperative hen; what is more, she is an unproductive hen. As long as she is broody she will refuse to lay eggs. As long as she is broody she will set on anything or nothing — on two eggs or one or an empty nest. She will drive other hens away from the nest and resist all efforts to get her into a different frame of mind. The reader will recall that one of the ancient writers on chickens recommended pouring water on broody hens, presumably as a kind of shock therapy and to cool them off. It makes some sense, but I have had no particular luck with the technique. The other ancient remedy, passing a feather through the hen's nostrils, I confess I have not the gumption to try. I am unnerved for such drastic measures by the feeling that the hen, after all, has a perfect right to be broody and my efforts to discourage her should be correspondingly restrained. My recommendation is to shut the broody hens up in a separate cage, halfheartedly pour a little water on them, and hope for the best.

So much for broody hens.

The final point to consider is that hens have a laying life of about three years, though a few may lay for six or seven. If they are not pressured and harassed and hurried to lay, they will produce eggs at a diminishing rate into their fourth or fifth year. Therefore, the chicken raiser whose interest is primarily in eggs should plan to rotate his small flock in such a way that he will have a new group of pullets coming along at the same time that his established layers are in the twilight of their careers.

What to do with hens that have come to the end of their laying cycle is one of those virtually insoluble problems like what to do with kittens. A young pullet that is worth between $2.75 and $3.25 at six months, three years later when she has had almost every possible egg extracted from her is worth about twenty-five cents for soup stock or pet food. She is too old and tough to be a good roasting hen but she is by no means useless. She will make an excellent soup, her legs will make jelly base, her liver will be tasty and her fat useful in a variety of ways. Against all that there is the matter of killing a creature whom you have gotten to know and who has faithfully produced perhaps three or four hundred delicious eggs for you and your family. Of course eventually the hen will die of natural causes, but she may live for ten years or more after she has laid her last egg and may consume a good deal of feed in the meantime.

One more cautionary word might be added here. Never make chickens into pets. (There is a large question in my mind whether in fact dogs and cats should ever have been made into pets.) Chickens are not pets; they are chickens; they are producers; they exist to lay eggs and to be eaten. Never name a chicken. To do so is merely cute — and silly — and an abuse of names. This does not mean that you cannot enjoy, admire, and love chickens individually and collectively; it just means that you must not sentimentalize and falsify your relationship to chickens. This, for the most part, is why I feel keeping chickens should involve killing chickens as well. Somebody or some machine has to kill chickens, so why shouldn't you, particularly if you are going to eat them?

Old hens past their laying days will often make good foster mothers. When an old hen shows signs of broodiness by trying to set on the eggs of younger birds you can place fertile eggs under her. She will hatch the eggs and raise a brood as well as any other hen and better than flighty young pullets. Moreover, the productive birds will not interrupt their egg laying for the time-consuming responsibilities of motherhood.

To know when to remove or "cull" a nonlaying hen and put her in a stew one needs, of course, to keep some rough account of the age of one's hens and have a notion of which ones have stopped laying. Some authorities say that when hens are laying their combs lack color and incline to pink rather than bright red. Certainly this is not observable in Leghorns, for example, whose vivid red combs are their most striking characteristic. A much more reliable test is to feel the pelvic bones of a hen. If they are soft and wide apart, the hen is laying. An even better check on a hen's productivity is a trapnest — a nest with a hinged door which the hen can enter but which then falls and traps her. The problem here is that the bird has to be confined in order for the procedure to work. If you have a small flock of unconfined hens, close observation is probably the best method to determine which hens have ceased to lay.

We might here leave to Angelo Poliziano the last word on the hen as mother:

Meanwhile the brooding hen cackles with a sharp
    sound.
The old woman takes up her eggs, marks the days
And watches with her lantern,
Keeping the dates of the growing moon.
When the hen clucks she places
An uneven number of eggs under her,
Turns them carefully, listens to them
To learn whether inside the shell
The chick is peeping, has broken the tender shell
With its soft beak and is trying to come out of the
    egg.

Researches have indicated that hens will not mate with cocks that have not established dominance over them. Thus it is unusual for a mature hen to allow a young cockerel to mate with her, although the same bird may mate readily with hens of his own generation.

It has also been noted that in all-male flocks, certain males dominate others and mount and tread them as though they were females; conversely, as we have mentioned earlier, in flocks of hens, the more dominant hens (those at the top of the so-called pecking order) will mount more submissive females.

When chickens are confined, where food and space is or appears to be scarce and must be competed for (space especially since food is usually in abundance), serious rivalries develop. Birds that have been hatchery-produced, and have thus not been inducted into the flock of "adult" chickens by a solicitous mother and had an eye kept on them by a dominant cock who preserves good order in the flock, have to establish an "order" and they have to do it under trying circumstances. In a commercial flock they are pressed for space (in order to keep them from exercising and losing weight if they are meat birds; in order to limit their activity to eating and laying if they are egg "producers" and to conserve heat by utilizing their own body heat).

The ratio of cocks to hens was accounted one to six by the ancients lest a cock wear himself out by "too much copulation." Actually a cock, in his prime, can take care of a good many more hens than six. Part of the problem is that if you have twenty-four hens, let us say, and three or four cocks, the cocks will fight constantly unless they are kept in separate cages. While it is true that most cocks will work out a kind of *modus vivendi* that accords leadership to a particular cock, usually on the basis of seniority, if a cock is withdrawn from the flock and segregated for breeding purposes for a few weeks, it will have to fight for its proper place all over again when it is returned to the barnyard. A new cock introduced into an established flock is a more serious matter. He will be engaged in a constant round of battles with the resident cocks or cock until he is killed or flees or acknowledges the dominance of the boss cock and (probably) his subordinates. Certainly such a newly introduced cock will make off unless it is confined. Aelian, who took note of this characteristic in cocks, proposes a ritual to cope with it. You put your dining room table in the middle of the barnyard and carry the new cock three times around it. He can then be released with confidence that he will never run away.

If you have cocks among your hens, most of the eggs you collect will be fertile eggs. The mark of that fertility will be an almost invisible thickness in the white of the egg.

On the freshness of eggs there is also much confusion. An egg, quite naturally, is freshest when it is still warm from the hen. If it is collected and chilled (not frozen, of course) at the end of a day it will remain "fresh" for days. If it remains outdoors several days in hot weather it will lose much of its freshness. The freshness of an egg can be measured by the size of the air pocket inside the shell. That pocket is smallest in the freshest egg; it grows larger as the egg grows older. This fact is, of course, of little use to the prospective eater of the egg since the information is hidden within the shell. It is readily discernible in a hard-boiled egg, and a simple home test is to put an egg in a pan of water. If the egg is old, the air chamber will be large enough to make one end of the egg rise about the other, thus indicating an egg that is "getting on," though not necessarily an egg that is bad or "rotten."

The fact is it takes an egg a long time to get "rotten." Eggs placed in "cold storage" will last for months, and eggs that are not fresh — that is eggs that are more than a week or so old — are perfectly satisfactory for cooking purposes. Indeed, it takes a rather sensitive palate to identify an egg that is, say, two weeks old, as opposed to one two days old. And, as we know, the Chinese prefer them a hundred years old.

I suppose something should be said about chicken diseases. A sick chick is one of the sickest looking of creatures. It is listless, its eyes are often cloudy or rheumy, but, more strikingly, it draws in its neck and hunches down, its feathers askew and its whole posture proclaiming its misery. If it is the victim of coccidiosis it generally has blood in its stool. Such birds should be isolated. While, as we have seen from the operations of giant breeding farms, there are many vaccines and medicines that have been developed for chickens, they are of little use to the amateur chicken keeper.

Besides isolating sick birds and insuring that like a human patient they have warmth, food, and water, one is best advised to let nature do its own healing. The sick chicken will get well or die. It may or may not infect others. Chickens are, on the whole, very sturdy creatures or they could not have survived the experiments that have been performed on them in the last fifty or seventy-five years in the name of scientific chicken raising. If a chicken has a genetic defect (and these are fairly common because of inbreeding), it is usually kinder to kill it. Similarly, if a sick bird does not recover within a reasonable period, say a week, it should be killed. Chickens may, like people, get cuts and abrasions. If these are severe they can be treated just like human cuts and abrasions. For a chicken, for example, that has been attacked by a cat or a dog, the cleansing of the lacerations, some mild disinfectant, and, where called for, some stitching up would constitute proper treatment. But primarily quiet and isolation.

Although chickens have lived in the closest proximity with man for thousands of years, often, in peasant communities, sharing the same quarters, they have an understandable wariness about their human neighbors. They are proverbially hard to catch. Men, and more especially women, have been chasing chickens since they were first domesticated with, on the whole, indifferent success. The particular chicken in a good-sized flock that one has in mind to eat or sell or simply to put in a cage to breed or to fatten, seems to know instantly that it has been singled out for special attention, however artfully casual the approach to it may be. If unconfined, it immediately makes itself as scarce as possible. If it is in a fenced-in yard it takes refuge behind every other chicken in the flock. If pursued, it darts and dashes with the skill and unpredictability of a broken-field runner, meanwhile squawking as though the devil were after it and setting the whole flock to an excited clamor. The wisest course is to wait until your chicken has gone to roost. Then, when she is drowsy and almost comatose, you may, with a little care, pluck her from her roost. Indeed, chickens at night have poor eyesight and fall into a state close to hibernation.

If it is necessary to catch a chicken in the daytime, considerable agility plus a net with a long handle are helpful. It is possible also to make or buy a chicken-catcher with a wooden handle on one end and a metal hook on the other. With this device, which should be about three and a half to four feet long, you can, with some practice, hook a chicken's leg. The "hook" should be approximately a quarter-inch width from the shank and some two inches long, with a blunt or curved open end. The trick is to catch the bird's leg, the hook being too narrow for a foot to slip through.

The ancients recommended doping the chicken with asafetida mixed with crushed wheat and honey. But that seems a bit like putting salt on a bird's tail to catch it. If you can get a particular bird to eat your bait you could probably just as easily snare it. And how is one to prevent other chickens from eating the same feed? Another ancient means, especially effective in robbing a roost, was burning henbane under the nose of roosting hens, upon which "they are so seized with madness that they not only forget to move away from their perches but even fall and make it easy to capture them." This was the favorite means of the gypsies (the ancients called them "Egyptians"). Gypsies were also reputed to use hooks to steal hens, ducks, geese, and rabbits, snaring them so swiftly that they had no time to sound the alarm or even flap their wings.

But smoke of various kinds has been the preferred method for chicken thieves for several millennia. When Mark Twain was invited to become a member of the American Poultry Association, he wrote accepting the honor and declared that he had been a chicken "raiser" since his youth. He had found that the best and least expensive way to raise chickens was to take a sack and some sulfur matches on a dark night, light a sulfur match under the beak of the intended victim, and then quickly "raise" the bird and stuff it into the bag.

The language of chickens is perhaps more varied than that of any other bird. In the Reverend Mr. Dixon's words: "The language of Fowls, though inarticulate, is sufficiently fixed and determined for us to know what some of it means."

The crow, of course, by no means exhausts the cock's repertoire of sound any more than the cackle is the only utterance of the hen. The cock clucks and even gives an odd squeak at times. He has sounds that tell of his discovery of a particular morsel, a worm, or a nest of grubs that he has turned up. He has a shrill sound of warning if things threaten to get out of hand (or beak or claw) in the barnyard. He has a mating sound when he begins his dance, wing extended, round the hen; and he has a warring sound when he is squaring off against another cock. Most striking of all, he has a scream of utter anguish and terror if he is seized in the night when he is dormant and vulnerable. A hen, seized by a thief, or a coon, or fox, may give a kind of muffled despairing squawk, but the cock will split the night and rouse his master and mistress from a slumber as deep as death if an enemy lays hold of him.

As for the hen, she is rich in comfortable sounds, chirps and chirrs, and, when she is a young pullet, a kind of sweet singing that is full of contentment when she is clustered together with her sisters and brothers in an undifferentiated huddle of peace and well-being waiting for darkness to envelop them. The chick, of course, peeps — peeps of various tones and intensities. In the words of Aldrovandi, "The cock sings always practically the same song; however, those cocks who are more courageous sing more deeply, as Aristotle says. . . . The hen changes her voice to suit various actions. She makes one sound as she walks, another when she is laying [I have never heard her make any sound at all when she is laying], another when she is rearing her young."

Aldrovandi reports that in a certain quarter of the city of Thessalonica the cocks never crow, being a particular voiceless breed. Modern geneticists could doubtless develop a similar breed (if such a one ever existed) for modern city dwellers but it is hard to feel that a crowless cock would be a real cock. The Italian naturalists also remind us that chickens chirp. It is also true that both hens and cocks croak on occasion, and we may even hear sometimes a sound that Gilbert Longolius describes as follows: "She does not cackle, she sobs. For with this word Varro imitates the sound of a hen, broken and formed within her beak." In Aldrovandi's words, "The hen . . . shapes a thin little infirm cry when the cock is about to mount her."

While ancient writers disagreed on the question of whether hens sing, Aristotle, while inclined to reserve that word for the crowing of the cock, adds, "Nevertheless, sometimes the song of a female is heard. By women it is commonly taken as a bad omen, to such a degree that they wish to kill the hen that sings," and Terence likewise testified to the fact that "when a hen sang (or crowed) it was considered a portent," classifying the fact as a prodigy: "A hen has crowed; the soothsayer has forbidden it." Certainly hens crow much in the fashion of cocks. They do so indeed quite frequently without, so far as I have observed, anything worse than usual happening.

The balance of my remarks on raising chickens are addressed to those chicken raisers who are fortunate enough to be able to maintain *polli ruspanti,* chickens that are, for all practical purposes, free. Of course much of what I have had to say about confined chickens will apply also to free-ranging chickens. But here we are dealing only with our third alternative. Anyone who wishes to have *polli ruspanti* should begin with a cock and two or more mature hens. A half acre (or possibly less) can accommodate a cock and a dozen hens unconfined. The procedure with the trio is as I have earlier described it. They should have a simple coop with a roost in it and they should be kept in it for a week or so with plenty of food and water until they are thoroughly accustomed to it, and a simple nest made of a box with low sides and some straw in it should be provided. If one of the hens shows an inclination to set she should be allowed to do so. It of course will take more than a week to determine whether one of the hens will become broody.

Chickens will go to roost at sundown. Old birds usually go to bed early; young birds, like young children, like to stay up until the last possible moment and, being flighty by nature, after the last pullet or cockerel has entered the henhouse and you are ready to shut the door he or she may dash out to search for a final morsel of food. If you have a cock who takes his responsibilities seriously, he will shoo his wives off to bed at a respectable hour and see that they are all inside the coop before he takes up his own post, sometimes alone, sometimes beside a favored spouse.

Where chickens are free-ranging, the immemorial question at issue between the gardener of the establishment and the custodian of the chickens is whether to fence in the chickens or to fence in the garden. Chickens can make a shambles of a garden in short order, especially when it is young and tender. When it is well grown, with a fairly dense cover so that the ground cannot easily be scratched up, chickens can be turned into the garden to search for bugs. However, since they love green things and will eat the leaves off many plants and vegetables, this is an operation that needs to be carefully superintended in order to determine whether the ultimate effect will be positive or negative. The chicken fancier will of course take the line that it is far cheaper and simpler to fence the garden unless, of course, it is too extensive for that to be practical. The gardener will, almost invariably, take the opposing position. I have nothing to add except to say that, generally speaking, whether the chickens are fenced in or the garden is fenced will depend largely on whether the gardener or the custodian of the chickens has the stronger personality.

Let us assume here that it is the chicken fancier, so that the chickens are free to wander as the spirit moves them. During the day the greatest enemy of mature chickens will be transient dogs; of chicks, stray cats. If you have cats or dogs they will usually accommodate themselves quite readily to the introduction of chickens when you make clear to them that the chickens are an official part of the family "unit." If a dog falls into the habit of chasing chickens it may be difficult to break him of it. One rather Draconian remedy is to tie around a dog's neck the particular chicken that he has killed and leave it there until it is thoroughly offensive. The problem here is that you, presumably, live with the dog (or the dog with you), and such punishment may be as hard on the owner as on the dog. Indeed, this is a cure more for a dog that chases other people's chickens than one that chases your own. A dog may chase a chicken with one of two objectives in mind: to eat it, or simply *pour le sport*. It is difficult for the chicken to know in which spirit it is being chased and it, naturally, has a panic reaction. Even if the dog is "only funning," it is hard for a hen to keep her mind on laying eggs. But animals that are forced to occupy the same space usually, as I have said, come soon to some reasonable accommodation.

Unconfined chickens find their own food, for the most part, in summer, and do not need to be fed except when they are being fattened for eating, and in the winter months when foraging is meager.

The basic point to emphasize is that chickens, like all living creatures, love to be free. They are much happier roaming about than shut up in cages. It does not, of course, follow that they lay more eggs (rather the reverse), but it is certainly true that they enjoy laying them much more, that they lay better eggs, and, for the most part, they are much easier "keeping."

So *polli ruspanti* are, one trusts, clearly the happiest and most contented chickens and have the happiest and most contented masters or mistresses.

But as in all good things there are, of course, problems and complications. A free life is, for chickens as well as for people, in some ways more arduous and more dangerous than a confined life. (Otherwise people would not wish to live in cages and it would not occur to them to put other living creatures in cages.) Many people, as distinguished from animals, prefer to trade freedom for boredom. They would rather be bored than free, and so a vast portion of our energy and money is devoted to coping with the ubiquitous problem of boredom, which, perhaps above all things, characterizes our society.

An unconfined chicken, as we have noted, has a penchant for gardens and green things. It loves dust baths and would gladly turn the whole world into an enormous dust bath if it could. Once it has started to dig a comfortable depression to fit its body, it often seems to get carried away by the sheer pleasure of digging and makes a hole big enough for a hippo's wallow. Chickens love a big bush where they can rest in the shade; they like to creep under things; they are endlessly curious, and, displaying an almost human perversity, they persistently seek to penetrate those places where they are forbidden to go — like gardens.

About their egg-laying they are usually quite offhand. They lay eggs, for the most part, where it has been suggested to them that it would be accommodating to lay their eggs because it is an essential part of a hen's nature to be accommodating. Thus, a hint in the form of a glass egg, or in the absence of glass, a plastic egg, will usually suffice to get them started in a particular spot. (Incidentally, a glass or plastic egg should be filled with sand so that it has the approximate weight of an egg. The egg will thereby better simulate a real egg and better delude the hen. It is also less likely to be knocked out of the nest.) One of the advantages of using artificial eggs rather than real ones as nest eggs is that real eggs attract egg-eaters — rats, snakes, skunks, jays, and so on. I have several times found plastic eggs covered with scratches and teeth marks where some furious animal has tried to eat them.

Since hens are not at all possessive about nests, except when setting, most hens will be content to lay in one or two nests. Of course, if you fail to designate a nesting spot, your hens will find their own. If you find it and strip it of all its eggs, they will get discouraged and look for another nest. Therefore, if you do not have glass or plastic (or marble) eggs (the last are hard on a hen's bottom because they are so cold), you should leave several eggs in a nest. You can mark these eggs and leave them there more or less permanently, or you can rotate them so that no eggs grow stale.

Since hens have minds of their own, there is no guarantee that your hens will respond to your hint or hints. Despite your tactful intimation of an appropriate spot, they may, and often do, find their own nest spot or general nesting area. Here again, you should leave an artificial egg or two, the notion being, I suppose, that hens can't count and that as long as there is an egg in the nest each hen will assume that it is her own and will continue to lay there.

As we noted in the chapter on the egg, hens lay in a cycle or series. At the beginning of the series they start early in the morning, and each successive laying day — a day or so apart normally — they lay approximately fifteen or twenty minutes later. So the first egg in a particular series may be laid at seven o'clock in the morning and the last at five or six o'clock in the evening. When a particular series of eggs has been laid, the hen takes a break for a few days, then "resets her clock" and begins the new series early in the morning. Such, at least, have been the findings under laboratory conditions. My own observation is that for free hens the middle of the day between the hours of eleven and one is the period when most eggs are laid. The reason for this may be that birds in cages with a constant supply of food and water lay eggs on the described schedule, whereas free hens get up in the morning, so to speak, and spend several hours searching for food to fill up their uncomfortably empty craws (another reason for giving them some grain in the morning when they are let out of the henhouse) and follow their impulses, which may suggest a dust bath or a little sunning before getting down to the serious business of laying an egg.

It is clear there is a large element of the volitional in egg-laying. A hen does not *have* to lay an egg if she doesn't wish to. How many eggs she lays and when she lays them depends on a variety of elements important undoubtedly to the hen if inscrutable to her keeper. The fact that more than one hen lays in a particular nest indicates that hens are highly suggestible birds. The cackle that announces an egg laid (sometimes it only announces the intention) calls the attention of other hens to the event, and, indeed, to the particular spot, and commonly another hen hurries up and occupies the vacated nest.

As I have said, when a hen is broody she will often set anywhere. If there are four or five eggs in a nest, none of them hers, she may add an egg of her own and then resolutely refuse to vacate. More typically she will, when she is ready to set and raise a batch of chicks, seek out an ingeniously hidden spot and there, very quietly, without any fuss or feathers, without any betraying cackles, lay a secret clutch of eggs. During the time she is laying, she will be as casual and noncommittal as you please, coming and going like all the other hens in the flock until she has laid the number of eggs she desires to set on — seldom fewer than twelve or more than twenty. Then she disappears without a trace. When you count your hens on their roost at night or at feeding time she is simply missing, and then suddenly she appears, every feather betraying her broodiness. She looks puffed up with the importance of her impending motherhood and she is all business. She comes for the feeding trough on the dead run, giving a squawk or two to warn any idlers to clear the path. She eats in great haste, drinks her fill, and then looks about. If there is anyone around who has no business knowing where her nest is, and that is most typically, of course, her owner, she ambles off with an air of studied casualness as though she were just an average, ordinary hen looking for a bug or two. But she has excellent eyesight, and she never for a moment loses track of the curious observer. She knows that she must get back to her nest promptly or her eggs will chill and the embryos die, but she is determined not to give away their hiding place. So she saunters here and there, occasionally dashing off in a direction deliberately intended to deceive and then doubling back to find out if she has lured the observer into following her and betraying thereby his presence. (One hen quite literally led me around the barn three times. Finally, watching through a knothole, I saw her give a final look around and then, convinced that the coast was clear, dart into a pile of underbrush. When I came up with her she looked both furious and undone and I felt guilty as I always do, in ousting her from her nest and gathering up the carefully hidden eggs.)

I would say that the principal problem in having free-ranging chickens is the matter of finding the nests of broody hens. The reader might very well ask, "Why not leave the hen to hatch her chicks?" For one thing, the hen may be a pullet. For another, the chicken raiser wishes, usually, to control the breeding of his birds. It is simply common prudence to insure that the best hen mates with the best cock. Moreover, if your flock of chickens is made up of mixed breeds or varieties, you will wish to control the mating of the different birds.

Assume, for the moment, that your flock is of the same breed and that the hen that is setting is one of your best hens, a suitable mother for an increase in your flock, and you are therefore pleased to have her set, it is still important to search out the nest, tedious as this may be. If you leave her to her own devices, she may well be discovered by a predator. This is especially true if you live in an area inhabited by raccoons or 'possums — many fairly heavily settled and even suburban areas have these predators. Raccoons and 'possums will often search out a setting hen, make off with her, and eat her eggs. If they fail to come upon her while she is setting, they will most invariably find her after her chicks are born; they will be guided by the peeping of the babies. If, therefore, you wish to have the mother hen hatch her eggs and raise the chicks, you should locate the nest, wait until dark, and then take a box filled with straw and a soft cloth. Place the cloth over the hen, lift her off the nest, remove the eggs and, if possible, a portion of the existing nest, place them in the box, put the hen on that nest, and then put the box, eggs, and hen in the chicken house, taking pains to be sure that there is no hole or aperture in the structure through which the slender, prehensile fingers of a 'coon could penetrate. I have lost valuable hens because I did not find their nests soon enough and put them in a safe place. I have lost chicks because the cages in which I placed them were of wire, and raccoons were able to reach in and pull the baby chicks through the wire, tearing them to pieces in the process. I have also had 'coons reach through heavy wire, seize the leg of a roosting chicken and eat it off, the chicken of course dying of shock and loss of blood.

The raccoon is the most implacable enemy of the chicken, especially a mother raccoon with young ones. The fact is that chicken predators have a kind of schedule through the night. At dusk foxes and feral cats are on the prowl; at that hour a fox will often grab a dilatory bird that is late in going to roost. Cats are deadly to young chicks. They will seldom disturb a mature hen or cock. Then come the skunks, who love eggs, and later at night the 'possums and finally the deadly raccoon. If birds are roosting in trees, they may be attacked by owls. Hawks are apt to be about just as the light is fading, and I have caught one in my henhouse when I have gone to close it up for the evening. A large 'coon, or the less agile 'possum, may shake roosting birds out of a tree and then catch them on the ground, where they stumble about helplessly in the dark.

So a setting hen needs the protection of a henhouse. There is a popular belief that a hen will abandon a nest that has been disturbed. If the nest is changed about during the daytime that is likely, although some hens are far more tenacious in sticking to their nests than others. I have never had a hen, transferred at night, when she is practically in a state of hibernation, refuse to stay on her new nest.

With *polli ruspanti* life takes on somewhat the character of a perpetual egg hunt. This does not seem to me onerous. I enjoy matching wits with chickens, and there is a special sensation of pleasure in discovering a nest where hens have been laying (but not setting), confident that they had found an out-of-the-way spot. It is like discovering a treasure.

Which brings me to the whole matter of collecting eggs. That seems to me one of the most agreeable of all domestic tasks. The eggs are sometimes still warm from the chicken; they are almost always clean-shelled, and they have a mysterious weight and density; they lie in the hand solid and yet fragile, of an ineffable, always recurring, always different beauty, a color of infinite delicacy and promise — white, mauve, brown, a faint pink. The particular egg that rests in your hand recapitulates life, even as it contains a far more mundane promise for your breakfast. It is such a simple, elemental act to pick up a freshly laid egg from the nest in which the hen has recently deposited it. Is not that perhaps the most common, graceful, and gracious gesture that the human species has known in the four or five thousand years that chickens have shared their strange bounty with men — picking up an egg, holding it in one's hand, and placing it in a basket?

Finally, one must note that the temperament and personality that chicken raisers once observed in their individual charges persist. Chickens have their own distinct personalities, and when they are free-ranging these qualities become evident. Some, for one example, are much tamer than others and some are much more enterprising or ingenious. Some are more industrious layers and some, as we have seen, are particularly disposed to motherhood. Sometimes such qualities are represented most clearly in certain breeds, but even within breeds there is a considerable range of difference among members of the same flock. Perhaps the most conspicuous difference is in the pattern of dominance and subordination, but this is minimized, as we have noted, when birds are at large.

At this point the prospective keeper of chickens may find consolation in E. B. White's *Basic Chicken Guide:*

"Be tidy. Be brave. Elevate all laying house feeders and waterers twenty-two inches off the floor. Use U-shaped rather than V-shaped feeders, fill them half full and don't refill until they are empty. Walk, don't run. Never carry any strange object into the henhouse with you. Don't try to convey your enthusiasm for chickens to anyone else [a rule which he and I have broken]. Keep Rocks if you are a nervous man, Reds if you are a quiet one. . . . Never give day-old chicks starter mash for the first couple of days — give them chick feed, which is fine cracked grain. Don't start three hundred chicks if all you want is eight eggs a day for your own table. Don't brood with electricity unless you are willing to get out of bed at 3 A.M. for a thunderstorm and a blown fuse. Do all your thinking and planning backwards, starting with a sold egg, ending with a boughten starter. Don't keep chickens if you don't like chickens, or even if you don't like chicken manure. Always count your chickens before they are hatched. . . . Use clean sawdust for nest material and renew it often. Never use straw for litter unless it is chopped. Tie your shoelaces in a knot in the morning when you get dressed, since hens are under the impression that shoelaces are worms. When you move birds from a broodhouse to a range shelter, keep them locked up in the shelter for two nights and one day before letting them out to play."

So much, then, for the keeping of chickens. You are not keeping them, of course, to make or even to save money. You are not keeping them as pets. You are keeping them for the simple pleasure of their company and the beauty and tastiness of their eggs and their meat. You are raising them because you wish to strike a modest blow for the liberation of the chicken — and, indeed, of all living things on earth.

Just as a rose is a rose is a rose, an egg is an egg is an egg. So perhaps our final word should be in praise of the egg. Elemental and ultimate, it is, I would guess, the most famous and familiar shape in the world. Without putting too fine a point on it, I would say *that*, after all, is what it is all about — the raising and maintaining and nurturing of chickens: it is about the egg. I believe it is not entirely preposterous to say that a good many disordered lives might be re-ordered around the motif of the egg, of collecting eggs and experiencing in each splendid, immaculate shape the strange bounty of nature, who treats us so much better than our deserts if we only let her. I seldom gather my eggs of an evening, grumbling if my charges have been skimpy, negligent or deceitful, delighted if they have been generous, that I do not allow myself the fantasy that the world may in some arcane way be redeemed by the egg, the genuine, authentic, nonindustrial egg, emerging from the genuine, authentic, nonindustrial chicken. Until we get right with the chicken and with the egg, until we get them right and get back into the old, the true and proper relation to them, what matter world councils, international monetary systems, capitalism, Marxism, and all the world's vanities and pretensions? We must start with something ancient and simple and beautiful, something like the egg. That's asking a lot of the egg, I suppose. Or a lot of mankind. The noncommercial egg is a very modest and very fragile vessel for the redemption of the world. And yet, and yet, I say, as I gather up my eggs, one must, for a certainty, begin somewhere and I will begin with the egg. I will leave it to philosophers to construct new cosmologies; I will collect fresh eggs.

On Keeping
Chickens

342

I T WOULD BE PRESUMPTUOUS to say that the chicken was born to be eaten. Indeed we have already suggested that the *raison d'être* of the chicken is the egg. Yet the chicken is undoubtedly the most universally eaten of all meats. Some societies, as we have seen, keep chickens but refrain from eating them for religious reasons. Most of the peoples of the world who have kept chickens have done so primarily for their eggs — or, of course, for fighting. Eggs were too valuable a product of the chicken to justify killing the hen that laid the egg. Those chickens that were killed for food were thus young cockerels, caponized cocks, or hens past laying or at least at the end of their cycle. In many cultures a chicken was killed and cooked as a special delicacy for an honored guest. "This creature," Aldrovandi wrote, "almost alone is our chief resource when friends or guests arrive suddenly and unexpectedly; we owe to the chicken all the splendor displayed by a rich table or by one that is modestly supplied or by that which is slenderly laden. If there is need for an elegant and groaning board, you have in the chicken the most praiseworthy meat, both boiled and roasted, and eggs that are better than those of other birds, which can also furnish you with various courses. But if your table must be modestly laden, as in those days [of fasting] when the eating

The Culinary
Chicken
(*and Egg*)

343

of flesh is forbidden by sacred law, eggs alone will suffice for you. If your table must be scantily provided, as is suitable for sick people, whence, I ask you, can you find a safer and more pleasant diet than this animal provides?"

In countless American households in the nineteenth and well into the twentieth century, chicken on Sunday was a treat and the mark of at least moderate prosperity. (There was even a nostalgic book entitled *Chicken Every Sunday*.)

By divorcing the production of eggs from the sale of chickens for food, Americans, and the citizens of those countries which have followed our technological lead, can have chicken virtually every day. It is no longer a luxury; it is far cheaper and more available than pork or beef, and it is high in protein. That the industrial production of chickens has produced an abundance certainly cannot be denied. That they are genuine chickens is much less certain.

In any event, there are literally thousands upon thousands of recipes for cooking chicken, beginning with the ancient Greeks (and earlier) and extending to every part of the world.

Indeed, there is, in most instances, a national chicken dish characteristic of virtually every country (for America, for instance, it would certainly be fried chicken, Kentucky or straight). The Spanish have *paella valenciana*, the Russians *kurnik*, the Hungarians chicken paprika, the Italians as many classic chicken dishes as there are Italian cities, beginning perhaps with the famous *pollo alla diavola* of Florence and proceeding to chicken *cacciatore* and *pollo ravellino*. Georgians dote on *chakhokhbili*, Austrians on *Backhuhn*, Indians on chicken *tandoori*, the Indonese on *sambal hati-hati*, the French on *coq au vin*, the Chinese on dozens of delicious dishes, the Moroccans on *bastelah*, the Scotch on cockyleeky, the Japanese on chicken *teriyaki*, chicken *tempura*, and, especially, *oyako domburi*.

Special recipes have been associated with historical figures as diverse as Caesar, St. Francis, Napoleon, and Thomas Jefferson. The opera singer Tetrazzin. was honored with a dish named after her, as was the composer Rossini. Marie Leszczynska, wife of Louis XV, is reputed to have been the queen in whose honor *bouchées à la Reine* was created. *Poulet Marengo* was concocted to honor a great Napoleonic victory and *salade Bagration* for one of his rare defeats.

Unfortunately, just as it is necessary to break a perfect egg to make an imperfect omelet, it is necessary to kill a chicken to prepare it for the table. Thus we come to what is certainly the least pleasant part of the discussion of chickens — the killing of them. There are several methods, the most common being cutting off the head with a hatchet or axe or breaking the neck. Wringing a chicken's neck was once a common way of killing a bird. A quick snap is perhaps the simplest method, but it involves a technique, and the average amateur is, I suspect, disinclined to experiment with an area that is unnerving enough in the best of circumstances. A chicken's throat can be cut, a method which has an advantage over breaking the neck in that the dead bird is allowed to bleed. My preference is for a sharp axe or hatchet. Those who study refinements in such matters recommend hypnotizing a chicken before killing it, since a chicken is easily hypnotized.

The fact is no matter how a chicken is killed, it will, in common with those snakes from whom we are told it is descended, thrash and flop about after it is dead, in a thoroughly demoralizing way. I can only say that one becomes more or less accustomed to this in time, and if we are to eat meat it is essential, in my opinion, that we understand at first hand that this means killing creatures, which is never pleasant or easy. But it is better that we do it ourselves, at least occasionally, and do so in relation to our own eating of meat than that it simply be done by machines or by specialists in killing.

Experts profess to be able to kill chickens by piercing their brains with a needle-sharp instrument in such a fashion as to cause the sockets of their feathers to relax for a period of a minute or so, during which time the feathers can be much more easily plucked than would otherwise be the case.

There are, again, various other techniques for plucking chickens, including the use of hot wax, but these are of more historical than practical interest. If a freshly killed chicken is dipped into a pail of hot water, it can be quite quickly and easily plucked, ten or fifteen minutes to a chicken at the outside, I would say. The butchering of a chicken is no more complicated than cleaning a fish. Indeed, with a little practice it can be done very simply and rapidly.

The parts of the chicken that one saves depend primarily on one's taste. Certainly, one would hope, the livers for chicken livers on toast with bacon or liver pâté, the feet, the back, and the neck for soup stock, and so on.

Following the historical system of this work, it seems appropriate to begin with the recipes of the ancients for the cooking of chickens. Here it must be said that precise measurements — ½ cup olive oil, 2 teaspoonfuls of melted butter, etc. — are modern inventions, the *Boston Cooking School Cookbook* claiming to have been the first cookbook to give exact measurements. Be that as it may, classical recipes are notably vague. The Greeks, for example, were fond of a hen cooked with olives and a white wine sauce. The body cavity of the bird was filled with water and olive oil during cooking.

Of course, chicken broth or soup is the oldest as well as the most universal manner of cooking a chicken, and, as we have seen, its medicinal properties have been as highly esteemed as its culinary ones. Antagoras of Rhodes, a poet, was so fond of chicken broth that when he had boiled a hen, he abstained from going to the bath, which he dearly loved, for fear the boys in the household would drink the broth in his absence.

In ancient Egypt chicken broth was popular as a beauty aid. Since plumpness was much admired, Egyptian ladies drank chicken broth made from fat black hens while taking their luxurious and interminable baths, hoping thereby to grow fat and comely. In addition they doted on "a very fat black hen," stuffed with "pounded hazelnuts, sweet almonds, pistachios, pine nuts and peas. . . ."

A classical recipe for boiled chickens which seems to have originated with the Greeks (as so many things did) but was popular with the Romans called for a sauce made with dill seed, dried mint, asafetida root moistened with vinegar and supplemented with Jericho date, *liquamen* (sauce or gravy), a little mustard mixed with dried fruit and oil. The sauce was poured over the chicken as it cooked.

Another popular sauce with chicken called for a half-gill of olive oil, a bit of asafetida, a bit less than a gill of *liquamen* and an equal amount of vinegar, six scruples of pepper, one scruple of parsley, and a bunch of leeks (a scruple is a third of a dram [1.295 grams] or, more commonly, a small amount).

The ancients were particularly fond of milk-fed chickens, for these, according to Alexander of Aphrodisias, were "very large and easy to cook." Caponizing of young cockerels and their fattening for the table were common. For reasons that are obscure the Romans passed a law forbidding cocks to be caponized, but the law was generally ignored, and milk-fed capons were considered a special delicacy, as anybody who has had the good fortune to eat one can well understand.

The poet and physician Battista Spagnoli (Mantuanus) wrote in praise of the capon: "The greatest glory to you, cock, when you have lost your testicles, for then you are pleasing to sleep, to the stomach, to Venus, to Cybele."

In case an honored visitor caught a host without a milk-fed capon or hen, according to Horace, it was only necessary to dip a tough old bird into a basin of Falernum wine and water while still alive to soften it. The same purpose, we are told, could be served "with a fig placed in the creature's anus."

The Romans were fond of chicken boiled with pea pods. One recipe called for a boned chicken, cut into small pieces with chopped onion, coriander, and skinned brains added. This was then cooked in a sauce of oil and wine. Peas were then added, the ingredients placed in a suitable saucepan, and pepper, cumin, and chicken stock added. Two eggs were also mixed in. The remaining stock from the chicken was poured over whole boiled peas, and these were garnished with pine kernels. The dish was cooked over a low fire.

Chicken à la Varius was cooked in *liquamen*, oil, and wine, with leeks, coriander, and savory. When the chicken had cooked, pepper and pine kernels were added. A sixth-pint of *liquamen* with some cooking liquor was blended with milk and poured over the chicken. "Pour in beaten egg white to bind," the recipe concluded. "Put the chicken on a serving dish and pour the sauce over."

Another Roman recipe called, rather vaguely, for a boned chicken stuffed with cooked peas, brains, Lucian sausages, "and all the other usual things." Then freshly ground pepper, lovage, oregano, and ginger, moistened with a sauce of oil and wine; then raisin wine and cooking wine added. All these ingredients were to be arranged in alternate layers in the chicken as a stuffing. It was then wrapped in sausage casing, placed in a casserole, and cooked gently in the oven.

The combs and wattles of chickens roasted over hot coals and seasoned with pepper and orange juice were considered very tasty by Roman gourmets, and chicken livers similarly roasted on the coals and eaten with a cool white wine were guaranteed to revive "sagging strength in a short time."

Legend had it that in Prester John's fabulous kingdom of Ethiopia, "hens were served whose flesh, together with the bones, had been removed with the skin and filled with such great skill that nowhere appeared the place where the flesh was removed. . . ."

The medieval world made general use of classical recipes for chicken dishes and added a number of its own. One such was known as *"Potage* of Fowls with Green Peas." A chicken was boiled in stock. Green peas were cooked in a pan with butter or bacon fat. Both were stewed separately with greens and then mixed. Another recipe called for chickens covered "before and behind" with bacon, wrapped in vine leaves, and roasted. Since there was no refrigeration, chickens were often pickled with vinegar, salt, pepper, and lemon peel and then "left in their pickle till they be wanted." Then they were drained, fried in butter, and set to stew a few minutes in some of the pickle.

Aldrovandi, who is the source of most of our ancient recipes, had his own favorites. Chicken with almonds was one: "Take a half a pound of almonds, three small egg yolks, chicken livers, the finest wheat bread to the measure of two eggs, as much cream as can be bought for two pennies and the broth of an old hen very well cooked. Then press the crushed almonds through a sieve with the broth and serve. Or first place a cooked chicken in the broth thus prepared and boil it moderately so that it becomes rather thick. . . ."

Italians of Aldrovandi's day liked a roasted chicken

basted with butter and a little wine. "Some people," he wrote, "cook grapes with a chicken in a covered pot. . . . They crush the grapes, press them, and pour them back on the chicken with butter." Another popular recipe called for cooking the chicken "in the usual manner in a pot, pouring in wine and meat broth with a little salt and aromatic saffron as the bird cooked, thickening the gravy with a little toasted bread. This stock should be taken out, a crushed chicken liver added and then poured back and cooked completely with the chicken."

Sixteenth-century Italians collected the blood of chickens that were killed and drank it, a custom that has survived to modern times in rural communities in many parts of the world. A friend tells me that thirty years ago his father did likewise, and that the blood was considered a fine tonic.

According to Aldrovandi, in the German principalities a favorite dish was *Plutzhuhner*, roast chicken or capon cut up in pieces with sugar and spices or sweet wine. The bird was served cold. The French considered the rumps of cocks and hens an ideal food for the campaigning soldier, so that veteran soldiers were often called "fowl rumps."

Cocks' testicles were eaten for the virility that they were thought to infuse in the diner. Roasted with pine nuts, they were recommended for fishermen anxious to catch especially large fish.

The chicken recipes that follow are modern ones and, for the most part, more conventional (though not necessarily better) than most of those derived from earlier times. They are, with a few exceptions, recipes that the authors' wives or friends have cooked and served. Thus, out of the literally thousands of recipes available, these are the ones that have a personal flavor. *However, since amounts and procedures given are often imprecise, the reader will use his or her culinary instincts in trying them out.*

Again we might follow a roughly chronological line, starting with recipes from Colonial America. Brunswick Stew was one of the great American chicken dishes and a favorite of Thomas Jefferson. This recipe from the *Williamsburg Cookbook* instructs us to "cut up a three Pound Chicken (or two Squirrels) and put in a large Pan with three Quarts of Water, one large sliced Onion, one half Pound of lean Ham cut in small Pieces and simmer gently for two Hours. Add three Pints of Tomatoes, one Pint of *Lima* Beans, four large *Irish* Potatoes diced, one Pint grated Corn, one Tablespoon Salt, one fourth Teaspoon Pepper, a small Pod of Red Pepper. Cover and simmer gently for one more Hour stirring frequently to prevent Scorching. Add three ounces of Butter and serve hot."

Brunswick Stew is ideally suited for picnics and large social gatherings, since it can be best made in quantity. Consequently, it has probably been consumed at more community church and road buildings than any other dish, so much so indeed that it was known in many parts of the country as "Church Builder Chicken."

Another recipe from Colonial Virginia was Smothered Chicken: "Singe a young Fowl and split it down the Back. Draw it, then lay the Chicken, with inside downward, in a Baking-pan, breaking the Breast Bone to make it lie flat. Spread the Breast with Butter, dredge it with Pepper. Put Salt and about one half Cup of Water in the Bottom of the Baking-pan, place in a hot Oven, cover with another Pan, let bake for half an Hour, basting every ten Minutes. Remove upper Pan, turn Fowl, baste well on the Inside, cover again and bake for another half Hour. When done place it on a hot Dish; put Pan in which it was cooked on Top of Fire to brown, add Flour and stir until smooth and brown, then add a half a Pint of Milk and stir until it boils. Add Salt and Pepper and send up your Gravy in a Boat."

It is important, of course, for one who keeps and kills his or her own chickens to be well stocked with recipes for tough cocks or old hens. This can perhaps best be done by precooking a tough bird in a pressure cooker for twenty to thirty minutes. In the absence of a pressure cooker, steaming the chicken, while it takes longer, is almost as effective. Boiling a tough fowl in water before frying it will only make it rubbery.

A more exotic eighteenth-century preparation was Cock Ale, made with "ten gallons of ale and a large cock the older the better. Parboil the cock, flea [flay] him, and stamp him in a stone mortar until his bones are broken. You must craw and gut him when you flea him. Put him into two quarts of sack and put to it 3 pounds of raisins of the sun stoned, some blades of mace, and a few cloves.

"Put all these into a canvas bag, and a little while before you find the ale has done working, put the ale and bag together into a vessel. In a week or 9 days' time bottle it up, fill the bottles just above the necks, and leave the same to ripen as other ale." The authors do not endorse this potion.

The Boston Cook Book, which appeared in 1883, was written by Mrs. D. A. Lincoln and dedicated to the president of the Boston Cooking School "in recognition of her zeal in every good work for the benefit of woman and to the Pupil, Past and Present. . . ." It was the first modern "scientific" cookbook and its pride was in its comprehensiveness and exactness. It might be appropriate to borrow from it a recipe for fried chicken. "Singe; cut at the joints; remove the breast bones. Wipe each piece with a clean wet cloth; dredge with salt, pepper, and flour, and sauté them in hot salt pork fat till brown and tender. . . . Arrange on a dish with boiled cauliflower or potato balls, and pour a white sauce over them. Or dip in egg and crumbs, and fry in a deep hot fat, and serve with tomato sauce."

Gertrude Harris, a fine cook and author of *Manna: Foods of the Frontier*, vouches for a roast capon (or chicken) recipe that starts with a four-to-six-pound capon, stuffed with "7 slices of toast soaked in cream and mixed with 1 cup tiny shrimp, tablespoon of finely minced onion and the same amount of celery.

"Set on a grill in a roasting pan. Put into a preheated 400-degree oven for 15 minutes. Turn the bird, reduce heat to 350 degrees and continue roasting for 1 hour more.

"Baste frequently with pan juices. Turn the bird once or twice. Test for doneness by piercing the thigh; if liquid runs out and is pinkish, continue cooking until no liquid runs out at all; bird is tender and nicely browned."

The same friend offers us a Stuffed Roasted Chicken à la Grandma Tobias, a creation of her Hungarian mother-in-law. This starts with potato pancake batter and a five-pound chicken.

Stuffed Roasted Chicken à la Grandma Tobias

Five-pound chicken	7 eggs
4 tablespoons butter	¼ cup minced onion
1 stalk celery with	3 teaspoons salt
leaves chopped	¼ teaspoon pepper
1 cup chicken broth	2 tablespoons cracker
	meal
POTATO PANCAKE BATTER	1 tablespoon chopped
3 large raw potatoes,	parsley
peeled and grated fine	

Mix the batter ingredients in the order given. Butter and salt the chicken thoroughly and stuff it lightly with the potato pancake mixture. Sew the opening closed or skewer it. Spread the chopped celery over the bottom of the roasting pan and put the chicken on top. Roast in a moderate oven (350°) for 2½ hours, turning occasionally. Baste with broth.

French recipes for chicken seem to be without end. Here is our favorite.

Poulet à la Stanley

Large lump butter	1 cup milk
2 large, finely chopped onions	1 tablespoon tomato paste
1 cut-up chicken	½ teaspoon curry powder
Salt and pepper	
1 cup thin cream	½ tablespoon paprika
1 tablespoon butter	2 teaspoons lemon juice
3 level tablespoons flour	3 mushrooms, sliced

Melt a little butter in a pan. Add the onions and cook slowly without browning for 6 to 8 minutes. Add more butter, the chicken, salt and pepper, and cream. Cover and cook for thirty minutes. Remove the chicken but keep it warm.

Melt 1 tablespoon butter in a small pan, stir in flour, and add milk. Stir and bring to boil. Stir into the onion mixture. Add tomato paste and rub the sauce through a strainer. Add curry powder and paprika, lemon juice, and mushrooms that have been sautéed in butter. Bring slowly to a boil. Replace the chicken and simmer for 10 minutes. Arrange the chicken on a dish and pour the sauce over.

Poulet à la Kiev is another favorite of mine but it is a common enough recipe and we will not reproduce it here but I cannot resist two other French recipes, *Poulet Marengo* and *Poulet à la Regence.*

Poulet Marengo

2 broilers
Hot butter
2 tablespoons hot sherry
1 tablespoon tomato
  paste
2 tablespoons flour
1½ cups stock
3 mushrooms, finely
  chopped

4 or 5 tomatoes, skinned
  and sliced
1 bay leaf
Salt and pepper to taste
Lobster meat, cooked
Croutons
Fried eggs

Cut up the chicken and brown it well in hot butter; pour on the hot sherry. Remove the chicken and add to the pan the tomato paste and flour. Stir until smooth; pour on the stock. Stir over the fire until the mixture comes to a boil; add the chopped mushrooms. Put the chicken back in the pan, adding the tomatoes, bay leaf, salt, and pepper. Cover and cook rapidly for about forty-five minutes. Remove, arrange chickens on serving dish and place on top slices of lobster meat. Pour over the sauce and garnish with lobster shells, croutons, and fried eggs.

Poulet à la Regence

2 three-and-a-half-
  pound chickens
Butter
2 tablespoons brandy
1 teaspoon meat glaze
1 tablespoon tomato
  paste
3 teaspoons potato flour
1½ cups stock

Salt and pepper
1 bay leaf
2 or 3 slices bacon,
  cooked and shredded
24 small white mush-
  rooms, sautéed
24 green olives, stoned
24 ripe olives, stoned

Brown the chickens in hot butter. Pour brandy over them and remove them from the pan. Place in the pan the meat glaze, tomato paste, potato flour, and stock. Stir over heat until the mixture comes to a boil. Add salt, pepper, and bay leaf. Put the chicken back in pan breast side down, cover and cook slowly for 35 to 50 minutes, until just tender.

Remove skin from one chicken. Remove breast from each side; cut in halves lengthwise. Remove remaining meat from this chicken and cut in fine shreds. Add the bacon, mushrooms, green olives, and ripe olives; arrange on a flat platter. Arrange the whole chicken on top. Place the breast of chicken at each side. Pour over the sauce and serve.

A recipe for Baked Chicken Rosé comes from Mrs. Joseph Concannon, Jr., of the Conconnon Vineyard in Livermore via a friend, Beth Brown. It is one of the best chicken dishes I know.

Baked Chicken Rosé

1 three-pound chicken,
   quartered
Seasoned flour
4 tablespoons butter
2 tablespoons flour
¾ cup chicken bouillon
½ cup California rosé
   wine

¼ cup green onions,
   including tops, sliced
½ cup mushrooms,
   sautéed
1 nine-ounce package
   of frozen artichoke
   hearts, cooked as
   package directs

Dust the chicken with the seasoned flour. Melt 2 tablespoons of the butter in a shallow baking pan. Place the chicken in the pan. Bake uncovered for 45 minutes at 350°. Melt 2 tablespoons of butter in a saucepan. Stir in the flour. Add the bouillon and wine; cook, stirring constantly until the mixture is smooth. Turn over the chicken sprinkle it with the onions, mushrooms, and the cooked artichoke hearts. Pour the sauce over it. Return the chicken to the oven and bake it 30 minutes longer.

Serve with rice Milanaise with chicken sauce on top and fresh asparagus.

Chicken in Orange-Wine Sauce comes to us from our friend Frances Rydell, a gourmet cook.

Chicken in Orange-Wine Sauce

2 fryer chickens, about two-and-a-half pounds apiece

⅓ cup flour

½ teaspoon salt

½ teaspoon pepper

½ cup butter

3 medium onions, sliced thin

1 can sliced black olives, drained

SAUCE

¼ cup thawed orange juice concentrate

½ cup dry white wine

1 teaspoon salt

1½ teaspoons thyme

Wipe the chickens dry. Coat them with flour, salt and pepper, and brown them in butter in a large ovenproof frying pan. Set pieces aside as they are browned.

Add onions to the pan and stir until they are lightly browned; stir in flour left from coating the chickens. Return the chickens to the pan, pour in the orange-wine sauce and mix lightly, cover and bake in a 375° oven for 1 hour. Remove the birds to a platter and keep them warm. Add the olives to the pan juice. Boil vigorously until the sauce thickens. Pour it over the birds. This will serve 6.

For the hostess or host with a penchant for the spectacular there is boned stuffed chicken covered with gold leaf.

An almost equally exotic dish is stuffed chicken

breasts in clay, the clay being, most commonly, a hard salty dough.

Stuffed Chicken Breasts

BREAD STUFFING

Celery and onion
  browned in butter
French or plain bread
Dressing seasoning
Salt and pepper to taste
Paprika
Parsley
1 egg

Hot water

CHICKEN

4 whole chicken breasts,
  boned
Flour
Paprika
Salt
½ cup butter

Toss together the stuffing ingredients. Put a bit of stuffing on each chicken breast, then fold and tuck, starting at the "V" end of the breast, making a pocket for the stuffing. Skewer the pocket together; try to keep the skin spread out as much as possible around the breast.

Roll the chicken pieces in flour seasoned with paprika and salt. Melt the butter and roll the floured breasts in it to coat them. Sauté in butter for 10 minutes.

Then the "clay."

Baker's Clay (Ekman Version)

4 cups flour   1½ cups water
1 cup salt

Combine the ingredients and mix with your fingers until the mixture is smooth. Keep it covered (a Tupperware cake bowl works nicely) and be sure to use it within one hour. Knead it until smooth on a well-floured board. Roll it out on waxed paper to a 9-inch square. Set a chicken breast in the center. Bring the clay around the breast and seal it completely. Repeat this process for each piece.

If you prepare chicken breasts the day before, the cooking time will be cut almost in half. Wrap them in foil and chill them overnight. Make the clay and wrap them early in the day. Once the clay has been placed around them it should be painted in various bright colors with food coloring. Bake about 1½ hours at 325°.

Sauce for Chicken Breasts

2 tablespoons butter	½ cup heavy cream
½ small onion, minced	½ cup sour cream
½ pound mushrooms	Salt and pepper to taste
2 heaping tablespoons flour	

Melt butter in a saucepan. Halve each mushroom. Sauté the minced onion and the mushrooms until soft, not brown. Cover the saucepan and cook for 10 minutes over low heat. Carefully stir in the flour. Add the heavy cream, sour cream, salt, and pepper. Heat almost to the boiling point, but do not allow the sauce to boil.

Barbara Embree's Liver Pâté

1 pound fresh chicken livers	Salt and pepper to taste
1 bunch green onions with tops, chopped	Dash of dill (pounded seeds or green foliage)
Garlic	1 teaspoon rosemary
¼ pound butter	½ teaspoon dry mustard
⅔ cup white wine	2 tablespoons brandy
	Black olives, sliced

Sauté the chicken livers, onions, onion tops, and garlic in butter. Cook until the livers are delicately browned, then add the wine, salt, pepper, dill, rosemary, and mustard. Simmer for 10 minutes. Put all in a blender with brandy. Pour into a pot. Chill overnight; decorate with sliced black olives.

Since the Chinese are perhaps the only rivals to the French in the variety and delectability of their chicken dishes, it is appropriate to conclude the section of cooking chickens with four recipes given me by my student Michael Woo.

Rock Salt Chicken is one of the oldest methods of cooking chicken in China, and is still a favorite of gourmets. It is not done so much in households here, but it is widely sold now in Chinatown delicatessens.

Rock Salt Chicken (*Yim Goke Gai*)

About ⅔ of a 5-pound sack of rock salt	1 broiler, about 3 pounds (Be sure skin is unbroken.)
Soy sauce	
Salt	3 or 4 slices fresh ginger
Dash of sugar	Green onion
	Chinese parsley

Using a wok or a large Dutch oven, heat the rock salt until it is very hot. There must be enough of it to form a bed for and completely smother the chicken.

Lightly rub the cleaned chicken, inside and out, with a mixture of the soy sauce, salt, and sugar. Inside the cavity of the chicken place ginger slices, onion, and parsley. When the rock salt is sufficiently hot (about 10 minutes), place the chicken in the middle of it, and cover it completely with more hot rock salt. Cover the pot, turn off the fire, and let it stand for 20 minutes.

When it is done, remove it from the salt bed, chop it up, and serve it hot.

Soy Sauce Chicken (She Yau Gai)

This is one of the simplest ways of preparing chicken in China. A great favorite, but also not done in households much because it requires a big pot of soy sauce, though the sauce can be reused several times. This chicken is also widely sold in Chinatown delicatessens.

Soy sauce
Shoa Hing wine (a
   light cooking wine),
   equal amount
Whole Star anise
   (available at Chinese
   groceries)

1 pound rock sugar
Piece of dried tangerine
   peel the size of a
   half-dollar
1 3 or 4 pound chicken

Using a large pot with a cover, cook together the soy sauce, the wine, the anise, the rock sugar, and the tangerine peel until the mixture boils. Immerse the cleaned chicken into this hot sauce, cover the pot, and turn off the heat. Let the pot stand, covered, for about 20 minutes.

Remove the chicken to a platter when it is done; chop it up to serve.

Lemon Chicken

1 broiler, whole
2 or 3 tablespoons
   sesame oil
Soy sauce
Wine
1 clove garlic, crushed
Onion
Fresh ginger
Juice of one lemon

¼ cup sugar
Salt to taste
2 tablespoons chicken
   stock
2 more tablespoons wine
Cornstarch
Peel of ½ lemon, sliced
   thin
Grated onion or parsley

Marinate the chicken in soy sauce and wine. Using a large pot, heat oil. Add crushed garlic, onion, and ginger and brown for 12 or 13 seconds, and then add the chicken, browning it evenly all over until it is golden yellow. Then add the lemon juice, sugar, salt, chicken stock, and wine. Cover and cook over low heat for 15–20 minutes.

When it is done, remove the chicken to a platter until it is cool enough to chop up. Thicken the remaining liquid in the pot with a little cornstarch. Pour this sauce over the chopped chicken; garnish with grated onion or parsley.

Steamed Mushroom Chicken

1 small chicken, chopped up	A sprinkle of sugar
Soy sauce	Fresh ginger, crushed
Sesame oil	1 clove fresh garlic, crushed
Salt	6 medium-sized dried mushrooms, reconstituted with water
3 teaspoons cornstarch	
2 tablespoons Hoy Sin sauce or 3 tablespoons oyster sauce	

Marinate the chicken in the soy sauce, sesame oil, salt, and cornstarch. Work the mixture well into each piece (if not enough cornstarch is used, the chicken becomes soggy when cooked). Then add Hoy Sin or oyster sauce, sugar, crushed ginger, and crushed garlic. Place chicken and sauces in a deep dish for steaming. Slice the mushrooms and place them evenly over the chicken. Top this with cut pieces of onion and parsley. Cover the dish and steam for 15 minutes over high heat. About 5 minutes before it is done, uncover and turn over the chicken pieces so that they will cook evenly.

Recipes for cooking eggs, like recipes for cooking chicken, are almost infinite and, again, we can only hint at their range and variety. Indeed, the egg is, if anything, more essential to the cook than is the chicken. In the words of the French chef, Stacpoole: "All cookery rests on the egg. The egg is the Atlas that supports the world of gastronomy; the chef is the slave of the egg. What is the masterpiece of French cookery, the dish that outlives all other dishes, the thing that is found on His Majesty's table no less than upon the table of the bourgeoisie — the thing that is as French as a Frenchman, and which expresses the spirit of our people as no other food could express it? The omelet.

"Could you make an omelette without breaking eggs? Then cast your mind's eye over this extraordinary Monsieur Egg and all his antics and evolutions. Now he permits himself to be boiled plain, and even like that, without frills, naked and in a state of nature he is excellent. Now he consents to appear in all ways from poached to *perdu;* now he is the soul of a vol-au-vent, now of a sauce.

"Not a pie-crust fit to eat but stands by virtue of my lord the egg, and should all the hens in the world commit suicide, tomorrow every chef in France worthy of his name would fall on his spit, for fish is but a course in a dinner, whereas the egg is the cement that holds all the castle of cookery together."

Aldrovandi, though less lyrical, was equally emphatic. "We prefer hens' eggs," he wrote, ". . . to all the rest, especially if they are eggs which the hen has conceived by a cock." Those conceived by the wind — wind eggs or zephyr eggs — were said to taste less good, to be smaller and "more humid." By the same token fresh eggs were infinitely to be preferred over old ones, "since the freshest are the best and the oldest are the worst. . . . Fresh eggs are very easily distinguished from the old. The fresh eggs are full; old eggs are usually empty in the wider part."

One of the most frustrating experiences in boiling an egg is having the white adhere to the shell so that when one peels the egg much of the white is lost. To prevent peeling of the white and to preserve the flavor, place the eggs to be boiled in a pan of lukewarm water with a tablespoon of salt, bring the water to a boil, then turn down the heat and cook for ten minutes. Turn the heat off and let the eggs stand for fifteen minutes and then put them under the cold water tap for four or five minutes. Let stand another ten minutes and then peel. Laborious perhaps, but not so much so as having to contend with adhering whites.

If you raise your own chickens under natural conditions you will have a period, sometimes as long as five months, without eggs, and when your chickens are laying you will have a glut. It is therefore important for the amateur poultry keeper to know how to preserve eggs, especially for cooking. Eggs absorb odors through their shells and the process of deterioration in an egg goes on by means of the pores of the shell. Eggs should thus be cooled (but not frozen) as soon as they are collected. On the other hand, it should be said that a fertile egg will remain capable of germinating after three or more weeks of warm weather, so that it is in no sense rotten. By the same token an egg fresh from the nest should be allowed twenty-four hours or so to set up, especially if it is to be cooked (rather than used in cooking or eaten raw). Eggs turned up in a barnyard cache of uncertain age can be put aside for cooking and the fresher eggs used for eating.

Before refrigeration a variety of techniques was used to keep eggs so that they would be available when hens were not inclined to lay. Fertile eggs can be kept for six weeks or two months by packing them in bran and keeping them at a temperature of about 60 degrees. They can *then* be put under a setting hen and hatched. Pliny recommended bran or bean meal to keep eggs for long periods and Varro wrote that prior to being stored they should be rubbed with fine salt. Lime water was widely used to preserve eggs for as long as six to eight months, but I wouldn't recommend it.

St. Kilda is a tiny island off the northwest coast of Scotland where the few hundred inhabitants had, in earlier times, little to eat but barley cakes and eggs. A visitor to the island in 1698 reported that the standard ration for an islander was a barley cake and eighteen eggs a day. Since the eggs were to be had fresh only during the summer, the islanders saved the surplus, packed them in ashes, and placed them in pyramids, thereby preserving them for six or seven months.

The Irish, on the other hand, used to preserve eggs by coating them with butter. The Reverend Mr. Dixon preferred pork lard, rubbing it into the pores of the egg to close them and placing the eggs, end down, in an old butter firkin. An alternative was to pack the eggs in an earthen vessel and pour warm sheep tallow over them. Before the year-round production of commercial eggs — a phenomenon of the last twenty-five years or so — eggs were commonly preserved by being placed in water glass, potassium silicate, or sodium silicate. This can be bought in powder form and mixed with nine parts water to one part sodium silicate, the eggs completely submerged, and the jar kept in a cool place. So treated, eggs last six to eight months or even as long as a year. But who needs a year-old egg?

To freeze eggs, select a plastic ice cube tray that has individual cube segments. Break an egg into each compartment and freeze. Pop them out into a plastic bag and put the bag into your freezer. The eggs can be thawed on a saucer and easily slipped off into a warm buttered pan for fried or poached eggs, or they can be separated. They also can be beaten in any quantity and frozen for scrambled eggs or for baking, and so on.

Perhaps the last word on preserving eggs may be left to a great English farmer and politician, William Cobbett, who wrote, "Preserved Eggs are things to run *from*, not after."

In the ancient world, salad was usually the first course of a meal, followed by an egg dish, usually two eggs to a plate. That diners often skipped their salad is suggested by Cicero's comment, "I bring my hunger intact to the eggs. . . ." The Greeks liked scrambled eggs (the Greek word for them was *exapheta*, or "dispersed") and poached and fried eggs were also popular, although Galen, the physician, inveighed against fried eggs because, as he put it, "Fried eggs descend through the stomach slowly, have bad juice, and corrupt even the foods mixed with them, and are considered among the worst of those edibles which cannot be cooked together." They were, nonetheless, popular with "the common people . . . nor do the higher classes abstain from them." Perhaps it was some such distinction that Alexander Pope had in mind when he wrote many centuries later: "The vulgar boil, the learned roast an egg."

There was a division of opinion — and always has been — over where eggs should be opened. Aldrovandi reports that the Jews of his day opened their eggs at the round end and discarded any that showed blood. The Italians, on the other hand, opened them at the sharp end and the Germans opened them on the side.

While eggs in the ancient world were often cooked in warm ashes, like chestnuts, boiling was the preferred method. Poached eggs on toast were considered most suitable for sick people and an omelet, typically, was made of oil and wine "mixed together and shaken." The Greeks called soft-boiled eggs *trometa,* or "trembling eggs."

Italians in the sixteenth century used hard-boiled eggs to garnish salads, and Aldrovandi assures us that the practice was a common one throughout Europe. He confessed he liked his eggs "cooked without shells . . . because they are more healthful for my own daily use and for a taste that is delicate, especially if some fresh butter is poured over them."

Cheese omelets and custards were also known to the ancients. A popular recipe for custard called for eggs, milk, and honey, five eggs to a pint of milk. A cheese omelet was made by mixing water and milk with eggs and beating until the mixture was light and fluffy, then adding grated cheese and cooking with oil and butter: "They will be pleasanter," the writer of the recipe noted, "if they are not cooked too long and if they are turned while being cooked." An excellent omelet could also be made with beet leaves or rock parsley, "juice of buggloss [bugloss] or ox-tongue, mint, marjoram or sage" were used and another recipe that survives calls for the same herbs cut fine and fried in oil or butter. In addition there were pancakes made from eggs, and "eggs on a griddle." The latter recipe called for eggs beaten and poured into a pan and folded in four folds, cut into squares, then covered with fresh eggs, sugar, and cinnamon — a *crêpe,* in other words. *Verzuzum* was made with four egg yolks, four ounces of sugar and the same amount of orange juice, a half-ounce of cinnamon, and two ounces of rosewater.

All of which bring us to the egg in modern times and a few concluding recipes. Here we begin with Gertrude Harris's omelet.

4 eggs
4 tablespoons of water
(or milk)
½ tablespoon salt
Freshly ground pepper
to taste
1 tablespoon finely
minced parsley

1 teaspoon chive stalks,
minced
2 tablespoons fresh sweet
butter
12 chive blooms (fully
opened but still fresh)

Break eggs into a bowl and beat them to blend the yolks and whites. Add water, seasoning, parsley, and chive stalks. Melt the butter in a heavy iron skillet over medium heat. Beat the egg mixture and pour it into the skillet. When the eggs begin to set, lift them and, tilting the skillet, let the uncooked part run underneath. Sprinkle on the blossoms and fold the omelet. Slip the omelet from the skillet onto a warmed platter. Serves 3–4.

Eggs Chimay

4 hard-cooked eggs
8 teaspoons heavy cream
1 teaspoon chopped
sautéed mushrooms
4 tablespoons Worcester-
shire sauce

Pinch of salt
Pinch of pepper
4 teaspoons grated Edam
cheese

Split egg lengthwise; remove yolk. Mix yolk with mushrooms and cream. Blend the Worcestershire sauce with salt and pepper to taste. Stuff the whites generously. Place them on a buttered cookie sheet, brush with a little cream, and sprinkle the cheese on them. Place under the broiler long enough to turn the cheese to a glaze.

Eggs Bordeaux

2 tablespoons butter
1½ tablespoons
  Parmesan cheese
Pinch of salt
Pinch of cayenne pepper
10 eggs

¾ cup Bordeaux wine
½ cup grated Gruyère
  or other soft white
  cheese
4 slices dry toast

Melt the butter, stir in the Parmesan cheese, add the salt and cayenne pepper. Stir until the mixture is smooth. Beat the eggs with the wine and Gruyère cheese. Pour the mixture in the pan and scramble until fairly firm; serve over toast.

Here are two Indian recipes.

Baked Spiced Eggs

2 large onions
2 garlic cloves
1 small bunch fresh
  coriander leaves or
  watercress
1 green pepper
2 ounces cooking fat

1 tablespoon vinegar or
  Worcestershire sauce
4 eggs
½ teaspoon cumin
  powder
1 teaspoon sugar
½ teaspoon salt

Thinly slice the onions. Finely chop the garlic cloves, the watercress, and the green pepper. Mix the vinegar (or Worcestershire sauce) and sugar. Fry the onions in the fat until they are almond-colored. Add the garlic, green pepper, and watercress to the onions. Fry for 3 minutes, stirring all the time. Beat the eggs and add to the onions in the saucepan. Add the cumin powder. Remove from fire and pour in the vinegar mixture and salt. Stir well. Pour the mixture into an ovenproof dish and put in preheated oven (400°) for 30 minutes or until set.

Egg Bhurji

2 medium onions	Salt to taste
2 green chilis	2 ounces (4 tablespoons)
4 or 5 large eggs	butter
Coriander, mint, or	
parsley to taste	

Slice the onions. Chop the chilis. Beat the eggs, add salt, chilis, and coriander. Heat butter in frying pan and fry onions until brown. Add eggs and stir with a fork until set. Do not overcook.

From China we have a recipe for Tiger-Skin Eggs. (Beware: the measures are approximate.)

Tiger-Skin Eggs

5 hard-boiled eggs	6 water chestnuts
8 cubes bamboo shoots	3 teaspoons soy sauce
8 mushrooms	Salt to taste

Fry the boiled eggs in deep fat until they are brown. Remove, and boil them with the vegetables for fifteen minutes. Cut each egg into halves and fasten a piece of water chestnut with a toothpick to cover the egg yolk and prevent it from dissolving in the liquid.

And, finally, for dessert, from Gertrude Harris again, a great recipe for Zabaione or Zabaglione. A heavy saucepan is needed.

Zabaglione

For each serving, allow 2 egg yolks, with 2 teaspoonsful of sugar and 2 tablespoons of Marsala.

"Beat the yolks and sugar together until frothy,

then stir in the Marsala and set over a low heat. Stir steadily (and, say the Italians, always in the same direction) until it is nice and thick, but not so thick it will not bear stirring easily. (It must not boil.) As soon as it thickens, pour into warmed wineglasses and serve promptly. Eat with a silver spoon. Good for what ails you. And as good a note to end on as any. *Bon appétit*, lovers of eggs and chickens."

The Culinary
Chicken
(*and Egg*)

371

Adams, Christian, "Frank Perdue Is Chicken," *Esquire* (April, 1973).

Aldrovandi on Chickens: The Ornithology of Ulisse Aldrovandi (*1600*) Volume II, Book XIV, translated from the Latin with introduction, contents, and notes by L. R. Lind, Norman, Oklahoma, 1963. Aldrovandi's book is the classic work on chickens.

Ali, Salim, and S. Dillon Ripley, *Handbook of the Birds of India and Pakistan,* Bombay, 1961.

Burnham, George, *The History of the Hen Fever,* Boston, 1885.

Carson, Jane, *Colonial Virginians at Play,* Williamsburg, Va., 1965.

Carter, George F., "Pre-Columbian Chickens in America," in *Man Across the Sea: Problems of Pre-Columbian Contacts,* edited by Carroll L. Riley et al., Austin, Texas, 1971, pp. 178–218.

Cobb, Ernest, *The Hen at Work: A Brief Manual of Home Poultry Culture,* New York, 1919.

Collais, N. E., E. C. Collais, D. Hunsaker, and L. Minning, "Locality, Fixation, Mobility and Social Organization within an Unconfined Population of Red Jungle Fowl," *Animal Behavior,* 14 : 550–559.

Corning, Gardner, *Corning Egg Farm Book by Corning Himself,* Bound Brook, N.J., 1912.

Dixon, Edmund Saul, *A Treatise on the History and Management of Ornamental and Domestic Poultry,* London, 1849.

———, *A Treatise . . . , With Large additions* by J. J. Kerr, M.D., Philadelphia, 1851.

Dryden, James, *Poultry Breeding and Management,* New York, 1928.

Evans-Pritchard, E. E., *Witchcraft among the Azande,* London, 1937.

Fithian, Philip, *The Journal and Letters of Philip Fithian,* edited by H. D. Farish, Willamsburg, Va., 1965.

Foucault, Michel, *The Order of Things: An Archaeology of the Human Sciences,* New York, 1970.

Geertz, Clifford, "Deep Play: Notes on the Balinese Cockfight," *Daedalus* (Winter, 1972).

Goodenough, Erwin R., *Jewish Symbols in the Greco-Roman Period,* vols. 7 and 8, Bollingen Series, XXXVII, Princeton, N.J., 1958.

Guhl, A. M., "The Social Order of Chickens," *Scientific American* (February, 1956).

Halpert, Herbert, *American Speech,* vol. 26.

Hogan, Walter, ed., *The Call of the Hen,* Mountain Grove, Mo.,
1913.
Hurd, Lewis, *Modern Poultry Management,* New York, 1928.
Jull, M. A., "The Races of Domestic Fowl," *National Geographic*
(April, 1927), pp. 379–452.
Kligender, Francis, *Animals in Art and Thought,* Cambridge,
Mass., 1972.
Lewis, Harry, *Productive Poultry Husbandry,* Philadelphia, 1913.
———, "America's Debt to the Hen," *National Geographic* (April,
1927), pp. 453–467.
Lewis, S. H., *The New Book of Poultry,* London, 1912.
Lewis, William M., *The People's Practical Poultry Book,* New York,
1917.
MacDonald, Betty, *The Egg and I,* Philadelphia, 1945.
Martin, Joseph Plumb, *A Narrative of the Sufferings of a Revo-
lutionary Soldier,* New York, 1968.
Moreau de St. Méry, Médéric Louis Elie, *American Journey [1793–
1798],* translated and edited by Kenneth Roberts and Anna M.
Roberts, New York, 1947.
Morse, H. B., *The Chronicles of the East India Company Trading
to China, 1635–1834,* 5 vols, reprint vol. I, Taipei, 1966.
Poultry Culture: A Text Book on Poultry, Ashland, Ohio, 1930.
Schauss, Hayyim, *Guide to Jewish Holy Days,* New York, 1962.
Schjelderup-Ebbe, T., "Social Behavior in Birds," in *Handbook of
Social Psychology,* edited C. Murchison, Worcester, Mass., 1935.
Scott, George Rypley, *The History of Cockfighting,* London, 1957.
Thompson, Stith, *Motif-Index of Folk Literature,* Bloomington,
Ind., 1961.
Willeford, Charles, *Cockfighter,* New York, 1972.

Magazines and Journals (a sampling of thousands)

Canadian National Poultry Record
Grit and Steel
Kimber Chicks: General Catalogue
Kimberchik News
The Leghorn World
Nulaid News
Pacific Egg and Poultry Association Yearbook and Directory
Petaluma Weekly Poultry Journal
Petaluma Argus and *Argus-Courier*
Poultry Tribune
University of California, Agricultural Experiment Station, *Circulars*

Africa, 30, 32, 35–36, 61, 67, 75
Alabama, 107
Albertus Magnus, 21, 57
Aldrovandi, Ulisse, 41–51; viewpoint, 4–5, 49–50; studies, 43–45, 49, 227; on hens, 43, 45–47, 143, 162–163, 213, 334; on cocks and cockfighting, 43, 56, 57, 60–61, 65–66, 71, 74, 334; advice on chicken raising, 47–48, 312, 319, 325; on eggs, 48, 166, 187, 367, 370–371; medicinal advice, 45, 49, 130–132; cooking advice, 347–348, 353–354, 367, 371; mentioned, 55, 64, 149, 167, 218, 228, 302n
America. *See* Latin America; United States
American Poultry Association, 228–229, 333
anatomy, 45, 168–177, 181–183. *See also* embryology
Andalusians, 273
Araucanas, 31
Aristotle, 17–18, 20, 21, 23, 41, 43–45 *passim*, 50, 213, 218, 334
Arizona, 105–106
Arkansas, 106
Aseels, 27, 110
Asia, 67. *See also* Near East; Southeast Asia, specific countries
Australoup, 311

Bantams, 19, 27, 229
Barred Plymouth Rocks, 221, 262, 273, 310
behavior. *See* cocks; hens; peck order
Black Sumatras, 27
Boston Poultry Show, 207–208, 219
Brahmas, 27, 49, 76, 209, 222, 273, 311
breeding: control, 178, 236, 341; nineteenth-century mania, 205–212, 218–233; scientific, 205, 226–228, 232–233, 236, 249, 268–269, 271; types, 216–217, 219–221, 228, 229, 233, 301, 310–311; amateur, 311. *See also* hybridizing; production; specific breeds
brooders, 239, 311, 344
broodiness, 20, 46, 48, 141, 181–183, 217, 238–239, 318–322, 325–326, 335, 340
Brunswick Stew, 355
Buddhism, 34
Buff Orpingtons, 311
by-products, 284–285

California, 237, 270, 278, 288, 289, 292–293, 300; cockfighting, 104–107, 109, 116, 118. *See also* Petaluma, Calif.
Capon (or Chicken), Roast, 357
Capons, 22–23, 126, 281, 310, 325, 351–352, 356

Caribbean Islands, 29, 118
catching chickens, 331–333
Chalcidians, 19
Chicken, Fried, 356
Chicken, Lemon, 365–366
chicken-or-egg argument, 45, 169–170
Chicken, Rock Salt (Yim Goke Gai), 364–365
Chicken, Smothered, 355
Chicken, Soy Sauce (She Yau Gai), 365
Chicken, Steamed Mushroom, 366
Chicken à la Grandma Tobias, Stuffed Roasted, 357–358
Chicken Breasts in Clay, Stuffed, 362–363
Chicken in Orange-Wine Sauce, 361
chicken raising, amateur, 307–346. *See also* breeding; production
Chicken Rosé, Baked, 360–361
chicks, 25, 46, 235–236, 246, 272, 309–313, 320–324. *See also* embryology; hen: maternal characteristics
China, 12–13, 14, 27–30, 32, 35, 75–76, 184, 205; eggs, 35, 256–258, 330; recipes, 364–366
Chinese Silkies, 49, 217
Chittagongs. *See* Cochin Chinas
Christianity, 41, 50, 52, 62–64, 67, 73–74, 161–162, 184–185. *See also* Protestant Ethic; Puritanism
Cochin Chinas (Chittagongs; Shanghais), 12–13, 27, 34, 49, 76, 205–206, 209, 216–217, 219, 221, 273, 311
cock: symbolism, 38–39, 51–52, 54–55, 60, 62–63, 66–67, 70, 72, 73, 121, 159, 223; power and bravery, 52, 55, 66, 137; military significance, 57, 58–59, 66, 71, 73; behavior in flock, 65–66, 223–225, 227, 268, 280, 324–325, 328–330, 335; methods of control, 268, 280–281, 310, 324–325, 351–352; effect of industrialization, 268,

281, 283. *See also* cockfighting; language; sexual connotations
cockfighting: origins and history, 11, 13, 17, 19, 27, 29, 69–80, 87–92, 95–104; illegality, 11, 95–97, 105–110, 114, 116–117, 119, 123; cultural, social and religious aspects, 67–68, 70, 72, 73, 75–77, 86–88, 95–97, 99–104, 115, 119–124; breeds, 70, 110–112, 217; spurs, 71, 84–86, 94, 101, 107, 115, 117, 121; feeding and training, 71–72, 80–83, 116, 121; cockpits, 78, 89, 104, 118; mains (fights) and betting, 80, 83–84, 86, 88–91, 101–102, 104, 108–109, 121; in U.S., 80, 85n, 98–114, 116–118 *passim;* treatment of injuries, 86–87, 118, 121; universality, 114–118
Columella, 18–20, 22–24, 41, 46, 47, 73, 213, 218, 322n
combs, 12, 39, 62, 174, 328, 353
confinement, 232–233, 258, 267–269, 271–272, 275, 302, 325, 328, 329. *See also* breeding: scientific
Connecticut, 98
"Connecticut Strawberries," 103
cooperatives. *See* production

disease and lice, 24, 258–259, 267, 271–272, 275–276, 289, 296–301, 317, 319, 330–331
divination, 29, 32–33, 36–37 *passim,* 58–60, 69
Dixon, the Rev. Edmund Saul, 9–11, 70, 132–133, 208–218, 223, 225, 227, 267, 308, 317, 323, 333, 369
domestication, 11, 33, 38, 69–70
Dominiques, 137, 217, 273
Dorkings, 16, 19, 209, 217, 273, 311
dream interpretation, 136, 167

Egg Bhurji, 374
Egg City, Calif., 293, 300

Eggs: history, 11–15, 19, 28, 31–33, 35; false nest eggs, 21, 319, 338–339; fertile, 21, 34, 192–193, 268, 315, 330, 367; shell, 31, 179, 197–200, 262, 277, 294; preserving and shipping, 35, 233, 369; as medicine, 33–34, 126–131, 133–134; in proverbs, 135–143, 146–147, 156, 168; symbolism and decoration, 162–167, 184–187, 214; practical uses, 166–167; description and size, 166, 189–190, 192, 343; praise for, 166, 187–188, 343, 345–346; development and ovulation, 170–177, 193; yolk, 172, 174, 184, 193–196, 313; Easter, 185–186; nutritional and cholesterol factors, 193–197, 252–253; processed, 196, 232, 256, 273; private supply, 307, 314–315, 318, 326, 344; freshness, 318, 330, 367–368; cooking and preserving, 347–348, 367–375. *See also* embryology; food, use as; hen: laying and reproductive effort; incubation; production

Eggs, Baked Spiced, 373
Eggs Bordeaux, 373
Eggs Chimay, 372
Eggs, Tiger-Skin, 374
Egypt, 13–16, 27, 31, 36, 37, 52, 184, 351
embryology, 17, 43–44, 168, 192–195, 200–203. *See also* eggs: fertile
Europe, 12, 13, 15, 27, 30, 75, 85n, 101, 114. *See also* Great Britain, Greece, Italy, Rome
experimental use, 163–166, 168

Fabergé, Carl, 186–187
Far East, 27, 34, 35, 67, 94. *See also* China; Japan; Southeast Asia
feed, 242, 248–249, 254, 260, 274, 276, 280–284, 288, 291–292, 312; of free-ranging chickens, 47, 313–314, 337. *See also* feed companies

feed companies, 242, 244, 248–249, 251, 276, 291
fertilization. *See* eggs: fertile
Florida, 105–106
folklore, 66–67, 135, 147–156. *See also* proverbs
food, use as: meat, 22–23, 32, 40, 233, 237, 262, 271, 280–284, 347–348; cock, 22–23, 145, 281, 310, 325, 347, 351–352, 354, 356; eggs, 34, 35–38, 193–197, 232, 252–253, 256, 273, 302, 347–348, 367–375; taboos, 34–38, 40, 193, 226, 347; recipes, 348–375
free-ranging chickens, 165, 176, 181, 215–216, 232, 244–245, 267, 280, 313, 316–317, 335–344. *See also* confinement
Frizzleds (Frieslands), 217

Geertz, Clifford, 119–124
Georgia, 98
Great Britain, 16, 205–207, 217, 221, 227, 311; cockfighting, 74–75, 77–81, 83–84, 87–92, 95–98, 105, 114
Greece, 13, 15–18, 21, 32, 40, 52–54, 56–57, 60–62 *passim*, 67, 126, 350–351, 370, 371; cockfighting, 13, 16, 70–72, 81, 82, 103; proverbs, 135–136, 160
Grey Jungle Fowl, 70
Grit and Steel, 85n, 107, 110–113
Guelderlands, 209, 217

Hamburgs, 209, 217, 273
hatching and hatcheries, 20, 235–236, 238, 246, 321–322. *See also* incubation
Hawaii, 28–29, 117
hen: behavior, 18, 21, 143, 163, 173, 176, 266–267, 323, 328–329; maternal characteristics, 19–20, 46, 137, 159–162, 182–183, 212–213, 227, 238–239, 319–324, 327–328; productive period, 23, 47, 238, 326–328; laying and reproductive effort, 23, 173, 176–177, 179–

hen (*Continued*)
181, 189–191, 216–217, 237–239, 264–265, 267–269, 280, 307, 314, 326–328, 338–341; Protestant and Victorian attributes, 153, 162, 212–213, 223, 266–267, 273; industrialized behavior, 267–268, 272, 316; non-productive, uses for, 326–327. *See also* broodiness; eggs: development and ovulation; embryology; folklore

henhouses, 24–26, 47, 210, 248, 307–309, 312, 335

Hindus, 34, 37, 69, 114–115, 184

history, 10–31, 33, 35–38, 41–42. *See also* cockfighting; eggs

Hollands, 273

Houdans, 311

hybridizing, 271, 280–281, 288, 300, 310. *See also* breeding

Illinois. 241

incubation, 14–15, 19, 20, 22, 35, 48–49, 201, 234–235, 238–239, 242–243, 272, 319–320. *See also* hatching and hatcheries

India, 10, 12–13, 27, 30, 32, 34, 35, 61, 70, 75–76, 91–95

Indonesia, 10, 12, 37, 68, 76, 115–116, 119–124

industrialization. *See* production

Iowa, 241

Iran. *See* Persia (Iran)

Italy, 42, 46, 49, 114, 221, 353–354, 370, 371

Japan, 13, 35

Javas, 11, 27, 217

Judaism, 37–39, 61–62, 67, 193, 370

Jungle Greys, 11

Jungle Reds, 11

Kansas, 107

Kentucky, 107

Kerr, J. J., 11, 208–209, 215–216, 227

killing and plucking, 283, 325, 327, 349–350

Kimber, John, and Kimber Farms, 270–272, 279–280, 285–290, 300

language, 333–336; crowing and cackling, 23, 39, 52, 55–58, 61–63 *passim*, 66, 140, 224, 315–316, peeping, 320–321, 323–324

Langshans, 27

Latin America, 29–31, 86, 117–118

Leghorns, 221, 236, 239, 240, 252, 262, 271, 272–273, 280–281, 310, 328

literature. *See* folklore

Liver Pâté, Barbara Embree's, 363–364

magical properties. *See* religious and magical functions

Malays, 27, 209–210, 217

manure, 255, 272, 275, 278, 284–285, 309, 312, 314

marketing. *See* production

Maryland, 107

meat. *See* food, use as

Medians, 19

medicinal properties, 17, 18, 32–33, 43, 45, 49, 54, 55, 61–62, 67, 125–134

Middle East, 67, 94. *See also* Persia (Iran)

military significance. *See* cock

Minorcas, 221, 273

Missouri, 241

Mohammedans, 34, 35, 39, 61, 116

molting, 12, 161, 267, 279–280

Near East, 35, 70, 94

nests, 48, 173, 321–322, 338–343, 344; trapnest, 236, 328

New England, 98, 262

New Hampshire Reds, 310

New Jersey, 241

New York, 98, 103, 113

Ohio, 241

Old English Game Fowls, 87

Omelet, Quaker Blue Flower, 372

Oregon, 105–107
Oriental crosses, 110
ornamentation, 29, 32, 38, 220, 229

peck order, 141, 163–165, 316, 318, 329, 344
pecking, 139, 268, 272, 296, 316. *See also* peck order
peeping. *See* language
Perdue, Frank, 283
Persia (Iran), 35, 61, 70–71, 92, 184
personality, 218, 343–344
Petaluma, Calif., 233–235, 239–246, 250–257, 259, 260, 278, 293–295
pets, 54, 60, 327
Philippine Islands, 31, 68, 86, 90, 116–117
Pliny the Elder, 18–22, 41, 51, 53, 57–59 *passim*, 127–129 *passim*, 130, 131, 218, 369
Plymouth Rocks, 221, 262, 273, 310, 344
Polish, 209, 217, 273, 311
Polynesia, 13, 28–32, 34, 36, 37, 94, 117
Poulet à la Regence, 359–360
Poulet à la Stanley, 358
Poulet Marengo, 359
Poultry Producers of Central California, 250–251
prophecy. *See* divination
production: egg, 171, 177, 199, 225, 232–234, 236–242, 246, 248, 250–262, 264–269, 271, 273, 277, 279–281, 285, 287–288, 291–300, 302; small poultry business, 232–251, 260–262, 266, 269–270, 273–274, 277–279, 286–300, 329; industrialization, 14–16, 232, 263–265, 267–269, 270–273, 275–290, 292–293, 295–303, 348; marketing, cooperatives and cost, 250–261, 274, 276, 291–293, 300, 302–303. *See also* breeding: scientific; feed companies; food, use as; shipping

protection, from predators, 324, 336–337, 341–343
Protestant Ethic, 153, 162, 212–213, 284, 293, 295
proverbs, 135–147, 168. *See also* folklore
pullets, 279, 317–318, 320
Puritanism, 75, 95–96, 98, 107, 119, 138, 284. *See also* Protestant Ethic

recipes, 348–375. *See also* specific recipes
Red Jungle Fowl, 10, 11, 70
religious and magical functions, 16–17, 18, 29, 31–40, 49, 52–53, 55, 58–61, 66–70, 121–124, 159, 160, 166, 184–185, 226–227
reproduction. *See* embryology; hen
research and journals, 247–249
Rhode Island Reds, 221, 262, 273, 310, 344
Rhodians, 19
Rome, 15–16, 18–26, 32, 41, 52–55, 58–61, 62, 67, 135, 351–353; cockfighting, 13, 19, 72–73, 81
rooster, 51n, 137, 138. *See also* cock
Rose Comb Black Bantams, 27

science. *See* breeding: scientific
Sebrights, 229
sexing chickens, 260, 281, 310
sexual connotations, 36, 39, 122, 164, 173, 328–329; of cock, 51n, 53–54, 56, 57–58, 60–61, 72, 82, 115, 120, 127, 146, 223–225, 280, 283, 329, 354
Shanghais, 76, 205–206, 209, 216–217, 219
shipping, 35, 233, 236, 248, 369
Society for the Preservation of Poultry Antiquities, 311
South America. *See* Latin America
South Carolina, 98
Southeast Asia, 10, 27, 30, 32, 33–34, 36, 37, 61, 70, 75–76, 86, 115. *See also* Indonesia

Spanish, 19, 217, 273
Standard of Perfection, The,
229
Sultans, 273
Sumatras, 209, 273
superstitions, 33–34, 52, 60, 140–
143 *passim,* 160–161. *See* religious and magical functions
Sussex, 273
symbolism. *See* cock; egg; hen;
religious and magical functions; sexual connotations

Taboos. *See* food, use as
technology. *See* breeding: scientific; production
Texas, 113
time telling, 32, 56–57
*Treatise on the History and
Management of Ornamental*

and Domestic Poultry (Dixon), 9, 208, 223

United States: chicken raising, 15, 205–212, 218–221, 226–
230, 232–233, 242, 290, 295,
296. *See also* cockfighting;
production; specific states

Varro, Marcus Terentius, 18–
25, 47, 218, 322n, 334, 369
Vermont, 107
Virginia, 100–102

weather forecasting, 57, 141–
142, 160–161
Wyandottes, 221, 273, 311

Zabaglione, 374–375
Zoroastrians, 61